M000313158

The nascent field of Memory Studies emerges from contemporary trends that include a shift from concern with historical knowledge of events to that of memory, from 'what we know' to 'how we remember it'; changes in generational memory; the rapid advance of technologies of memory; panics over declining powers of memory, which mirror our fascination with the possibilities of memory enhancement; and the development of trauma narratives in reshaping the past.

These factors have contributed to an intensification of public discourses on our past over the last thirty years. Technological, political, interpersonal, social and cultural shifts affect what, how and why people and societies remember and forget. This groundbreaking series tackles questions such as: What is 'memory' under these conditions? What are its prospects, and also the prospects for its inter-disciplinary and systematic study? What are the conceptual, theoretical and methodological tools for its investigation and illumination?

Palgrave Macmillan Memory Studies
Series Standing Order ISBN 978–0–230–23851–0 (hardback)
978–0–230–23852–7 (paperback)
(*outside North America only*)

You can receive future titles in this series as they are published by placing a standing order. Please contact your bookseller or, in case of difficulty, write to us at the address below with your name and address, the title of the series and the ISBN quoted above.

Customer Services Department, Macmillan Distribution Ltd, Houndmills, Basingstoke, Hampshire RG21 6XS, England

Journalism and Memory

Edited by

Barbie Zelizer
University of Pennsylvania, USA

and

Keren Tenenboim-Weinblatt
Hebrew University of Jerusalem, Israel

TO Vince —
with fond
regards —
missing you!
Barbie

palgrave
macmillan

First published 2014 by
PALGRAVE MACMILLAN

Palgrave Macmillan in the UK is an imprint of Macmillan Publishers Limited, registered in England, company number 785998, of Houndmills, Basingstoke, Hampshire RG21 6XS.

Palgrave Macmillan in the US is a division of St Martin's Press LLC, 175 Fifth Avenue, New York, NY 10010.

Palgrave Macmillan is the global academic imprint of the above companies and has companies and representatives throughout the world.

Palgrave® and Macmillan® are registered trademarks in the United States, the United Kingdom, Europe and other countries.

ISBN 978–1–137–26392–6 hardback
ISBN 978–1–137–26393–3 paperback

This book is printed on paper suitable for recycling and made from fully managed and sustained forest sources. Logging, pulping and manufacturing processes are expected to conform to the environmental regulations of the country of origin.

A catalogue record for this book is available from the British Library.

A catalog record for this book is available from the Library of Congress.

Typeset by MPS Limited, Chennai, India.

Contents

List of Figures and Table

Figures

Table

Notes on Contributors

Kari Andén-Papadopoulos is Associate Professor at the Department of Journalism, Media and Communication, Stockholm University, Sweden. She has published internationally on photojournalism in times of crisis and war, with particular interest in amateur visual practices and new social media. Her forthcoming book, *Global Image Wars: Geopolitics and Post-9/11 Visual Culture*, considers the increasingly important role that visual images and practices play in the conduct and critique – and later memory – of global political affairs. She is currently engaged in an international research study, *I – Witnessing: Global Crisis Reporting Through the Amateur Lens* (funded by the Swedish Research Council), which examines how the contemporary proliferation of citizen-created imagery – documenting breaking news events as they happen – is recasting the production, reception and recollection of global crisis news.

Daniel A. Berkowitz is Professor, School of Journalism and Mass Communication, and Associate Dean, Graduate College, at the University of Iowa, USA. His research involves social and cultural approaches to the study of news, journalists and journalism, with a focus on mythical narrative, collective memory, professional boundary work and news of terrorism. He is editor of *Cultural Meanings of News: A Text-Reader* (2011) and *Social Meanings of News: A Text-Reader* (1997). He has published more than 40 articles in journals and edited books.

Matt Carlson is Assistant Professor of Communication at Saint Louis University, USA, where he teaches and researches in the area of media and journalism studies. His work examines public discourse about journalism with a focus on the cultural construction of journalistic norms and practices and competition over journalistic boundaries. He is author of *On the Condition of Anonymity: Unnamed Sources and the Battle for Journalism* (2011) and co-editor of *Journalism, Sources, and Credibility: New Perspectives* (2011). In addition, his work has appeared in *Critical Studies in Media Communication, Journalism, Journalism Studies, Journalism Practice, New Media & Society, Journal of Communication Inquiry* and *Media, Culture & Society* among others. Carlson holds a PhD from the Annenberg School for Communication at the University of Pennsylvania.

Paul Connerton is the author of *The Tragedy of the Enlightenment: An Essay on the Frankfurt School* (1980), *How Societies Remember* (1989), *How Modernity Forgets* (2009) and *The Spirit of Mourning: History, Memory and the Body* (2011). He has been a Visiting Fellow at the Australian National University, Canberra, and a Simon Senior Research Fellow at the University of Manchester. He is currently Research Associate in the Department of Anthropology at the University of Cambridge, and Honorary Fellow in the Institute of Germanic and Romance Studies in the University of London.

Jill A. Edy is Associate Professor of Communication at the University of Oklahoma, USA. Her academic interests include collective memory, political communication, public opinion and journalism studies. She is the author of *Troubled Pasts: News and the Collective Memory of Social Unrest* (2006). Other recent publications include 'The Democratic Potential of Mediated Collective Memory,' in *On Media Memory* (Palgrave Macmillan, 2011) and (with Shawn Snidow) 'Making News Necessary: How Journalism Resists Alternative Media's Challenge,' *Journal of Communication*, 61(5) (2011), 816–34.

Robert Hariman is Professor of Rhetoric and Public Culture in the Department of Communication Studies at Northwestern University, USA. He is the author of *Political Style: The Artistry of Power* (1995) and *No Caption Needed: Iconic Photographs, Public Culture, and Liberal Democracy* (2007), which is co-authored with John Louis Lucaites. He has published three edited volumes and numerous book chapters and journal articles in several disciplines, and his work has been translated into French and Chinese. He and co-author John Lucaites post regularly at nocaptionneeded.com, their blog on photojournalism, politics and culture.

Andrew Hoskins is Interdisciplinary Research Professor in Global Security and Director of the Adam Smith Research Foundation, University of Glasgow, UK. His research focuses on the theoretical and empirical investigation of today's 'new media ecology' and the nature of/ challenges for security, and individual, social and cultural memory in this environment. He has an established record of leading externally funded empirical research into the shifting relations between media, war and terrorism, media and radicalization, and media and memory. He is founding editor-in-chief of *Memory Studies*, founding co-editor of *Media, War & Conflict*, co-editor of the Palgrave Macmillan book series *Memory Studies* and co-editor of the Routledge book series *Media, War & Security*.

He has given invited lectures and keynotes in 20 countries. His books include *War and Media: The Emergence of Diffused War* (2010, with Ben O'Loughlin) and *Radicalisation and Media: Connectivity and Terrorism in the New Media Ecology* (2011, with Awan and O'Loughlin).

Susana Kaiser teaches Media Studies and Latin American Studies at the University of San Francisco, USA. Her research focuses on communication, cultural/political memory and human rights. She has written about the communication strategies developed by the mothers, grandmothers, and children of the disappeared in Argentina, the construction and transmission of memories of political violence, and the role of film and popular music in writing memories of state terrorism. Her book *Postmemories of Terror: a New Generation Copes with the Legacy of the 'Dirty War'* (2005) explores young Argentineans' memories of the last dictatorship. Other publications include 'Memory Inventory: The Production and Consumption of Memory Goods in Argentina' (in *Accounting for Violence: Marketing Memory in Latin America*, 2011), 'Singing, Dancing and Remembering: The Links Between Music and Memory' (in *Inhabiting Memory: Essays on Memory and Human Rights in the Americas*, 2011) and 'The Struggle for Urban Territories: Human Rights Activists in Buenos Aires' (in *Ordinary Places/Extraordinary Events: Citizenship, Democracy, and Urban Space in Latin America*, 2008).

Carolyn Kitch is a Professor of Journalism at Temple University's School of Media and Communication, USA, where she is also a faculty member and the former director of the doctoral program in Media and Communication. Her research and teaching areas include media history, memory studies, magazines and women in journalism. She has published four books: *The Girl on the Magazine Cover: The Origins of Visual Stereotypes in American Mass Media* (2001), *Pages from the Past: History and Memory in American Magazines* (2005), *Journalism in a Culture of Grief*, co-authored with Janice Hume (2008) and *Pennsylvania in Public Memory: Reclaiming the Industrial Past* (2012). Additional scholarship has appeared in *Journalism & Mass Communication Quarterly, Journalism History, American Journalism, Journalism: Theory, Practice and Criticism, Journalism Studies*, the *Journal of Popular Culture, Critical Studies in Media Communication* and *Memory Studies*. Kitch is a former writer and editor for *Reader's Digest, Good Housekeeping* and *McCall's* magazines.

Carolyne Lee is a Senior Lecturer and Researcher in the Media and Communications program in the School of Culture and Communication at the University of Melbourne, Australia. Her research area is predominantly media language, and she has been published in academic journals in Australia, France, the UK, the USA and China. She is the editor or author of four books, the most recent of which is *Our Very Own Adventure: Towards a Poetics of the Short Story* (2011).

John Louis Lucaites is Associate Dean for Arts and Humanities and Professor of Rhetoric and Public Culture in the Department of Communication and Culture at Indiana University, USA. He is also an Adjunct Professor in American Studies. He is the co-author of *Crafting Equality: America's Anglo-African Word* (1993) with Celeste Condit and *No Caption Needed: Iconic Photographs, Public Culture, and Liberal Democracy* (2007) with Robert Hariman. He has published two co-edited volumes, as well as numerous journal articles and book chapters. He co-hosts the blog nocaptionneeded.com with Robert Hariman and is a contributing editor at the blog BAGnewsNotes.com.

Oren Meyers is a Senior Lecturer in the Department of Communication at the University of Haifa, Israel. His research interests focus on journalistic practices and values, collective memory and the security discourse in the Israeli media. Meyers is co-editor, with Motti Neiger and Eyal Zandberg, of *On Media Memory: Collective Memory in a New Media Age* (Palgrave Macmillan, 2011). His recent publications include 'Past Continuous: Newsworthiness and the Shaping of Collective Memory' (with Zandberg and Neiger, *Critical Studies in Media Communication*, 2012); 'Journalists in Israel' (with Yariv Tsfati, *The Global Journalist: News People around the World*, 2012) and 'Purity and Danger: Newsworthiness, Framing of Image Crises and the Kishon Diving Investigative Report' (with Asaf Rosen, *Media Frames: Israeli Journal of Communication*, 2013). He is currently working with Roei Davidson on an Israel Science Foundation sponsored research project looking at the professional life histories of Israeli journalists.

Motti Neiger is the Dean of the School of Communication, Netanya Academic College, Israel. His academic interests include media memory, popular culture and journalism during conflicts. Among his recent publications (together with Oren Meyers and Eyal Zandberg) are the edited volume *On Media Memory: Collective Memory in a New Media Age* (Palgrave Macmillan, 2011) and the articles 'Past Continuous: Newsworthiness and the Shaping of Collective Memory' (2012, *Critical Studies in Media Communication*), 'Tuned to the Nation's Mood: Popular Music as a Mnemonic Cultural Object' (*Media, Culture & Society*, 2011), 'Structuring the Sacred: Media Professionalism and the Production of Mediated Holocaust Memory' *Communication Review*, 2011), 'Communicating Critique: Towards a Conceptualization of Journalistic Criticism' (*Communication*,

Culture and Critique, 2010) and 'Prime Time Commemoration: An Analysis of Television Broadcasts on Israel's Memorial Day for the Holocaust and the Heroism' (*Journal of Communication,* 2009). He served as the president of the Israel Communication Association (2006–09) and as the founding editor of the Association's journal, *Media Frames: Israeli Journal of Communication.*

Jeffrey K. Olick is Professor of Sociology and History at the University of Virginia, USA. He is author of *In the House of the Hangman: The Agonies of German Defeat, 1943–1949* (2005) and *The Politics of Regret: On Collective Memory and Historical Responsibility* (2007), and most recently, editor of *The Collective Memory Reader* (2011) as well as editor and translator of two critical editions of Frankfurt School work on public opinion. His current work addresses the problem of theodicy in contemporary culture.

Anna Reading is Professor of Cultural and Creative Industries at Kings College, University of London, UK. She was Professor of Communication at the University of Western Sydney (2011–12), where she is now an Honorary Visiting Professor and member of the Institute for Culture and Society. She founded and was Head of the Centre for Media and Culture Research at London South Bank University, UK, 2009–11, and is an Honorary Visiting Professor in the Department of Social Sciences at the University of Loughborough and a Research Associate at the Centre for Cultural Policy Research, University of Glasgow. She is currently writing a book on how new media technologies are changing gendered memory through 'the globital memory field,' and co-editing a book on memories of nonviolent struggle. She is the author of *Polish Women, Solidarity and Feminism* (1992) and *The Social Inheritance of the Holocaust: Gender, Culture and Memory* (2002), researched *Communism, Capitalism and the Mass Media* (with Colin Sparks, 1998), and is a joint editor of *The Media in Britain* (1999) and *Save As...Digital Memory* (with Andrew Hoskins and Joanne Garde-Hansen, 2009). She is a joint editor of *Media, Culture & Society* and is on the boards of *Memory Studies,* the *Journal of Media Studies,* the *Philosophy of Photography* and the *Journal of Media Education Research.*

Michael Schudson is Professor of Communication at the Columbia Graduate School of Journalism, USA, and Adjunct Professor in the Department of Sociology. He was a founding member of the Department of Communication at the University of California, San Diego where he taught from 1981 to 2009. He is the author of seven books, co-editor of three books, and author of many articles and reviews in both professional and popular journals. His most recent books are *The Sociology of News* (2003), *Why Democracies Need an Unlovable Press* (2008), *The Good Citizen* (1998) and the co-edited *A History of the Book in America, volume 5: The Enduring Book* (2009). He is currently working on a book on the history of the emergence of 'transparency' as a cultural norm and social practice in the United States, focusing on the 1950s–1980s.

Barry Schwartz, Professor Emeritus of Sociology, University of Georgia, USA, is author of numerous articles and seven books, including *Abraham Lincoln and the Forge of National Memory*, which traces popular views of Lincoln from 1865 to the 1920s. His second volume, *Abraham Lincoln in the Post-Heroic Era: History and Memory in the Late Twentieth Century*, tracks Lincoln perceptions from the Depression decade to the turn of the twenty-first century. He is now working on *The Gettysburg Address in American Memory*, a book-length treatment of the original and changing meanings of Lincoln's famous eulogy, documented in part by national surveys. Schwartz's research on collective memory addresses many issues in many national cultures, including memories of shameful and exemplary events in the United States, Europe, the Middle East and Asia. His most recent book, with Mikyoung Kim, is *Northeast Asia's Difficult Past* (2010). Barry Schwartz's recent work also addresses the problem of Jesus in first-century Christian memory through the lens of twenty-first-century research and theory. These works develop common themes: the resistance of memory to distortion, the academy's emphasis on memory's imperfections, history's dependence on memory, the functions of forgetting, memory as a source of national unity and disunity, the tension between mnemonic continuity and social change, and the enduring need of individuals to find orientation and meaning for their lives by invoking, assessing, embracing, rejecting, revising and judging the past.

Keren Tenenboim-Weinblatt is Assistant Professor at the Department of Communication and Journalism, The Hebrew University of Jerusalem, Israel. Her research focuses on cultural and political dimensions of journalism from a comparative perspective, news temporalities, media and conflict, and the intersection of journalism, political communication and popular culture. Her award-winning work has appeared in *Communication Theory*, *Media, Culture & Society*, *Political Communication*, *Journalism*, *International Journal of Communication*, the *Communication Review*, and *Communication & Critical/Cultural Studies*, among others. Her most recent articles are: 'Bridging Collective Memories and Public Agendas: Toward a Theory of Mediated Prospective Memory' (*Communication Theory*, 2013) and

'The Path to Political Substance: Exploring the Mediated Discourse Surrounding Controversial Media Texts' (*Political Communication*, 2013).

Ingrid Volkmer is Associate Professor, Media and Communications Program, University of Melbourne, Australia. She has taken up visiting positions at the University of Vienna, the LSE, London, and the University of Amsterdam. She has published widely in the area of global political communication and implications on journalism, satellite cultures and generational 'world' perceptions. Volkmer has directed one of the first international studies on the construction of mediated memories in three generations, results are published in *News in Public Memory* (2006). Volkmer currently leads an international study on 'Global Youth & Media,' is the editor of the *Handbook of Global Media Research* (2012) and her book *The Global Public Sphere* is forthcoming.

Eyal Zandberg is a senior lecturer at the School of Communication, Netanya Academic College, Israel. His academic interests focus on the interrelationships between popular culture and collective memory and on journalism during conflicts. Recent publications (together with Motti Neiger and Oren Meyers) include the edited volume *On Media Memory: Collective Memory in a New Media Age* (2011) and the articles 'Past Continuous: Newsworthiness and the Shaping of Collective Memory' (*Critical Studies in Media Communication*, 2012), 'Tuned to the Nation's Mood: Popular Music as a Mnemonic Cultural Object' (*Media, Culture & Society*, 2011), 'Structuring the Sacred: Media Professionalism and the Production of Mediated Holocaust Memory' (*Communication Review*, 2011), 'Communicating Critique: Towards a Conceptualization of Journalistic Criticism' (*Communication, Culture and Critique*, 2010) and 'Prime Time Commemoration: An Analysis of Television Broadcasts on Israel's Memorial Day for the Holocaust and the Heroism' (*Journal of Communication*, 2009).

Barbie Zelizer is the Raymond Williams Professor of Communication and Director of the Scholars Program in Culture and Communication at the University of Pennsylvania's Annenberg School for Communication, USA. A former journalist, Zelizer is known for her work in the area of journalism, culture, memory and images, particularly in times of crisis. She has authored or edited thirteen books, including the award-winning *About To Die: How News Images Move the Public* (2010) and *Remembering to Forget: Holocaust Memory Through the Camera's Eye* (1998), and over ninety articles, book chapters and essays. Recipient of a Guggenheim Fellowship, a Freedom Forum Center Research Fellowship, a Fellowship from Harvard

University's Joan Shorenstein Center on the Press, Politics, and Public Policy, and a Fellowship from Stanford University's Center for Advanced Study in the Behavioral Sciences, Zelizer is a fellow of the International Communication Association and a Distinguished Scholar of the National Communication Association. She is also a media critic, whose work has appeared in *The Nation*, the *Jim Lehrer News Hour*, *Newsday*, the *Huffington Post* and other media organs. Co-editor of *Journalism: Theory, Practice and Criticism*, her work has been translated into French, Spanish, Hebrew, Portuguese, Italian, Romanian, Chinese and Korean. She is a past president of the International Communication Association.

Journalism's Memory Work

Barbie Zelizer and Keren Tenenboim-Weinblatt

Since Marcel Proust first noted that the remembrance of things past is not necessarily the remembrance of things as they were, the question of how memories form has produced multiple answers. So too with the positioning of the platforms by which memory takes shape. Though the recognition of collective memory clearly implicates some notion of institutional presence, which institutions are central has never been clear. And though one of the most productive take-away points of collective memory studies is that institutions with no direct connection to memory in their remit are engaging in memory work all the time, journalism is nowhere in these discussions.

This book aims to remedy that neglect, by tracking the ways in which journalism and shared memory mutually support, undermine, repair and challenge each other. How is journalism's address to memory different from that of other institutions, such as education, politics or the legal system? How does it resemble other institutional engagements with memory? Bringing together journalism scholars who have charted journalism's memory work and memory scholars who have investigated the broad trappings of collective memory, *Journalism and Memory* makes explicit the longstanding and complicated role that journalism has played in keeping the past alive. From anniversary issues and media retrospectives to simple verbal and visual analogies connecting past and present, journalism incorporates an address to earlier times across the wide array of its conventions and practices. How it does so and what this suggests about our understanding of collective memory constitute the charter of this volume.

Ever since memory studies coalesced as a recognizable field of inquiry, its reliance on a wide array of institutional settings has been an implicit part of understanding how collective memory works. Journalism's relative absence from those settings, however, has left journalism's status as a primary recorder of a shared past both unsettled and unarticulated. Though the very surfacing of collective memory depends often on a wide range of institutional engagements, more so today than perhaps ever before, the neglect surrounding journalism's role in the establishment and legitimation of shared memory leaves a curious hole in our understanding of memory's trappings.

Journalism has not made it easy to consider its forays into the past. Long touted as the first draft of history, journalism has typically exhibited a reticence to move beyond the topical, novel, instantaneous and timely. Undergirding the sense of self by which journalism has kept itself distinct, the play to the temporally proximate has remained journalism's defining attribute. But in an era of increasingly blended performative domains, of recycled narratives, pictures and impulses that are no longer identifiably tethered to one point in time, of information that seems to come from nowhere, a recognition that journalism regularly and systematically looks backward is long overdue. It is important not only for understanding the complex temporal nuances by which the news works but for understanding journalism's central role as a primary repository of collective memory in every society in which it finds itself.

In large part, the kinds of ellipses reflected in journalism's understated placement in memory studies can be found in nearly all instances of knowledge acquisition. As Thomas Kuhn (1964) argued long ago, what we know has a social life that privileges certain ways of knowing. Inquiry depends on consensus building and on developing the kinds of shared paradigms that name and characterize problems and procedures in ways that are recognized by the collective. As individuals battle over definitions, terms of reference and boundaries of inclusion and exclusion on the way to achieving consensus, they classify what emerges along already proven lines. In other words, what we think has a predetermined shape and life-line, one that privileges community, solidarity, and power.

This has clear implications for the centrality, or lack thereof, of journalism in collective memory studies. Once scholarship started to amass and journalism was nowhere inside it, it became more difficult to find a place to include journalism down the line. And yet, the lack of consonance between how we think memory works without journalism and the evidence by which journalism engages in shaping our version of the past is troubling. It exposes a significant hole in our understanding of how enmeshed journalism and memory are, particularly in the contemporary moment.

On trajectories and domains

Relevant to the processes by which collective memory studies have evolved are the broader processes of knowledge acquisition. And perhaps there are no aspects more central to our acquisition of knowledge than the temporal and spatial dimensions by which knowledge unfolds. Though time and space have been applied to understanding phenomena as diverse as global markets, agricultural models and language systems, their relevance to knowledge systems and the ways in which we acquire knowledge have been less documented.

This is curious, for the twinning of space and time is not new. Long central to work in anthropology on primitive cultures, to Einstein's theory of special relativity and to notions of time-space in physics, it has more recently been implied across the curriculum, specifically in the work of Giddens (1981), Harvey (1990) and Virilio (2000); and this evolving recognition that time and space are necessarily related – though not always in parallel ways – suggests that unpacking the stuff of knowledge as it organizes along temporal and spatial lines might be a worthwhile exercise.

As a type of knowledge, memory is no exception to these circumstances. Two constructs – trajectories and domains – are relevant to understanding how ideas about memory, and the practices that accompany them, have unfolded, and both have clear temporal and spatial biases. Though not mutually exclusive and separated here more for heuristic value than because they tell us something about the memories that result, they nonetheless serve to elucidate what has been obscured in the relationship between memory and journalism.

Trajectories, which signal the temporal aspects of memory, are defined as the paths of a projectile or moving body through space – in other words, time defined spatially. By contrast, domains, which signal the spatial aspects of memory, are defined as fields of action, thought or influence as they have evolved into some kind of recognizable form – in other words, space defined temporally. While trajectories offer a chronological unfolding of activity between two or more points in time, domains drive a focus on the concentration of efforts in a coherent plane of activity at one point in time. Taken together, they highlight what is most relevant about the acquisition of knowledge – that it evolves in some kind of recognizable fashion across time and that its particulars offer sufficient detail at one point in time. Temporal and spatial complexity, then, complement each other.

In this scenario, the study of memory might thus be approached through a disciplined set of procedures that reflect the temporal and spatial dimensions necessary for its establishment, legitimation and maintenance. *Journalism and Memory* reflects the logic of these two aspects of memory's unfolding. It first traces the trajectories of memory by which journalism has figured in uneven ways and then addresses a select set of domains of memory, by which mnemonic work takes on a particular shape within journalism.

Trajectories of memory

The questions of where memory comes from and how we know have been interrelated for longer than tends to be readily admitted. It is thus no surprise that the uneasy alliances through which memory and journalism have been set in place over time reveal varying and often illogical configurations regarding what they tell us about memory and what they suggest about its source environments.

The received trajectory about how collective memory surfaced as a concept tells the story of shared memory emerging in response to the inadequacies of the notion of individualized recall as a tool. Though it is difficult to generate agreement about this trajectory's particulars, it is clear that collective memory is presumed to have emerged from a perfect storm of circumstances – dissatisfaction with how individualized recall connected with complicated pasts, the changing nature of the historical record, burgeoning questions about interpretive authority, complicated events that forced a tentativeness onto the memories that engaged with them. Significantly, as the study of memory moved from individual to collective dimensions, institutions became increasingly relevant as a primary source environment for memory work. And as the polity, the market, education and religion began to figure in the transformation from individual to collective remembering, journalism was not part of that repository of knowledge that resulted.

Four vantage points in this book tackle the ways in which journalism and memory have connected in existing trajectories of memory; each of them considers what has been gained and lost in the evolving alliances between journalism and memory that ensued. In Chapter 1, 'Reflections on the Underdeveloped Relations between Journalism and Memory Studies,' Jeffrey Olick reflects on the barriers and biases that have inhibited analysis of the connections between journalism and memory. Part of the problem, he argues, resides in the respective scholarships – journalism studies and memory studies – and part resides in the ways in which journalism and memory entail each other. Olick first explores these disciplinary blinders and their origins, outlines aspects of journalism's memory work and addresses memory's dependence on journalism. Maintaining that the practice of journalism involves both individual and social memory, he considers how it also constitutes an archive of social memory that provides an immediate record, is implicated in forms of commemoration, and acts as a site of memory itself.

In Chapter 2, Barbie Zelizer tracks the chronology of journalism's placement in ideas about memory from early conceptualizations of mnemonic work up to the present day. In 'Memory as Foreground, Journalism as Background,' she reminds us that though memory studies has long argued for the importance of a wide variety of institutional settings engaging in memory work, journalism has not typically been one of them. But evidence suggests that early work on collective memory always attended to journalism, even if its reliance was not articulated as such. Zelizer revisits four main stages of thinking about memory in which central notions of memory implicated journalism's presence to varying degrees. Showing how central the journalistic record was to the evolution of the field of memory studies, she asks whether collective memory could exist without some journalistic function and maintains that it could not. In so doing, she considers how the backgrounds of academic inquiry impact the shape of what we think we know.

Ingrid Volkmer and Carolyne Lee orient the discussion of memory's trajectories toward the global landscape. In Chapter 3, 'Shifting the Politics of Memory: Mnemonic Trajectories in a Global Public Terrain,' they show that despite the fact that journalism in today's networked contexts has a transnational reach, memory studies mainly focus on the national model of journalism practice. Based on qualitative interviews with international students in Australia, Volkmer and Lee identify a new memory space situated across multiple public spheres. That space, they contend, is not only of relevance for identifying cosmopolitan civic identity but also for national journalism in a globalized context. In particular, it requires new forms of journalistic practice, which can open up the narrowly defined frameworks of public memory to a wider range of narratives and communicative modes.

In 'Collective Memory in a Post-Broadcast World' (Chapter 4), Jill Edy demonstrates how the current transformation of journalism has important implications for the ways in which societies remember. While the mass media era made plausible the idea that journalism could create a shared public understanding of the social world and was therefore instrumental in creating shared public memory, today's media environment suggests otherwise. Selective exposure to media content and particularly news content, she claims, produces a public with less common ground than it had in the broadcast era and brings into question previous assumptions about mediated collective memory. Edy maintains that what has been particularly troubling is the continued resonance of outdated concepts like 'dominant' and 'alternative' memory and the potential emergence of memory silos, in which groups of people within a social system share a collective memory exclusive to them, unaware that this memory is atypical or even unknown beyond the boundaries of their group. Such silos, Edy offers, likely strain community decision-making processes.

Each of these four views troubles and complicates the received trajectory of memory's connection with journalism. Taken together, they show not only the multifaceted, uneven and at times disputed nature of this connection over time but also map out the terrain for future trajectories in the study of journalism and memory.

Domains of memory

Despite the uneasiness of journalism's incorporation within ideas about memory, there is ample evidence of memory work unfolding within a wide array of journalistic settings. Existing work on memory has long foregrounded the domains through which versions of the past are shaped, disseminated and maintained, and this book focuses on three such domains. Though not the only aspects of journalism in which memory surfaces, they reflect three aspects of the news – narrative, visual and institutional parameters – that are both reflective of journalism itself and central to distinguishing journalism from other kinds of mnemonic settings. Narrative and visual memory each incorporates the conflicting impulses of journalism – the referential versus the symbolic, information versus ritual. Together – at times consonant and at times dissonant with one another – they constitute the primary discursive domains for the construction of memory in journalism. The institutional domain connects journalism's verbal and visual memory work to the unique and contingent values, histories and authority of journalism as a social institution.

Journalism and narrative memory

The centrality of narrative – the verbal record by which events both past and present become known – has always been a distinguishing feature of the news apparatus. Similarly, ever since the inception of collective memory as a concept, narrative has been viewed as one of the major devices in its social construction. We can thus expect that storytelling would constitute an important link between journalism and memory. Given the inherent temporality of social narratives, it is also not surprising that cultural critic Douglas Rushkoff recently identified 'the collapse of narrative' as one of the first casualties of what he sees as a social reorientation to the present in the twenty-first century (Rushkoff, 2013: 7). The three chapters in this section challenge this observation, while disentangling the intricate relationship between journalism, narrative and memory. Focusing on the diverse uses of memory in the creation and management of news narratives, as well as the application of journalistic storytelling devices in the construction of collective memories, they expand and systematize the conceptualization of narrative memory in journalism. In so doing, they also demonstrate the sustained presence of temporal narrative in public discourse, with journalism constituting a central site for the social construction of narratives that span from past to future through the nexus of the present.

In Chapter 5, 'Journalism as a Vehicle of Non-Commemorative Cultural Memory,' Michael Schudson discusses what it means to say that journalism is our most widely distributed and easily accessible storehouse of memory. Scholars have long noted the role of news in commemorating persons and events, but its role as an agent of 'non-commemorative memory' may be even more important. With examples drawn from the *New York Times*, Schudson argues that journalists make news a mechanism for non-commemorative memory in three ways – by referencing the past to show the rarity or uniqueness of an occurrence to justify front-page prominence, by using the past as a context to help explain a news event, and by showing how people act in ways that incorporate a sense of past or future, of aging or of impending death. In all these ways journalism makes itself a vehicle of cultural memory without aiming to commemorate.

Keren Tenenboim-Weinblatt extends the discussion of narrativity toward an explicit engagement with the temporal domain. In Chapter 6, 'Counting Time: Journalism and the Temporal Resource,' she suggests that while we tend to think of time as a factor which shapes and constrains journalistic practices, time also serves as a rich discursive resource for managing news stories. Drawing on a study of the media coverage of stories of kidnapping and captivity around the world and focusing in particular on the mnemonic practice of counting time in the news, she discusses the multilayered functioning of time as a discursive and narrative resource for journalists. She argues that such temporal practices allow journalists to both sustain continuous stories in the news and discursively enact a rich array of mnemonic roles, associated with both retrospective and prospective remembrance. Within this framework, Tenenboim-Weinblatt suggests that the challenge facing journalism may not be how to overcome its temporal inferiority in relation to new media actors but how to claim time as a resource for creation and re-imagination.

Motti Neiger, Eyal Zandberg and Oren Meyers address the intersection of commemoration and narrativity. In Chapter 7, 'Reversed Memory: Commemorating the Past through Coverage of the Present,' they show how temporality works in the reverse direction of present to past: new details or developments regarding significant past occurrences become the main focus of the news narrative, while the historical details of these past occurrences are pushed to the background. Naming this narratological device 'reversed memory,' they discuss how the past is commemorated by means of narration of the present and reversed memory enables the creation of narratives that qualify both as news items and commemorative tools. Drawing on an analysis of Israeli media coverage of the Remembrance Day for the Holocaust and the Heroism across the past decade, they offer a typology of reversed memory components. These narrative practices, they contend, are most pronounced at the intersection of national commemorative rituals and everyday news production and dissemination.

Journalism and visual memory

Some notion of visuality has long been a central part of journalism's workings, even if it has been largely absent from its rhetoric. It is precisely this absence, combined with the mnemonic power of images, which has made visual memory a particularly useful starting point in scholarly explorations of journalism's memory work. Digital culture, marked by a profusion of visual technologies of memory and visual archives, has further challenged longstanding assumptions about visuality in journalism, while raising new questions on journalistic authority and values. This section offers four perspectives on visual memory within journalism. Ranging across diverse visual practices and different types of interactions between journalists and other agents of visual memory, the four chapters in this section complicate our understanding of journalistic practice and journalism's unique contribution to public culture in a changing media landscape.

In Chapter 8, 'Hands and Feet: Photojournalism, the Fragmented Body Politic, and Collective Memory,' Robert Hariman and John Louis Lucaites demonstrate how photographs featuring only hands or feet productively offset the idea that images provide fragments of the past that are incidental or harmful to the narrative continuity of collective memory. Arguing that the isolated body part can fulfill an elocutionary function by creating gestures that communicate emotions and provide an iconography for democratic speech, Hariman and Lucaites contend that such gestures articulate a vision of the body politic and its implication as a trope of political imagination and memory. Because the body is shown in ways that are increasingly fragmented and heterogeneous, its representation lends a vitality and representativeness toward what it signifies. They argue that by accepting the incompleteness, plurality and pathos of collective memory, one can reconsider the relationships between image, narrative, fragmentation and community.

In Chapter 9, Kari Andén-Papadopoulos takes the discussion of visual memory toward contemporary videography. In 'Journalism, Memory and the "Crowd-Sourced Video Revolution,"' she considers how journalistic memory work changes the so-called 'new memory ecology.' As smartphone-carrying citizens increasingly replace professional journalists as eyewitnesses to breaking news, they produce images that linger as historical markers of disruptive events. Analyzing the mobile footage of the killing of Neda Agha Soltan, Andén-Papadopoulos traces a shift in the representation of authenticity in crowd-sourced images of news events, recasting professional crisis reporting as a political, affective space that exceeds normative renderings of impartiality and detachment. As news organizations become more reliant on citizen eyewitness images that claim partiality and subjectivity as the route to 'truthfulness,' so too might a different kind of journalism emerge that is more audience-centered and cognizant of the limitations of objectivity and impartiality. While crowd-sourced footage now endows the news with a new moralizing potential, professional journalists add value to crowd-sourced content, giving it global visibility and significance and mitigating the issues of reliability, accuracy, verifiability, security and dignity that are raised in the new circulatory memory-scape.

In Chapter 10, 'The Journalist as Memory Assembler: Non-Memory, the War on Terror and the Shooting of Osama Bin Laden,' Anna Reading deconstructs the news of the shooting of Al Qaeda leader Osama Bin Laden in May 2011 by US security services, as it was first broken via Twitter. Showing how Twitter feeds coincided with the simultaneous withholding of video and photographs by US authorities, with no images of the shooting or the dead body released to news sources or shown to the general public, Reading demonstrates how journalists and non-journalists reassembled and reworked available information to fill the void, focusing on an image entitled 'The Situation Room.' She argues that this example – of journalism and 'non-memory' – shows how journalistic practice can be understood as a process of assemblage within 'a globital memory field.' It embodies the ways in which the professional work of the journalist now intersects with that of non-journalists as they 'assemble' and 'reassemble' witnesses to the story, even in the absence or withholding of digital witness images.

Andrew Hoskins, in Chapter 11, 'A New Memory of War,' orients the discussion of visual memory to war journalism. Following the increased pervasiveness and accessibility of digital technologies, devices and media in a 'post-scarcity culture,' he asks which conditions now shape a journalistic vision of warfare. He identifies two incompatible memorial trajectories – a diffusion of memory, by which everything is connected, remediated and networked in a journalism liberated from its profession, and maintenance of traditions in which the continuity of the past is constantly referenced and re-referenced. This coupling of Big Media's projection of twentieth-century warfare with the more recent depictions of catastrophes and conflicts together generate a 'new memory' of warfare. Hoskins argues that the media are engaged in a complex meshing of forces, where some memory technologies appear to bring audiences closer to the frontline (helmet cams and online archives), while some warfare technologies appear to move military action out of journalistic reach (drones and computer viruses). Under these conditions, Hoskins asks, what will endure of the memory of both warfare and journalism?

Journalism and institutional memory

The notion of institutional memory permeates the contemporary imagination. In an episode of popular NBC television series *The West Wing* titled 'Institutional Memory,' the newly elected president offers one of the series regulars the opportunity to continue serving in the new administration, because, in the president's view, 'institutional memory is an invaluable commodity.' No surprise, then, that in the end, considerations of journalism invariably rest in part on its institutional presence and that not unlike new fictional administrations, journalists draw on institutional memory to meet the challenges of the time. The four chapters in this section demonstrate how institutional memory is strategically mobilized by journalists across time and place, and how changing institutional parameters of journalism are shaping memories of key historical events.

In Chapter 12, Matt Carlson and Dan Berkowitz discuss the commemorative lore that helps shape the institutional culture of journalism. In 'The Late News: Memory Work as Boundary Work in the

Commemoration of Television Journalists,' they examine how the US television news community uses the memory of deceased journalists to construct symbolic boundaries delineating acceptable forms of practice. Surveying news coverage surrounding the deaths of several television journalists, including Walter Cronkite, Edward R. Murrow, David Brinkley, Peter Jennings and Mike Wallace, they show how in this professional moment mediated remembrances turn from the external world to gaze inward, anchoring current practice firmly in place and legitimating a boundary shift for future practice. In essence, this rite shores up cultural authority in the face of a tumultuous present and an uncertain future; by doing so, memory work becomes boundary work.

Barry Schwartz transports the discussion of institutional memory to early American journalism. In Chapter 13, 'American Journalism's Conventions and Cultures, 1863–2013: Changing Representations of the Gettysburg Address,' he recounts how most American newspapers in April 1863 ignored or made no comment on the Gettysburg Address, and how the few journalists who responded split along party lines. Yet, he argues, as an interpretive framework, Lincoln's speech had to be drastically reworked before issues involving racial integration could be keyed to it. Schwartz shows that not until the twentieth century did the Gettysburg Address come to occupy a prominent place among American political symbols, when a new journalism conveyed to the public a new perspective on history: Lincoln at Gettysburg had declared the war's purpose to be racial equality. Showing how this interpretation was linked to the emergence of an adversary culture – left-leaning, cynical of established authority, and committed to the well-being of minorities – Schwartz argues that a new Gettysburg Address, a new journalistic culture and a new history emerged simultaneously, in which Lincoln's words were deployed to gauge the meaning of strife over racial equality.

Carolyn Kitch, in Chapter 14, 'Historical Authority and the "Potent Journalistic Reputation": A Longer View of Legacy-Making in American News Media,' offers a similarly long view of the strategic uses of memory by news media, surveying two centuries of legacy American journalism. Tracing the uses of memory in media across an initial pursuit of cultural and commercial prominence, a period of influence and dominance and a contemporary struggle for relevance and survival, she argues that the success of news organizations has always rested in part on their ability to stake a claim to 'history.' In the nineteenth century, newspapers and magazines made frequent references to both the future and the past, describing 'American history' as they worked to establish brand-name recognition during a race for mass-circulation audiences. The twentieth century saw the rise and dominance of the mainstream news media, whose authority and influence were symbolized by iconic reporters and broadcasters. In today's beleaguered environment, those same 'legacy' institutions turn to summary journalism and reminiscence about their own great pasts; in the meantime, the newest forms of journalism now stake their own claims to public memory and historic importance.

Susana Kaiser turns the discussion of institutional memory in journalism toward the global South, where three decades after an Argentine dictatorship (1976–83) in which 30,000 people disappeared, hundreds of torturers and assassins are now on trial. In 'Argentinean Torturers on Trial: How Are Journalists Covering the Hearings' Memory Work?' (Chapter 15) she addresses the way in which the trials are taking shape within a dynamic process of memory construction. Using three sets of data – ethnographic observation of the hearings, assessment of newspaper coverage and interviews with journalists – Kaiser sees the trials as public spaces for the ongoing writing of memory, arenas for memory battles and forums where new knowledge about state terrorism continually emerges. Asking what memory work takes place at the hearings and how journalists use the raw material of memory, she examines the role of journalists as professional witnesses and memory agents and what their coverage of events reveals about the relationship(s) between journalism and memories of state terrorism.

On making journalism matter in memory studies

In bringing journalism to the forefront of collective memory studies, this book reveals the significance of journalism as an agent of memory and a repository of shared memory across time and space. It also sheds light on the ways in which shifting the gaze to journalism can facilitate the development of broader conceptual and theoretical frameworks in memory studies. Acting in the fashion of a transparency slide newly affixed to a longstanding – and previously familiar – set of visual data, these ruminations about journalism and memory complicate existing conversations in many ways. Not only do they offer new variables through which to think about memory, but they also suggest a retooling of some of memory studies' most steadfast components.

First, *how* journalism works suggests that memory may at times operate differently from the templates supported by memory studies. Journalism's unique location vis-à-vis the social nexus of time and the link between its memory work and its social role as a primary teller of current events help expose conceptual territories that may be less visible, though not insignificant, in the workings of other agents of collective memory. Among the examples discussed in this book are the practices of non-commemorative memory, prospective memory and reversed memory, each of which underscores alternative configurations of past and present that can illuminate the operation of memory across a wide swathe of institutional settings.

Second, *why* journalism works introduces new perspectives into the repository of knowledge about memory. Focusing on journalism – the strengths, weaknesses and contradictions inherent in its practices, values and aspirations – usefully refracts longstanding questions that have not been adequately resolved by existing scholarship in memory studies. These range from questions about the practices and processes of mobilizing, structuring and reproducing collective memories – as they take shape, for instance, across narrative and visual domains of practice – to the discursive modes, social interactions and cultural conditions that shape them in complex institutional settings. As shown in this book, examining these issues through the prism of journalism can substantially contribute to their development and refinement by taking into account contemporary temporal and spatial conditions. This reminds us that the margins of study often contain powerful impulses that can and should tweak its centers; otherwise, scholarship ossifies.

Third, *where* journalism works complicates what can be expected of memory. Though *Journalism and Memory* began with the supposition that memory studies has not taken sufficient account of mnemonic practices in journalism, these chapters show how energetically such practices vary in journalistic settings around the globe. The scholars gathered here – from the US, the UK, Sweden, Argentina, Israel and Australia – give diverse answers to the question of how journalism matters for memory studies and, vice versa, how memory studies matter to journalism, across different geographic and cultural contexts. From terror trials in the global South to Holocaust remembrance in the Middle East, all have attempted to clarify a temporal relationship whose spatial parameters have been insufficiently addressed in scholarship despite decades of engagement on the ground.

Fourth, *what we know* about journalism raises important questions about how we evaluate what we think we know about memory. The exercise at the heart of this volume raises questions that go beyond journalism's relevance to collective memory studies. Memory has been employed here as a gateway for addressing questions regarding the production of academic knowledge and the position of journalism in relation to other media players. How do we best differentiate between the study of journalism and memory and the study of media and memory? Is journalism, at best, one among a plethora of media institutions that mediate and generate memories, and, at worst, a dying institution of minor relevance to the production of memory? Or, as this book suggests, does journalism constitute a separate domain of inquiry, whose potential contribution to understanding is above and beyond the mediation processes it shares with other media actors?

What, then, ultimately is it about journalism that changes our understanding of the nexus between journalism and memory? Journalism's internal complexity, its symbiotic relationship with other institutions, its sense of service to the public, its necessary presence at the key events and issues that shape history – all of these help mold journalism in service to memory. But memory services journalism as well, through its fundamental malleability, its community building capacities, its visual and narrative resources, and its signaling and legitimation of specific events and institutions in the collective imagination. It is the singular attributes of that relationship, as they unfold at the intersections of temporal and spatial axes, that this book has tried to draw out. How can the study of memory be enriched through journalism's presence? And how would our understanding of journalism fall short without paying attention to memory? On its way to making journalism matter in memory studies, this book offers a start to addressing those questions.

References

Giddens, Anthony (1981) *A Contemporary Critique of Historical Materialism: Power, Property and the State*. London: Macmillan.

Harvey, David (1990) *The Condition of Postmodernity*. Cambridge, MA: Blackwell.

Kuhn, Thomas (1964) *The Structure of Scientific Revolutions*. Chicago: University of Chicago Press.

Rushkoff, Douglas (2013) *Present Shock: When Everything Happens Now*. New York: Penguin Group.

Virilio, Paul (2000) *Polar Inertia*, trans. P. Camiller. London: Sage.

Part I
Trajectories of Journalism and Memory

1

Reflections on the Underdeveloped Relations between Journalism and Memory Studies

Jeffrey K. Olick

In the 2008 inaugural issue of the journal *Memory Studies*, Barbie Zelizer claimed that 'memory's work on journalism does not reflect journalism's work on memory.' Her charge to colleagues was clear: 'As journalism continues to function as one of contemporary society's main institutions of recording and remembering, we need to invest more efforts in understanding how it remembers and why it remembers and why it remembers in the ways that it does.' In the pages that follow, I take up this charge, albeit in a rather schematic fashion: for as a memory scholar and historian of memory studies (Olick and Robbins, 1998; Olick, Vinitzky-Seroussi and Levy, 2011), I am one of the guilty who has not given journalism its due.

Preliminary issues

To begin, it is important to engage in some definitional clarification. Zelizer's essay, for instance, can be read as addressing at least two analytically distinct, though empirically related, issues: on the one hand, memory's work on journalism and journalism's work on memory, and on the other hand, memory *scholarship's* attention to journalism and journalism *scholarship's* attention to memory.

In the first case, journalists can be said to be interested in memory in a variety of ways. For instance, journalists cover memory science and memory politics, as well as commemorative events (for example, political anniversaries). Not only does journalism *cover* commemorations, it also celebrates them, for instance by publishing special issues of newspapers on anniversary occasions. It also has its *own* commemorations, for instance celebrating *journalistic* anniversaries, such as the twentieth year of a news show, or acknowledging the role of founding journalistic fathers, like Edward R. Murrow. In the second place, cultural and collective memory is not only shaped *by* journalism, but includes memories *of* journalism: as a society, we remember important broadcasts, iconic broadcasters, and even the media themselves (such as the look of a major newspaper's front page or the theme music of an evening news broadcast); collective or cultural memory includes journalism and journalistic events, as well as being shaped by journalism. Journalism and memory are clearly implicated in each other.

The question of the relationship between memory and journalism, however, is distinct from the issue of blind spots in their respective scholarships. On the one hand, there are excellent examples of both kinds of scholarship that have taken up the connection: journalism scholars have investigated the relationship between memory and journalism (for example, Zelizer, 1992; Kitch, 2005; Edy, 2006). Memory studies, too, has occasionally explored journalism as either a source or a site of memory (for example, Olick, 2005), though often it has done so under the broader rubric of media. On the other hand, it is also true that 'no main theorists of the field of collective memory included "news making" as an important component in their work that explored the field' (Neiger, Meyers and Zandberg, 2011: 7). Obviously, this has been consequential for the course of memory studies in its development as a field (see Olick et al., 2011).

Indeed, while memory and journalism as endeavors and practices focus on, as well as ignore, each other implicitly and explicitly in a variety of ways, it is the task of memory scholarship and journalism scholarship to catalogue and theorize these relations. By the same token, not only must we specify 'how [journalism]… remembers and why it remembers and why it remembers in the ways that it does.' We need also to explain the *scholarly* attention and inattention across the link. And the ways in which memory scholarship and journalism scholarship engage with or ignore each other and their objects (memory and journalism) are the consequence of historical and institutional factors that may or may not have to do with the primary relation between memory and journalism as practices.

A second preliminary issue emerges from the foregoing, namely the subsumption of journalism under the more general topic of media. For instance, had Zelizer replaced the term journalism with the term media – as in 'Why Memory's work on *Media* Does Not Reflect *Media's* work on Memory' – her argument would have been less convincing, though to be sure not entirely without merit. For, as Astrid Erll (2011: 113–14) has put it in her introductory survey of the field of memory studies,

'Cultural memory is unthinkable without media.' As a result, Erll continues, 'it is no surprise that cultural memory research is often simultaneously media research.' Indeed, the literature on media memory, media and memory, and media of memory is by now quite extensive. But it is unclear in what ways, to what extent, and for what reasons this scholarship has left *journalism* behind.

Often, for instance, media studies is preoccupied with so-called 'new media,' rather than the supposedly boring old media usually implied by the term journalism. Something could be said about journalism that is analogous to what Pierre Nora (1989) said about memory: namely, that 'we speak so much about memory because there is so little of it left': perhaps we speak so much about *journalism* because there is so little of *it* left. Of course, as just noted, we do not in fact speak as much about journalism when we are speaking about media today as we speak about other matters, so the equation does not quite work. Furthermore, Nora's statement about memory is itself debatable: is there really so little memory left, or have its forms and functions merely changed? If the answer is more the latter than the former, the same could be said about journalism: it is not that journalism is no longer an important medium or that the importance of journalism has diminished in an age of 'new' media; rather, it is that the forms and functions of journalism have changed within this new media environment. So too have the relations between journalism and memory changed, and in even more complex ways, since, as Nora's work makes clear, memory itself has clearly changed as well.

The foregoing leads directly to a third preliminary issue, namely that memory and journalism (to say nothing of media) share the quality of being imprecise and over-generalized categories. Journalism took its name from its traditional function, the recording of the events of the day as they happened – mostly in the form of the daily newspaper, itself often titled the such-and-such *journal*. With the advent and spread of broadcast media, however, the term expanded to include other forms of reporting on 'news,' though the spread did not fail to generate professional rivalries (Schudson, 1981; Starr, 2005). Such professional rivalries, moreover, are key to locating journalism as a practice and profession in the new media environment, when access to restricted means of dissemination (for example, printing presses or television stations) is no longer a defining characteristic of 'reporting' and 'commentary.' The bottom line is that 'journalism' is hardly an operational concept for social science, just as it is a porous and multivalent identifier for varieties of forms and practices, many of them novel.

Something similar, of course, must be said about memory. Already in this chapter, I have referred to memory, collective memory and cultural memory. These terms in turn refer to a wide variety of mnemonic products, practices and processes, including commemoration, recall and testimony, among others. Even with the lay and sometimes scientific term 'memory,' there are a huge number of different references, and psychologists routinely distinguish between semantic memory, episodic memory, procedural memory and others. The point is that any analysis of the relations of memory and journalism, and of memory scholarship and journalism scholarship, requires a great deal of care and a large number of caveats; which is not to say that nothing of a general order can or should be said about the issues. Both terms, I believe, retain probative value despite their multiplicity of possible referents. But we must be careful not to ignore that multiplicity.

Why memory studies has not paid sufficient attention to journalism

As I am not a journalism scholar, I have comparatively little to offer on the place of memory in journalism scholarship. Nevertheless, a few speculative comments may be permissible. First, while memory studies as a field has indeed grown exponentially since the early 1980s and has attracted attention from scholars from a wide variety of disciplinary backgrounds (Olick and Robbins, 1998), with perhaps the one exception of experimental psychology, it has remained a special interest within these disciplines. In journalism scholarship too, memory studies is a special interest. Therefore, we should not assume without further investigation that there is something special or extreme about journalism scholarship's purported neglect or marginalization of memory. Second, journalism scholarship has many important concerns that are not specifically addressed in or as memory, namely public discourse and deliberation, free speech, ideology and so on (though of course memory is not irrelevant to these topics). Journalism scholarship's neglect of memory may thus be unfortunate, but it is hardly fatal. Finally (though this by no means exhausts the issue), journalism scholarship is concerned with professional practice in a way that memory studies is not (though to be sure memory studies is relevant to politicians, archivists, public historians, museologists and preservationists, among others). The identities of professions depend at least as much on their distinction from other professional practices as they do on their relevance for them. The cliché may run that journalism is the first draft of history, but historians are very clearly invested in the claim that they are *not* journalists, and journalists are at least somewhat careful about this distinction and usually recognize what it entails. Journalism *scholarship*, in turn, is distinct from – which is not the same thing as uninterested in – *historiography*, just as writing journalism is distinct from writing history, however much they may be confused in popular contexts.

What, then, may be said from the other direction, namely about the neglect of journalism and of journalism scholarship in memory studies? As I already showed, Zelizer pointed out the absence of discussions of journalism in the seminal theoretical works in memory studies. But beyond what Zelizer claims about Maurice Halbwachs and others, not one chapter of Pierre Nora's massive seven volume encyclopedia (Nora, 1984–1992) *Les lieux de memoire* – surely next to the seminal texts of Halbwachs the single most significant 'lieux de memoire' of memory studies itself – identified journalism as a whole, or any particular newspaper, magazine, or broadcast, as a major 'lieu de memoire' in France. And the number of works in memory studies addressing journalism – rather than media more generally – is relatively low given journalism's importance to memory.

To begin, however, I would like to walk back this empirical assertion just one notch. One of the most generative works of recent decades – perhaps not explicitly a contribution to memory studies, but surely well-noted within it – for instance, is Benedict Anderson's (1983) book, *Imagined Communities*, which theorized 'print-capitalism' as a – if not *the* – central feature of the age of nationalism. According to Anderson, print, including daily newspapers and related enterprises, was central to the consolidation of national identities, which in turn were understood by Anderson, following Ernst Renan, as memory constructs. As Renan had argued (quoted in Anderson, 1983: 6), a central constitutive feature of national identities is 'the possession in common of a rich legacy of memories.' Indeed, based on this and related works, the connection between memory studies and the theory of nationalism was a hallmark of memory studies in the 1980s and 1990s. As I will suggest below, memory studies has at least in part responded to contemporary issues, and in the 1980s and 1990s, especially following the break-up of the Soviet Union, nationalism was clearly a central concern. It may be that, since then, a perception of journalism as mediation – and journalism in the new media environment – has absorbed some of that attention. As for the claim that memory studies has *utterly* ignored journalism, of course, this is likely too much. For sociologists at least, the works of Lang and Lang (1989), again of Zelizer (1992), of Schudson (1993), or of

Dayan and Katz (1994) and at least a few others are key references. And analyses of newspapers and other forms of journalism appear in many empirical works, both as sources of data and as important institutions for the processes being studied.

Nevertheless, there are a number of features of memory studies as it has developed and consolidated as a field that have indeed worked against a more extensive focus on journalism. In the first place, as Kristin Ross (2004: 1) put it in her study of *May '68 and its Afterlives*, 'the whole of our contemporary understanding of processes of social memory has derived from analyses related to... World War II,' which, she argues, has 'produced the memory industry in contemporary scholarship...' Memory studies, for Ross, is thus marked by 'parameters of devastation – catastrophe, administrative massacre, atrocity, collaboration, genocide – [which] have in turn made it easy for certain psychoanalytical categories – "trauma," for example, or "repression" – to attain legitimacy as ever more generalizable ways of understanding the excesses and deficiencies of collective memory.' This characterization of the origins of memory studies is certainly overstated, but it is not entirely incorrect. And it suggests in part why journalism – rather than, say, psychiatry or conflict resolution – has not been center stage in memory studies. Long-term trauma and repression born of war and genocide are hardly the bread and butter of daily reporting, which is more inclined to the coverage of events than conditions, especially old conditions: that Holocaust survivors suffered long-term trauma is hardly 'news,' in any sense of the word.

In the second place, the changing conditions of both journalistic media and memory may give at least some reason to believe that whatever neglect of the relations between journalism and memory there may have been in the past was at least partly inscribed in the old media and old memory worlds, the implication being that the new media and new memory environment will 'naturally' lead to more exploration of the connections. Indeed, memory studies itself may be entering what Erll (2011) has identified as a third stage. The first stage of memory studies took place in the interwar period in the work of the sociologist Halbwachs (1925), art historian Aby Warburg (Gombrich, 1997) and psychologist Fredrick Bartlett (1995 [1932]), among others, each of whom independently theorized memory as a social or collective rather than entirely individual faculty. The second stage, according to Erll, was exemplified by Nora's theory about the role of 'lieux de memoire' in national identities, as well as the investigation of what Nora called 'the memory-nation nexus' more generally, as alluded to above in the discussion of Anderson and Renan. In the last ten years, a third wave has emerged. This has included work by Erll (2011) herself, influenced in part by post-colonial theory; work by scholars like Michael Rothberg (2009), which focuses on migration as a challenge to the clarity of the second stage's 'methodological nationalism'; and the arguments of, for instance, Aleida Assmann and Sebastian Conrad (2010) and Daniel Levy and Natan Sznaider (2005) which claim that memory of the Holocaust is an example of a new 'global' or 'cosmopolitan' memory. Taken together, this new scholarship is intent on showing how memory in the contemporary period transcends the 'container' of the nation-state. As such, these new developments in memory match – and are related to – developments in the new environment of media, which is characterized by fluidity, boundary-crossing and hybridity. The third wave of memory studies may thus hope to find connections with the state of the art in media studies that were not as apparent before. As Neiger et al. (2011: 2) put it in their volume *On Media Memory*, 'the intertwined globalization and localization of the media, numerous technological developments, and the audiences' ever-widening access to media texts dealing with the past, all call for an up-to-date discussion of the significance and implications of Media Memory.'

Yet another possible factor in the relative neglect of journalism by memory studies might stem from the liminal position of journalism, intellectually if not institutionally. From the perspective of historiography, for instance, journalism shares all of memory's suspect qualities. Because it is a mere 'first draft,' it is prone to error without revision. Journalism, like memory but in distinction to history, is fallible and ephemeral, and hence not corrected as carefully as historians would like. Journalism is, indeed, temporary by design. After all, who but a historian would read an old newspaper? At the same time, from the perspective of memory studies, journalism looks a lot like history: it is a professional enterprise, it is public, it values sources and rules of confirmation, and its residues are relatively permanent. In contrast, a great deal of memory studies has been interested in the validation of the authenticity of experience over the professionally produced, and in reception more than in production. Memory studies has also perhaps been more inspired by literary and other imaginative forms, in contrast to which journalism appears closer to historical scholarship than to the central concerns of memory scholarship. Again Neiger et al. (2011: 7): 'While fictional outlets were considered more closely related to imagined collective memory, news, journalism, and documentary were considered closely related to "true" historiography.' As such, they were not as obvious or as compelling topics for memory studies. Biases in memory studies have also included preferences for sites rather than media of memory (thus Nora), in commemoration rather than in the profane record (since, after all, the field had roots in Emile Durkheim's theories of ritual and of the distinction between the sacred and the profane), and in the vernacular rather than the institutional. Journalism expresses the opposite of most of these interests.

While perhaps none of these factors, alone or in combination, 'explains' the purported neglect of journalism by memory studies – a neglect that I have also suggested is at least slightly overstated – together they do characterize some tendencies that render the distance between the enterprises comprehensible. Surely, however, there must be other factors, not least among them institutional politics: for instance, as a field rather than a discipline, media studies is perhaps not inclined to link up with another enterprise that is also a field rather than a discipline (namely memory studies), though to be sure memory studies does not have the institutional permanence that media studies has; there are no departments of memory studies, to say nothing of schools of memory studies as there are schools of journalism and 'communication.' There are indeed real institutional goods at stake in such cross-fertilization, and real institutional reasons for neglecting it.

Again, though, my main concern is the view of journalism from memory studies, of which I am a practitioner, rather than of memory from journalism. By the same token, a complete picture of the relevance of journalism and memory – and hence of journalism scholarship and memory scholarship – depends on the view from both sides. I thus now turn to a schematic outline of some of the concerns that argue for a profound nexus between studies of journalism and studies of memory, akin to the nexus between studies of memory and studies of nationalism that constituted the uniquely important contributions of scholars like Anderson and Nora already discussed as forming the second period of memory studies.

Journalism's memory work

Before asking about the relevance of journalism to memory, I begin by laying out some of the ways in which journalism involves memory work, that is to say the relevance of memory to journalism.

Like everyone else, journalists clearly depend on memory in their work. They remember earlier events as well as earlier moments in their careers. Part of their professional knowledge is knowing – which means remembering – who to call or where to go. Moreover, as Gaye Tuchman demonstrated in her now classic study (Tuchman, 1980), journalists employ a variety of 'typifications' in their work. Typifications – a concept derived from sociological phenomenology (Berger and Luckman, 1967) – are habits, routines, assumptions and the like with which individuals approach any new situation (and indeed all situations are new in some respects). And typifications, which derive from past experience, are themselves forms of memory. Without them, no situation would be interpretable, and the actor would be paralyzed with information overload. In this regard, journalism, like any other kind of work, depends on rather ordinary memory of how to do the work, of what the work is about, of what counts as good work, what is part of the situation of the work and so on.

Individual journalists, moreover, employ what Tuchman called 'typifications of newsworthiness' – among other kinds of typifications – to identify what is worth covering. At the same time, typifications of newsworthiness – which are based on memory of what was considered newsworthy in the past – shape the routines not only of individual journalists, but of the organizations in and for which journalists work. News editors (who are also individual workers in journalism), for instance, prefer predictable events to unpredictable ones because they are easier to prepare for. In turn, news organizations are structured in ways that depend on such typifications, for instance through the assignment of reporters to beats, through the establishment of, and investment in, reliable sources, and in the very rhythm of journalistic production. All of these practices and structures are clearly mnemonic at their core, and thus can be understood through the lens of memory studies.

Beyond the individual and organizational forms of work memory, moreover, both individuals and the organizations in which they are employed use and are shaped by *social* memory – that is, by an awareness of history, of what is important to the group, and of where various events and themes came from and how they have developed over time. Typifications of newsworthiness, for instance, are not just expectations about where 'news' is likely to be happening, but of what will be received as relevant by the audience. These expectations depend on an awareness of what is important to the group. Journalists, for instance, view their professional work as reporting what is of public, rather than private, interest; while they may employ personal anecdotes – their own or from their sources – those anecdotes are in the service of relevance to the group. And this relevance may properly be understood as social memory. Why is a particular issue on the public agenda? Who counts as the public, what do they know, and what do they care about? Has something about that issue changed? What facts about the past are relevant to making the issue and is what is at stake in it comprehensible? What shared memory does the audience have and care about?

The issue of anecdotes, particularly those from reporters' sources, illustrates another way in which memory is relevant to journalism – namely, that journalism depends on the memories of its sources. When a reporter arrives at the scene of an event, for instance, he or she may interview eye-witnesses about what happened. And just as the journalist's own memory is fallible, so too is the respondent's memory. Understanding how memory, and in particular misremembering (memory distortion), work is thus essential to the journalist's professional practice. It is also essential to the scholar who studies that work: for instance in evaluating whether a journalist is presenting a biased account or whether journalism as a whole is biased, as well as in investigating the relationship between the elite, institutionalized versions of history's first draft and the immediate accounts on which such versions are based. The fact that journalism relies so substantially on interviews and recollection is part of what distinguishes it from academic history, though other factors distinguish it, for instance, from interview-based sociology.

As already mentioned at the beginning of this chapter, journalism also covers memory science, memory politics and commemorative events. The latter are obviously particularly important to understanding the memory-journalism nexus. In the first place, all the mnemonic issues that arise in the coverage of events – selecting what events are worthy of coverage, confirming information and checking sources, providing necessary background information and so on – are as important in the coverage of commemorative events as they are in the coverage of any other kinds of events. But the coverage of commemorative events is a particularly potent demonstration of the involvement of journalism with social memory and its politics. There are, for instance, more commemorative events than journalists cover, so how do they select which ones to report? And whose version of the commemorated events, and whose contributions to them, do journalists acknowledge and credit? What role do journalistic contributions play in the politics of memory overall?

Furthermore, journalists may be involved in the commemorative events themselves in a variety of ways (see especially Zelizer, 1992). Journalists are present at commemorative events, and indeed the commemorative events may be designed and performed with that presence in mind. Moreover, journalistic coverage may participate in sanctifying commemorative events, or at least in legitimating their marking.

Another feature of typifications of newsworthiness, for instance, is the identification of particular anniversaries, commemorations and other markings of time as publicly relevant topics.

Journalism, however, not only participates in commemorations of external events. It also commemorates itself. Like other organizations, for instance, journalistic organizations celebrate anniversaries of their own enterprise. Journalists refer to their predecessors, produce and consume professional lore, and advocate for their own role in history. Memory studies can thus illuminate the commemoration of journalism with tools used to understand commemoration in other institutions and fields. Is there something unique, for instance, to the identification and commemoration of iconic journalists in comparison to the commemoration of movie stars or politicians?

Finally, again with reference to the institutions of journalism, journalistic organizations are quite significant preservationists: news organizations have archives, very often comprised of materials they themselves originally produced or at least collected. These archives are useful not only for the work of the journalists themselves, but are often taken as historical sources. An awareness of the selectivity and relevance of these archives is obviously essential to evaluating their reliability and impact, and this requires understanding how archives work as and on memory.

Memory's dependence on journalism

Although I will come to it only at the end of this section, the issue of journalistic archives – the archives of historical materials that journalistic organizations have gathered and preserved, as well as, for instance, the historical archives of the news products themselves (that is, the collection of every previous edition of a newspaper) – leads directly to the question of the relevance of journalism to memory studies, the inverse of the question just addressed of the relevance of memory to journalism and journalism scholarship.

In the first place, it is clear that journalism could be considered a primary example of what Halbwachs (1925) – the founding father of memory studies – called a 'social framework of memory.' Both the autobiographical and historical memories of individuals are shaped in profound ways by journalism. We may, for instance, check the front page of the newspaper for the date or the weather and for a sense of what is going on in the world, and the awareness taken from doing so shapes the way we experience our day, week, or year. We may indeed mark the time of our own lives in units defined, or at least presented by, journalism. Beyond this, many scholars have demonstrated how cultural materials shape our experiences of the world. For example, Marita Sturken (1997) and others have argued persuasively that soldiers' experiences in the Vietnam War were shaped by their prior viewing of World War Two films. And if this is true of film, it is also true of journalism. Journalism scholars, moreover, have often referred to the 'agenda setting' and 'reality defining' roles of journalism and other mass media. Clearly, then, an understanding of these processes is essential to memory studies. Media not only provide the knowledge that shapes action, they also provide materials and frameworks that shape memories.

Psychological and other studies of so-called 'flashbulb memories' – memories formed by powerful events that occur out of the routine of everyday life – demonstrate that these events are often powerfully misremembered. That is, key events are not only particularly memorable, it turns out that they are particularly mismemorable: we will swear many years later that we remember exactly where we were during a particularly important event, but our strong faith in our memory is paradoxically connected to a high likelihood that our strong memory is mistaken. One of the main reasons our later memory of even the most powerful events is faulty is that such events have often received a great deal of attention from the media (including journalism), and our memories of them incorporate not only what we ourselves experienced but later reports and framings as well. Indeed, such an observation was clearly articulated in Halbwachs's early writing, when he noted that it is hard to say at a temporal distance whether what one remembers is what one really experienced or whether what one remembers has incorporated intervening materials and events. That Halbwachs was not attending directly to media or journalistic interventions does not alter the relevance of the basic observation to the discussion of the memory-journalism nexus.

Beyond these issues are two further points that have been touched on above. The first is that journalism is often a constitutive factor in events themselves. Journalism enters into the flow of events and shapes them, both actively and passively. Todd Gitlin (1981), for instance, has demonstrated how the needs of news organizations called forth a particular organization from protestors in the student movement of the late 1960s. As such, journalism was clearly going to be a constitutive factor in what of the movement has been remembered and how. Again, our memory of such events often incorporates the journalistic images of the events that journalism itself framed. Memory of public events is thus ultimately inseparable from their journalistic coverage and constitution. As a result, the objects of memory studies are almost always in some sense constituted by journalism whether memory studies is interested in the role of such constitution or not.

Second, journalism itself constitutes an interesting and important site of memory. We remember journalistic images and events, and these are major features of public memory. For instance, we do not really remember Willy Brandt's kneeling at the Warsaw Ghetto Memorial so much as we remember the photograph of him kneeling. Moreover, the history of journalism is an important and interesting part of public memory. As already noted, we can often picture even the format and lettering of a familiar newspaper, features that are themselves already memorial: after all it is not by accident that many newspapers employ old-timey fonts, particular in their names.

Finally, although this list in no way exhausts the relevant issues, we can return to the archive of journalism as a constitutive feature of collective memory. Many of us are old enough to remember going to the microfilm library to read the coverage of a historical event in an old newspaper. That such searches are now done on computers alters, but does not entirely transform, the archival resource this provides. However, we can also study such archives not for what they tell us about past events, but for what they tell us about the changing ways in which such events have been discussed. This comes from the information the journalistic archives provide as well as from the archives as phenomena in and of themselves – that is to say, we compare what a newspaper tells us about how people are thinking about an issue at different points in time, but we can also compare the different ways in which the newspapers present their coverage about the ways people are talking about a particular issue over time. Journalism is evidence of changes in memory while it is itself the change, especially as journalism concerns and forms change: all this is visible in the journalistic archives too. As such, journalistic archives are particularly rich laboratories for memory studies, although not necessarily for what they tell us about the history documented in them so much as for the changes in journalism itself evident there.

Conclusion

Perhaps the most important point, however, is that journalism is so central a part – rather than just a recorder – of collective memory that any memory scholarship that does not acknowledge its import is likely to be missing essential parts of the process. Not only is journalism a recorder of what is going on, not only does it provide an archive of what happened, it is itself archival in the sense meant by Jacques Derrida in his book *Archive Fever*: by the archival, Derrida meant culture itself, including the manifest and the latent, the actual and the potential, the past that will not pass away. In the modern period, there is no cultural or collective memory that is not at least in part journalistic. As Zelizer (1992: 214) writes, 'The story of America's past [or of any other contemporary past] will remain in part a story of what the media have chosen to remember, a story of how the media's memories have in turn become America's [or any other country's] own. And if not the authority of journalists, then certainly the authority of other communities, individuals and institutions will make their own claims to the tale ... It is from just such competition that history [and one might add, culture and memory] is made...'

References

Anderson, B. (1983) *Imagined Communities: Reflections on the Origin and Spread of Nationalism*. London: Verso.

Assmann, A. and Conrad, S. (eds) (2010) *Memory in a Global Age: Discourse, Practices, and Trajectories*. Basingstoke: Palgrave Macmillan.

Bartlett, F. (1995 [1932]) *Remembering: A Study in Experimental and Social Psychology*. New York: Cambridge University Press.

Berger, P. and Luckman, T. (1967) *The Social Construction of Reality: A Treatise in the Sociology of Knowledge*. New York: Anchor.

Dayan, D. and Katz, E. (1994) *Media Events: The Live Broadcast of History*. Cambridge, MA: Harvard University Press.

Edy, A.J. (2006) *Troubled Pasts: News and the Collective Memory of Unrest*. Philadelphia: Temple University Press.

Erll A. (2011) 'Travelling Memory,' *Parallax*, 17(4), 4–18.

Gitlin, T. (1981) *The Whole World is Watching: Mass Media in the Making and Unmaking of the New Left*. Berkeley: University of California Press.

Gombrich, E.H. (1997) *Aby Warburg: An Intellectual Biography*. London: Phaidon.

Halbwachs, M. (1925) *Les cadres sociaux de la mémoire*. Paris: Librairie Félix Alcan.

Kitch, C. (2005) *Pages from the Past: History and Memory in American Magazines*. Chapel Hill, NC: University of North Carolina Press.

Lang, K. and Lang, G.E. (1989) 'Collective Memory and the News,' *Communication*, 11, 123–9.

Levy, D. and Sznaider, N. (2005) *The Holocaust and Memory in the Global Age*. Philadelphia: Temple University Press.

Neiger, M., Meyers, O. and Zandberg, E. (eds) (2011) *On Media Memory: Collective Memory in a New Media Age*. Basingstoke: Palgrave Macmillan.

Nora, P. (ed.) (1984–92) *Les Lieux de mémoire*, 7 vols. Paris: Edition Gallimard.

Nora, P. (1989) 'Between Memory and History: Les Lieux de Mémoire,' *Representations*, 26, 7–25.

Olick, J.K. (2005) *In the House of the Hangman: The Agonies of German Defeat, 1943–1949*. Chicago: University of Chicago Press.

Olick, J.K. and Robbins, J. (1998) 'Social Memory Studies: From "Collective Memory" to the Historical Sociology of Mnemonic Practices,' *Annual Review of Sociology*, 24, 105–40.

Olick, J.K., Vinitzky-Seorussi, V. and Levy, D. (2011) *The Collective Memory Reader.* New York: Oxford University Press.

Ross, K. (2004) *May '68 and its Afterlives.* Chicago: University of Chicago Press.

Rothberg, M. (2009) *Multidirectional Memory: Remembering the Holocaust in the Age of Decolonization.* Stanford: Stanford University Press.

Schudson, M. (1981) *Discovering the News: A Social History of American Newspapers.* New York: Basic Books.

Schudson, M. (1993) *Watergate in American Memory: How We Remember, Forget, and Reconstruct the Past.* New York: Basic Books.

Starr, P. (2005) *The Creation of the Media: Political Origins of Modern Communication.* New York: Basic Books.

Sturken, M. (1997) *Tangled Memories: The Vietnam War, the AIDS Epidemic, and the Politics of Remembering.* Berkeley: University of California Press.

Tuchman, G. (1980) *Making News: A Study in the Construction of Reality.* New York: Free Press.

Zelizer, B. (1992) *Covering the Body: the Kennedy Assassination, the Media, and the Shaping of Collective Memory.* Chicago, IL: University of Chicago Press.

Zelizer, B. (2008) 'Why Memory's Work on Journalism Does Not Reflect Journalism's Work on Memory,' *Memory Studies*, 1(1), 75–83.

2

Memory as Foreground, Journalism as Background

Barbie Zelizer

Although memory studies has long argued for the importance of a variety of institutional settings engaged in memory work, journalism has not typically been one of them. But a brief revisit to memory studies' most central work and to the ways in which ideas about memory and journalism have developed alongside each other suggests that memory studies and the very notion of collective memory could not exist without journalism.

This chapter traces some early roots of the uneasy coexistence between memory and journalism and addresses memory scholarship in which journalism's presence was implicit but not duly noted. Demonstrating journalism's unarticulated relevance to the long duration of the study of memory, the chapter argues that according journalism more centrality in memory scholarship might facilitate greater understanding about the workings of collective memory. It also raises questions about the shape of academic inquiry.

The foreground of memory

In her comprehensive overview of scholarship on collective memory, Anne Whitehead (2009) observed that thinking about collective memory across time means recognizing that the settings emphasized in memory scholarship have not always reflected those in process on the ground. Perhaps nowhere has this been as much the case as with journalism. Though it constitutes one of memory's most active shapers, a lack of attention to journalism in memory scholarship has rendered it little more than a background to existing intellectual discussions.

Journalism has been largely missing from both the earliest and most recent ruminations about collective memory. Though journalism regularly and systematically looks backward in reporting about the present, its engagement with the past has gone unnoticed in discussions of memory. From writing about the arts of memory in ancient Greece and Rome all the way through scholarship on contemporary digital memory systems, journalism constitutes an afterthought.

This neglect has had multiple points of origin. They include uneven and changing understandings of the relationship between past and present, tensions over the kind of record that memory produces, and anxiety over the changing status of both journalism and memory in largely Western notions of modernity. Central too have been disciplinary alliances that force certain patterns of intellectual sharing, by which memory studies has focused on agents of memory other than journalism and journalism studies has emphasized the role that journalism plays in recording the present, not the past. Taken together, these circumstances have produced a deep hole in memory scholarship, through which the value of the connection between journalism and memory has fundamentally vanished.

The patterning of this uneven relationship emerges with particular clarity when surveying the intellectual conversations about memory that have surfaced over time, primarily in the West. Invoked here as part of a strategic exercise to elucidate notions that have been so tightly packed into longstanding intellectual discussions that they seem to have disappeared, it provides a heuristic for unpacking how and when journalism went backstage in discussions of memory and why that never changed. Four main stages of memory scholarship are illustrative in this regard. Though strategically selected and by no means reflective of all the vagaries in memory's intellectual work or the geographic singularities in journalism's spread, these stages – two of which reflect writings after the fact, two of which address writings during the period – provide a useful lens on how ideas of memory have sidestepped journalism's presence.[1]

Briefly, the chapter argues that these stages developed as follows. Discussions of the earliest forms of memory produced rich ideas about how memory worked, but journalism constituted a mere shadow to then popular currents of thought. When memory took a downswing during the evidentiary environment that came with modernity and the Enlightenment, memory and journalism were constituted as stark alternatives: journalism embodied modernity's promise, memory modernity's peril. In the foundational period, when ideas about collective memory accompanied notions of individual recall, journalism was positioned as the past's possible facilitator but remained vaguely relevant to its development. And finally, the contemporary period, with its increasing emphasis on the digital environment, has underscored journalism as a precondition for memory, but it has been framed as the work of mediation, writ broadly. Almost nowhere in these stages has journalism been called by name, suggesting that there are many ways to reside in the background of public and scholarly thought. This chapter thus raises questions about the patterning of intellectual inquiry, about how we decide what matters and about what happens to that which does not make the grade.

Early period: journalism as memory's shadow

The earliest conceptualizations of memory positioned journalism primarily as memory's shadow. During this period, which stretched from the earliest practices of memory in the classical era through those of the Renaissance, the relationship between memory and journalism remained fundamentally static. Journalism was existent, functional and patterned, but it was absent from ideas about how memory worked.

Though early discussions of memory suggest that it was seen mostly as an individualized activity, remembering was already recognized as an act that could be easily and fruitfully shared (Whitehead, 2009). Early forms of memory helped develop a productive platform for an elaborated set of cognitive, social, political and cultural activities involved with the past. Primarily though not exclusively oral in nature (Clanchy, 1979), memory was regarded as a source of inspiration for artists, a tool of argument for rhetoricians and a pathway toward intellectual refinement for philosophers. Associated among the Greeks with reason and as integral to the refinement of thought, and among the Romans with rhetoric and as central to the art of eloquent persuasion, the craft of memory – later aligned with the so-called 'arts of memory' (Carruthers, 1990; Le Goff, 1992) – was dependent on memory aids, highlighting an 'inextricable connection between memory and the means used to record that memory' (Whitehead, 2009: 15). This connection was implicit from the earliest practices of memory – Plato's notion of the wax tablet, the early prevalence of sarcophagi and shrines, the pyramids and tombs of ancient Egypt, and the development of complex visual symbols and place systems as venues in which to imagine memory work (Yates, 1966; Carruthers, 1990; Assmann, 2011). In each case, remembering depended on some form of mediation, where across the board media of recall were expected to facilitate three activities – recording, storage and retrieval.

Such ideas reflected what nascent forms of journalism were already beginning to provide at the time – an engagement with collective knowledge, recognition of its relevance for group functioning and a responsibility for disseminating it. Significantly, they suggested that the tasks widely seen as memory's core activities – recording, storage and retrieval – solidly paralleled journalism's own. Like memory, journalism remained centered on oral relay, and though its articulated mission was to address the present, a delicate line between past and present enhanced the possibility that journalism was already acting as an agent of collective knowledge regardless of temporality.

Thus early forms of journalistic relay often involved some sort of mnemonic activity even if rarely articulated as such. The original marathon, run in 490 BCE, brought news of victory to Athens by messenger (Stephens, 1988: 40), and commemorative activities ensued immediately in response. During the fourth century BCE, Plato's disciple Demosthenes pinpointed a preoccupation with spoken news, where continuous efforts to publicly 'fram[e] our several tales' provided a point of reference for Athenians gathering in the gymnasia to act upon their record of past action (cited in Stephens, 1988: 14). Roman handbooks on oratory famously recounted the story of a sole survivor of a building collapse who had used his mnemonic skills to recount exactly where everyone had been sitting, thus facilitating victim identification. Attributed in 55 BCE to Cicero (2001) as an example of mnemonic recall at its finest, the story mirrored what today would be easily recognized as journalism.

This patterning – taking activity that looked like journalism and calling it memory – continued across discussions of the Middle Ages and the Renaissance. As acts of remembering took the shape of pilgrimage routes, the sacred geography of commemorative worship and the development of memory theaters (Whitehead, 2009), memory became more visual and material. The embrace of mythological time gradually gave way to historical time, and an orientation to truth – already present during Plato's time – began increasingly to surface, positioning memory not only as the end product of perception but as the initiator of new knowledge acquisition (Carruthers, 1990; Whitehead, 2009). In this scenario, the mnemonic relevance of print-related projects ascended.

It is in this light that journalism became an important mnemonic platform. Town criers provided an ongoing public record of thirteenth-century Europe, circulating a record through which the community experienced itself collectively (Stephens, 1988: 40). In Rome, both the Forum and the public baths served as centers for news circulation, where Romans gathered to hear 'the latest news from the provinces' (Stephens, 1988: 40). During the Wars of the Roses, roadblocks were established to prevent bad war news from travelling onward lest the ensuing record stirred the people 'to commocions' (Armstrong, 1948: 434). Though each instance involved what was primarily news of the moment, these activities brought past events and present records into productive proximity.

From the 1500s onward, as a growing print culture revamped what it meant to remember, journalism's centrality increased while mirroring memory's own orientation toward visuality and materiality. The arrival of the printing press in 1476, the birth of the newspaper one hundred or so years later, and journalism's gradual evolution from oral relay to written technique all enhanced journalism's relevance in marking the past alongside the present. No surprise, then, that Milan of the 1500s produced special news sheets recounting the funerary details of prominent Italian individuals, which 'functioned less as sources of information... than as "souvenirs"' (Petta, 2009: 113–14), or that the so-called 'rebel songs' of the Dutch Revolt of 1568 received such extensive commemorative imagery over its eighty years of broadsheets that by the revolt's conclusion soldiers had moved in the public imagination from criminals to heroes and courtiers (Roberts, 2006). As snapshots of public events appeared across Italy, France, Germany and England of the 1600s – recounting gossip, satire, market news, court decisions, official edicts and military conquests – the relays provided a collective knowledge that put the past to strategic use.

In ideas about memory from this period, then, journalism thrived as an implicit agent of memory's workings, though it existed mostly in the shadows of memory work. The relationship showed much connection and parallel but received little recognition. Though there was a widespread intellectual investment in the nature of memory – it was complex, systematic and rule-bound – it was accompanied by a lack of attention to the range of possible agents of mnemonic work. Thus, writings focused on the most central mnemonic platforms and activity, leaving journalism out of the picture.

Evidentiary period: journalism as memory's other

Circumstances changed in the second stage of journalism's positioning in ideas of memory. This evidentiary period, which stretched roughly from the late seventeenth to the early nineteenth century, gave journalism the status of memory's other. Here the ascent of modernity and the Enlightenment squashed the opportunity to recognize journalism as even vaguely relevant to memory.

As modernity and the Enlightenment moved the West from a nostalgic view of the past to a progressive one (Le Goff, 1992), the earlier neglect of journalism's memory role was replaced by a triumphant (though overstated) celebration of the news. Through the writings of Locke, Descartes and others, the enterprises of reason, certainty, observation, objectivity, progress, rationalism and evidence came to be preferred over those involving emotion, subjectivity, the imagination and, of course, memory. These qualities, relevant to what was then seen as an optimum set of challenges for journalism, made the news an apt platform for forwarding modernity's promise. They helped position journalism as a driver of modernity, which was expected to advance rational and reasoned deliberation through full and complete information relay, to utilize clear judgment and reasoning, to produce value-free information and impartial, balanced prose, and to encourage a belief in productive civic engagement.

By contrast, the past turned into a bump on the road to progress. Though memory practices of the time accommodated the fact that 'there was a lot more of the past' to accommodate (Misztal, 2003: 37) – residing in new books and encyclopedias, driving the creation of museums and libraries, pushing secular and political rituals in place of those set by the church and crown, and legitimating newly invented traditions, like Bastille Day or labor rituals (Hobsbawm and Ranger, 1983; Gillis, 1994) – the past was riddled with entrenched platforms of tradition, custom and habit. While memory practices developed that were germane to Enlightenment aims, where commemorating the nation through medals, coins and holidays led mnemonic efforts (Misztal, 2003), the past nonetheless became aligned with the emotions, the imagination and the contingent, its traits of inconsistency, subjectivity and contradiction seen as suspect to progressive aims. Though modernity needed some sense of the past to move forward, it favored an impartial, distanced and authoritative version, one that could both legitimate its aspirations and naturalize a preferred assessment of what mattered about earlier times. This left memory out of the picture of what modernity valued, and it put memory and journalism on opposite sides of the neighborhood.

Drawing heavily on the rhetoric of modernity's promise, journalism developed practices that sought to promote a rational, reasoned and linear record of important events. While political satire, gossip and advice columns flourished, at their side developed practices to ensure provision of that record – reliable and unambiguous prose, corroborating sources, meeting deadlines, providing proof of authorship – all testament to what was thought to be an impartial account of events (Schudson,

1978). Notions of journalistic professionalism came to reflect journalism's role in encouraging reasoned deliberation (Hallin, 1992), securing for journalists a collective sense of self that adhered with modernity's promise. In this light, journalists no longer spoke explicitly of the past without a clear link to the present nor considered the past part of their purview, and it was roughly here that the logic of the now oft-cited dictum – that journalists write history's first draft – surfaced. Journalists were expected to provide the raw material for someone else's lasting, dispassionate and objective record.

What modernity thus expected of journalism was antithetical to the subjectivity, unreliability, inconsistency, contingency, hesitation and noise that characterized memory. This evidentiary period thereby displayed a downswing in the centrality of memory, and by the end of the eighteenth century, the arts of memory, so prevalent in earlier times, were seen as archaic. Projects long associated with memory – tradition, the nostalgic past, experience, intuition, imagination – fell by the wayside.

That is not to say that memory work disappeared altogether from journalism. As mediated platforms became increasingly relevant to disseminating knowledge of public life, journalism's mnemonic work began to cohere with Enlightenment aims, often marking patriotism and national identity. One of the earliest American editorial cartoons – a snake cut into eight pieces under the title 'Join or Die,' first printed in 1754 by Benjamin Franklin in response to the French and Indian War – was recycled multiple times over the following years as a symbol of American resistance to the British (Olson, 1987). Similarly, Thomas Paine's essay 'Common Sense,' which appeared on Philadelphia streets one morning in 1776, fashioned its plea for American independence on the back of biblical references and historical overviews of earlier English, French and Spanish monarchies (Paine, 1986 [1776]). Readers' commemorative letters to the editor pummeled American newspapers in the winter of 1799, when George Washington died (Kahler, 2008). And English and American newspapers first systematically displayed death notices, soon called obituaries, during the late eighteenth and early nineteenth centuries (Houlbrooke, 1998; Hume, 2000). Nonetheless, these practices were secondary to the significant thrust forward taken by journalism during this period, and it was a thrust toward modernity, away from memory.

In writings about memory during this period, then, journalism was established as an antidote to the weaknesses of mnemonic recall, a vantage point readily adopted by most journalists. Where memory failed, journalism prevailed. But positioning journalism as memory's 'other' did little to reflect the ongoing memory work that journalism of the time sustained, a reality helped along by the increasing background reliance on mediation. Though such a position cemented journalism's distinctiveness from memory, it celebrated ways of thinking about journalism that obscured the persistent parallels between journalistic and mnemonic work. Discussions also did not venture beyond the lingering focus on the nature of memory, whose workings and institutional venues still remained mainly out of sight.

Foundational period: journalism as memory's facilitator

The third stage of development was the foundational period, when journalism took on the role of facilitator to memory work. By the late nineteenth and early twentieth centuries, memory began to be conceptualized as a phenomenon of collective, not only individual, dimensions. As it drew interest from multiple academic disciplinary settings – among them critical studies, sociology, psychoanalysis, social history, psychology and philosophy – the application of new understandings enhanced the opportunity for thinking about memory's workings. In contrast, then, to the withering of memory that had accompanied the ascent of modernity and the Enlightenment, ideas of memory at this point began to be fruitfully and flexibly exported across the academic curriculum.

Ideas of memory were primarily developed here by disparate individuals who hoped to delineate some kind of shared capacity to recollect the past. Through the work of early precursors in the fields of psychology (Bartlett), the phenomenology and philosophy of time (Husserl, Bergson), art history (Warburg), critical studies (Benjamin) and psychoanalysis (Freud), thinking about memory began to pivot on some version of the idea that knowledge of the past could be situated in contemporary shared consciousness, refracting the act of recording the past through the contemporary aims it reflected. But each of these foundational attempts tried to map a certain disciplinary consciousness onto the act of collective remembering, creating what Terdiman (1993) later identified as the first full-blown memory crisis, when intellectuals tackled memory from multiple vantage points. Though it laid the foundation for studying memory as an interdisciplinary project, its parallel endeavors never quite saw eye to eye. As Schwartz (1991: 302) noted, the idea of collective memory became translatable into whichever terms were most available and recognizable, in many cases reduced to the familiar psychological terms of remembering and forgetting, a metaphor for society's retention and loss of information about the past.

It is here that disciplinary knowledge acquisition began to take hold, and this development had two related sources. On the one hand, ideas from this period challenged the certainty with which modernity and the Enlightenment had sought to establish themselves, and that was because modernity was beginning to be recognized as only minimally successful. The propensity of failed states, soft authoritarianism, transitional governments, widespread illiteracy, rampant malnutrition and illness, untold numbers of wars and conflicts all shed doubt on modernity's promise. On the other hand, questions surfaced about whether memory, and its associated subjectivity, inconsistency, emotions, imagination and contingency, had an as-yet unrecognized value. In particular, deep-seated questions about modernity's failure to deliver what it had promised – seen in that great challenge to modernity, the Holocaust – drove memory's reconceptualization from individual to collective terms and promoted it as an alternative frame for collective knowledge. Memory now came to be understood as a dynamic, shared and tentative address to partial pasts, all useful traits which offset the overly settled, authoritative and universal nature of modernity's claims.

It was no surprise, then, that as thinkers became invested in clarifying how shared memory differed from individual recall, they also pushed discussions of memory away from its nature and toward its workings. This shift drove further recognition of memory's mediated nature. As memory was seen as surfacing through the extra-rational activity that modernity had deemed suspect – using the institutional settings most associated with modernity to do so, such as the market, the polity, education and journalism – the implication that vast and intricate memory work could be accomplished by institutional settings that had little to do with memory per se brought the act of looking backward to the forefront of institutional public life.

Central to this scholarship was the work of Halbwachs (1992 [1950]). Though its centrality has been much debated, his orientation toward the institutions and processes of mnemonic work was particularly useful for orienting memory in the direction of journalism. Though not articulated as such, journalism was implicit in three aspects of his writings – memory's articulation through language, the social frames in which memory resides and the narrative nature of mnemonic activity.

First, Halbwachs insisted that memory must be articulated through language – a statement that could be a description of news itself, for journalism relies on nothing like it relies on language. Because memory did not exist, in his view, until it could be articulated and subsequently shared, language remained central throughout the processes involved: 'It is language and the whole system of social conventions attached to it, that allows us at every moment to reconstruct our past,' he wrote (Halbwachs, 1992: 173), praising 'verbal conventions' that provide 'the most elementary and most stable framework of collective memory' (Halbwachs, 1992: 45). Regardless of medium, journalism requires the systematic, patterned use of language to relay its information in verbal, visual or audio form, and multiple journalistic practices – editorial consults, group meetings, source corroboration, archival retrieval – all need conscious acts of articulation to unfold and sustain news-making.

Second, Halbwachs argued that collective memory needs some degree of social framing, insisting that social frames had to be set in place and circulated across groups in order for memory to operate. Here too a parallel with the news is obvious. Though much of the rhetoric of journalism maintains a naïve and non-interventionist engagement with its objects of coverage, critical views of journalistic practice emphasize the constructed nature of the classifications that journalists use as a natural part of their work – between hard and soft news, national and international news, mainstream and tabloid news, fact and opinion, front page and lifestyle news, chronicles and features, and the like. Journalism's salience as a frame in and of itself should be clear.

Finally, the nature of the mnemonic work that Halbwachs envisioned involves narrative activity that is patterned and systematic. 'If recollections reappear,' he observed, 'this is because at each moment society possesses the necessary means to reproduce them' (Halbwachs, 1992: 183), with narrative, and particularly stories, helping people 'evoke places and times different from those in which we find ourselves because we place both within a framework which encompasses them all' (Halbwachs, 1992: 50). Halbwachs's description echoes the work required of journalism – specifically the narrative activity by which journalists buttress interpretation, minimize inconsistency, validate facts, corroborate sources and confirm the information contained in their reports. All are accomplished through narrative.

On all three points, Halbwachs's writings thereby oriented toward journalism as a setting in which collective memory might unfold. Though he did not call journalism by name nor outline how it might work as a memory agent distinct from religion, class or the professions, his work offered a foundation for thinking about the processes of collective memory in institutional settings, writ large. It was left to others to surmise what might be distinct about the settings he did not mention.

It is worth noting that journalism of the time was packed with evidence of the mnemonic activity about which Halbwachs and others wrote. Because the period stretching from the late nineteenth to the middle of the twentieth century produced substantial growth in journalism's platforms – a small number of newspapers gave way to a vast and diverse mediated landscape, including radio, magazines, different kinds of newspapers and journals, broadcast and eventually cable television – mnemonic practices flourished exponentially across all available venues. They prevailed to such an extent that they became part of journalism's narrative apparatus – analogies and comparisons between past and present, story pegs crafted through the past, pictures of the past illustrating the present, events gauging the scale, magnitude or meaning of the present (for example, Schwartz, 1982; Zelizer, 1998). Some of journalism's more obvious mnemonic platforms surfaced and/or flourished during this period – historical timelines, updates and rewrites, revisits to old events, and commemorative or anniversary journalism (for example, Lang and Lang, 1989; Kitch, 2000, 2006).

Writings on memory thus reflected the growing background centrality of journalism, largely due to a growing reliance on mediation and an increasing intellectual preoccupation with mnemonic process and institutional settings. Yet journalism remained a largely unarticulated resident of memory's foreground, rarely, if at all, made explicit.

Contemporary period: journalism as memory's precondition

The fourth stage of journalism's relation to memory is the contemporary period, in which journalism has surfaced as memory's precondition. Since the 1980s, the study of collective memory has come into its own as scholars in multiple disciplines have acted upon the foundational suggestion of engaging with the processes and institutions by which collective memory takes shape.

This period has produced a plethora of new perspectives on memory, but it has also displayed a battleground for competing academic disciplines, each of which produces its own vision of what memory looks like. In sturdier times, such a focus might have certain advantages, but the uncertainty and instability of the current academic environment have positioned collective memory front and center in localized struggles to fortify disciplinary boundaries and enhance topicality. And though collective memory now regularly appears in curricula in literature, psychology, sociology, history, communication, anthropology and education, no discipline offers a sufficiently inclusive vantage point on memory's trappings.

Equally important, the sharing of vantage points extends in patterned ways across disciplines with an a priori tradition of sharing, such as American studies and English or comparative literature and German. The inclusion of journalism, which has long suffered from its own ghettoized knowledge (Zelizer, 2004), has fared unevenly in this scenario.

Such neglect is peculiar, for current ideas of memory now easily admit some degree of mediation in memory's workings. In part this stems from the orientation toward process and institutions initiated by Halbwachs. In part it results from the predominance of the digital environment across all disciplinary fields, where a consonance between memory and mediation – by which memory is necessarily though not exclusively shaped by mediated platforms – is widely regarded as a pre-condition for public knowledge of all kinds. As Erll (2011 [2005]: 113) remarked, 'cultural memory is unthinkable without media.'

Four tropes are relevant in this contemporary context – written memory, place memory, bodily memory and material memory. What follows are some brief comments about what they look like, for similar focal points are central to thinking about journalism (for example, Lang and Lang, 1989; Kitch, 2008; Zelizer, 2008; Tenenboim-Weinblatt, 2013).

Written memory

The centrality of written memory, or inscription, dates back to Plato and his notion of the wax tablet. But it has resurfaced in current thinking about memory practices, with work by Schudson (1992) and Zerubavel (1995) tracking what Connerton called 'something that traps and holds information, long after the human organization has stopped inform-ing' (1989: 73). Scholarship on the digital environment has centered on inscription from anew (for example, van Dijk, 2007). Journalism, whose fundamental activity is producing a written record, is clearly depend-ent on inscription: style guides, headlines, leads, writing cues, captions and note-taking practices all help to organize journalism's performance. This reliance is reflected in those discussions of journalism's mnemonic work that have appeared (for example, Meyers, 2007; Carlson, 2007). Fowler (2005), for instance, found distinct narrative categories of col-lective memory – dominant, popular and counter-memory – reflected in contemporary news obituaries.

Place memory

No less relevant has been the idea of place memory, or spatiality. While places dominated work on early memory practices (Yates, 1966) – positioning images within an imagined mental landscape – the reemer-gence of place in contemporary thought is largely aligned with Nora's notion of sites of memory or 'lieux de memoire,' which 'create archives, mark anniversaries, organize celebrations, pronounce eulogies and authenticate documents because such things no longer happen as a matter of course' (Nora, 1997: 7). Resonating in the work of Winter (1995), Wagner-Pacifici (2005) and Doss (2010), place memory has received renewed attention in studies of global memory (for example, Huyssen, 2003; Levy and Sznaider, 2005). Such a focus reflects the basic work of journalism, where the place of a news event, the beat or place of a reporter and the place of a news organization undergird newsmaking. Contemporary discussions, when they have appeared, show how place memory helps maintain distinctions between different kinds of journalistic practice (for example, Edy, 2006; Li and Lee, 2013).

Bodily memory

A third impulse relevant to memory work has been that of bodily memory, or incorporation. An early focal point in Aristotelian ideas of memory, today it features centrally in the work of Connerton (1989, 2009), Hirst and Manier (2008) and Narvaez (2012), who have articulated how mnemonic practices are shaped and inscribed on the body. News work can only take shape in response to individuals doing things with information – collecting, filtering, interviewing, writing, editing, distributing, consuming – and discussions of journalism have always privileged its somatic aspect. Bodily memory figures in notions of eyewitness news, the importance of 'being there,' the idea of the source, datelines that mark bodily presence and anchorpersons flown in to provide helicopter coverage at a disaster site. An address to news technology and the body further distinguishes the procedures involved across news media – a print news story needs to be sequentially drawn out, while radio is commonly called 'writing for the ear' – suggesting that even though bodily memory has been infrequently called by name (for example, Zelizer, 1992; Kitch, 2000), it is aligned with journalism in multiple ways.

Material memory

And finally, the impulse of material memory, or externalization, establishes how memory circulates through material objects. Though evident in the shrines and tombs that served among the earliest holders of memory (Yates, 1966; Carruthers, 1990; Assmann, 2011), it has resurfaced in the contemporary work of Hirsch (1997), Landsberg (2004) and Sturken (2007), each of whom have demonstrated how materiality changes what we remember. Nora (1989, 1997) aligned his notion of secondary memory specifically with journalism, which facilitates 'the return of the event' in historical recording by journalists acting as instant historians. It goes without saying that journalism relies on materiality, for radio shows, TV broadcasts, magazines and newspapers all shape the records – mnemonic or not – that ensue. Journalism's material nature is further enhanced by the links, posts and algorithms that characterize its digital environment (for example, Anden-Papadopoulos and Pantti, 2011; Garde-Hansen, 2011), reinforcing how journalism's development anticipates the future terrain of memory's study.

What does this contemporary work reveal about the relevance of journalism to mnemonic practice? It underscores the fact that journalism constitutes one of the few institutions to encapsulate contemporary memory's spread. But these four impulses are only part of the picture. The processes and contents of memory which have proved most relevant to the present moment are solidly situated in journalism's territory – witnessing, trauma, war, testimony, therapeutic discourse and mourning. All regularly and systematically covered by journalists, they further enhance journalism's centrality as a platform for considering memory.

However, despite all of this evidence, journalism still remains largely unarticulated as an agent of memory. Even though the signs of correspondence between memory and journalistic work have only become more marked over time, it is not journalism but mediation – or at times remediation – that tends to surface in contemporary discussions of memory. Thus, even at a moment in which journalism is clearly a precondition for memory's workings, it is still rarely called by name in contemporary memory scholarship.

This is critical. For as thinking about memory has accommodated a more complicated notion of what memory was and could be, journalism has become more and more central to its formulation. But it has moved little, if at all, in memory's discussion and conceptualization.

From background to foreground: naming journalism

The goal of this chapter has been to demonstrate three points:

1. that journalism has been doing mnemonic work since the earliest ideas about collective memory took hold and the very earliest evidence surfaced of its practice;
2. that some presence of journalism has been implicit in evolving ideas of memory, not at its margins but at its center;
3. that early and recent ideas of memory have been uniformly negligent by not articulating journalism's increasingly central mnemonic role.

What has emerged is a background with much nuance but very little recognition by its foreground.

Journalism has continued to occupy memory's background across multiple periods of thought, playing the role of shadow, other, facilitator and precondition to more generalized discussions of mnemonic activity. But almost nowhere has it been named as journalism. These facets of its longstanding background existence have obscured its perseverance in the shaping of memory and prevented its more representative recognition as an active and instrumental memory agent.

Why does this matter? First, the intellectual neglect addressed here has produced an erroneous picture of how memory works, and this perseveres despite the fact that journalism has increased, not decreased, in centrality. Journalism's attributes provide a certain landscape on which memory takes shape. But if we have not made a place for journalism as an agent of memory's workings, how can we make a place for how it shapes the memories that ensue?

Second, and no less important, this discussion reveals the underside of longstanding patterns of disciplinary knowledge acquisition that determine what matters in a field of inquiry. Often, they privilege the most proven, familiar and proximate knowledge in what has been already documented over the novel or strange, which is instead discarded as irrelevant. Numerous scholars – from Thomas Kuhn and Nelson Goodman to Mary Douglas and Michel Foucault – have argued that the act of knowledge acquisition is always accompanied by social arrangements that facilitate and hinder knowledge's spread. Surely, journalism is not the only bypass that characterizes contemporary studies of memory. What else has disappeared from inquiry and for what reasons? How would our understanding of memory change were we to admit the underemphasized and absent as much as we do that which gets readily circulated?

This chapter has shown that regardless of clear evidence to the contrary, journalism has not risen to the level of what matters in the study of memory despite the fact that it has mattered very much on the ground. As scholars, we can and should do better.

Note

1. Thanks to Nicholas Gilewicz for reading some of the works that follow with an eye to addressing the presence or absence of journalism within them, particularly the discussion of Halbwachs. Also thanks to the Humanities Institute at Stony Brook for the opportunity to present a version of the arguments contained in this chapter.

References

Andén-Papadopoulos, Kari and Pantti, Mervi (eds) (2011) *Amateur Images and Global News*. London: Intellect Books.

Armstrong, C.A.J. (1948) 'Some Examples of the Distribution and Speed of News in England at the time of the Wars of the Roses,' in R.W. Hunt, W.A. Pantin and R.W. Southern (eds) *Studies in Medieval History: Presented to Frederick Maurice Powicke*. Oxford: Oxford University Press, pp. 429–54.

Assmann, Jan (1995) 'Collective Memory and Cultural Identity,' *New German Critique*, 65, 125–33.

Assmann, Jan (2011) *Cultural Memory and Early Civilization*. Cambridge: Cambridge University Press.

Carlson, Matt (2007) 'Making Memories Matter: Journalistic Authority in the Memorializing Discourse Around Mary McGrory and David Brinkley,' *Journalism: Theory, Practice and Criticism*, 8 (2), 165–83.

Carruthers, Mary (1990) *The Book of Memory*. Cambridge: Cambridge University Press.

Cicero, M.T. (2001) *On the Ideal Orator*, trans. James M. May and Jakob Wisse. New York: Oxford University Press.

Clanchy, Michael (1979) *From Memory to Written Record: England 1066–1307*. Cambridge, MA: Harvard University Press.

Connerton, Paul (1989) *How Societies Remember*. Cambridge: Cambridge University Press.

Connerton, Paul (2009) *How Modernity Forgets*. Cambridge: Cambridge University Press.

Doss, Erika (2010) *Memorial Mania*. Chicago: University of Chicago Press.

Edy, Jill (2006) *Troubled Pasts: News and the Collective Memory of Social Unrest*. Philadelphia: Temple University Press.

Erll, Astrid (2011) *Memory in Culture*. Basingstoke: Palgrave Macmillan.

Fowler, Bridget (2005) 'Collective Memory and Forgetting: Components for a Study of Obituaries,' *Theory, Culture and Society*, 22(6), 53–74.

Garde-Hansen, Joanne (2011) *Media and Memory*. Edinburgh: Edinburgh University Press.

Gillis, John (ed.) (1994) *Commemorations*. Princeton, NJ: Princeton University Press.

Halbwachs, Maurice (1992 [1950]) *On Collective Memory*. Chicago: University of Chicago Press.

Hallin, Daniel (1992) 'The Passing of the "High Modernism" of American Journalism,' *Journal of Communication*, 42(3), 14–25.

Hirsch, Marianne (1997) *Family Frames*. Cambridge, MA: Harvard University Press.

Hirst, William and Manier, David (2008) 'Towards a Psychology of Collective Memory,' *Memory* 16 (3), 183–200.

Hobsbawm, Eric and Ranger, Terence (eds) (1983) *The Invention of Tradition*. Cambridge: Cambridge University Press.

Houlbrooke, R. (1998) *Death, Religion and the Family in England, 1480–1750*. Oxford: Clarendon Press.

Hume, Janice (2000) *Obituaries in American Culture*. Jackson: University Press of Mississippi.

Huyssen, Andreas (2003) *Present Pasts*. Palo Alto: Stanford University Press.

Kahler, Gerald E. (2008) *The Long Farewell: Americans Mourn the Death of George Washington*. Charlottesville: University of Virginia Press.

Kitch, Carolyn (2000) *Pages from the Past: History and Memory in American Magazines*. Chapel Hill: University of North Carolina Press.

Kitch, Carolyn (2006) 'Useful Memory in Time Inc Magazines,' *Journalism Studies*, 7(1), 94–110.

Kitch, Carolyn (2008) 'Placing Journalism inside Memory – and Memory Studies,' *Memory Studies*, 1(3), 311–20.

Landsberg, Alison (2004) *Prosthetic Memory: The Transformation of American Remembrance in the Age of Mass Culture*. New York: Columbia University Press.

Lang, Gladys and Lang, Kurt (1989) 'Collective Memory and the News,' *Communication*, 11, 123–9.

Le Goff, Jacques (1992) *History and Memory*. New York: Columbia University Press.

Levy, Daniel and Sznaider, Natan (2005) *The Holocaust and Memory in a Global Age*. Philadelphia: Temple University Press.

Li, Hongtao and Lee, Chin-Chuan (2013) 'Remembering Tiananmen and the Berlin Wall,' *Media, Culture and Society*, 35(7), 830–46.

Meyers, Oren (2007) 'Memory in Journalism and the Memory of Journalism: Israeli Journalists and the Constructed Legacy of *Haolam Hazeh*,' *Journal of Communication*, 57(4), 719–38.

Misztal, Barbara (2003) *Theories of Social Remembering*. Maidenhead: Open University Press.

Narvaez, Raphael (2012) *Embodied Collective Memory*. New York: University Press of America.

Nora, Pierre (1989) 'Between Memory and History: Les Lieux de Memoire,' *Representations*, 26, 7–25.

Nora, Pierre (1997) *Realms of Memory* (Volume 1). New York: Columbia University Press.

Olson, Lester C. (1987) 'Benjamin Franklin's Pictorial Representations of the British Colonies in America,' *Quarterly Journal of Speech*, 73(1), 18–42.

Paine, Thomas (1986 [1776]) 'Common Sense,' in Isaac Kramnick (ed.) *Common Sense*. New York: Penguin Classics.

Petta, Massimo (2009) 'Printed Funerals in 16th and 17th Century Milan,' in Elena Brambilla et al. (eds) *Routines of Existence*. Pisa: Plus-Pisa University Press, pp. 106–37.

Roberts, Benjamin B. (2006) 'The "Marlboro Men" of the Early Seventeenth Century: Masculine Role Models for Dutch Youths in the Golden Age?' *Men and Masculinities*, 9(1), 6–94.

Schudson, Michael (1978) *Discovering the News*. New York: Basic Books.

Schudson, Michael (1995) *Watergate in American Memory*. New York: Basic Books.

Schwartz, Barry (1982) 'The Social Context of Commemoration: A Study in Collective Memory,' *Social Forces*, 61(2), 374–402.

Schwartz, Barry (1991) 'Iconography and Collective Memory: Lincoln's Image in the American Mind,' *Sociological Quarterly*, 32, 301–19.

Stephens, Mitchell (1988) *A History of News*. New York: Viking Press.

Sturken, Marita (2007) *Tourists of History: Memory, Kitsch and Consumerism from Oklahoma City to Ground Zero*. Chapel Hill: Duke University Press.

Tenenboim-Weinblatt, Keren (2013) 'Bridging Collective Memories and Public Agendas: Toward a Theory of Mediated Prospective Memory,' *Communication Theory*, 23(2), 91–111.

Terdiman, Richard (1993) *Present Past: Modernity and the Memory Crisis*. Ithaca: Cornell University Press.

Van Dijk, Jose (2007) *Mediated Memories in the Digital Age*. Palo Alto: Stanford University Press.

Wagner-Pacifici, Robin (2005) *The Art of Surrender*. Chicago: University of Chicago Press.

Whitehead, Anne (2009) *Memory*. London: Routledge.

Yates, Frances (1966) *The Art of Memory*. London: Pimlico.

Zelizer, Barbie (1992) *Covering the Body: The Kennedy Assassination, the Media and Collective Memory*. Chicago: University of Chicago Press.

Zelizer, Barbie (1998) *Remembering to Forget: Holocaust Memory Through the Camera's Eye*. Chicago: University of Chicago Press.

Zelizer, Barbie (2004) *Taking Journalism Seriously*. London and California: Sage.

Zelizer, Barbie (2008) 'Why Memory's Work on Journalism does not Reflect Journalism's Work on Memory,' *Memory Studies*, 1(1), 75–83.

Zerubavel, Yael (1995) *Recovered Roots*. Chicago: University of Chicago Press.

3
Shifting the Politics of Memory: Mnemonic Trajectories in a Global Public Terrain

Ingrid Volkmer and Carolyne Lee

Conceptual debates about memory in the context of new transnational public sphere structures remain on the periphery of journalism research. Despite paradigmatic shifts toward the broader frameworks of information, digital or 'network' society, which increasingly situate national journalism in an enlarged spectrum of continuous viral flows across transnational public discourses, the role of collective memory as a discourse sphere within such a space is under researched. Given the increasing complexity of social media structures and the ontological centrality of public community, public memory could constitute an important layer of journalism within such an enlarged networked space. However, journalism research rarely incorporates spheres of memory and, as Zelizer remarked, is more concerned with the 'here-and-now' than the 'there-and-then' (Zelizer, 2008: 80).

This is surprising as the sphere of memory not only incorporates the subjective and/or subjectively shared collective past, thus informing political action, but, although often overlooked, is deeply interwoven into public spheres. In this constellation, journalism becomes an important discursive node; as Meyers has pointed out, journalists act as collective memory 'agents' when addressing national but also international events (for example, Meyers, 2007). Meyers argues that journalism's role as a public agent of framing memory implies three levels of journalistic practice: 'tell the public stories about realities', the coverage of 'the past within larger cultural and social contexts', and the narration of the 'past' and the shaping of social memories (Myers, 2007: 721). On a more abstract level, this role of journalism as a public agent relates to the politics of public memory through what might be called an amalgamation of the spheres of collective memory (what Meyers calls the 'narration of the past'), or what is perceived as 'history' in public discourse. This amalgamation

50

constitutes, as Habermas has repeatedly pointed out, an important moral category of societal reality, establishing and enforcing the legitimacy of a particular national 'frame' as a normative reflection of an assumed collective memory (Habermas, 1988). However, such a normative sphere of legitimation no longer reflects a collective narrative of a (national) past, but diverse multicultural, mobile and migrant legitimate 'pasts' in modern societies where diverse sets of normative memories negotiate history within new forms of collective memory. This discursive scope of memory politics constitutes an important area of journalism research as it legitimizes the past as the 'shaping of social memories' (Meyers, 2007: 721) not through a normative lens but through a cosmopolitan one.

Over recent years, various debates in journalism studies have addressed the implications of transnationalization in a variety of contexts. Some consider the national embeddedness of journalism in the larger macro-structural parameter of media systems (for example, Hallin and Mancini, 2012), while others address 'dimensions of influence' in the context of transnational journalism practice (for example, Hanitzsch and Mellado, 2011). A third debate highlights the transnationalization of journalism as seen through the 'networked' sphere (for example, Jones, 2012; Heinrich, 2011; McNair, 2006), relating it to issues of content convergence (for example, Robinson, 2011), the scope of social spaces of individual 'authentic' news production and competitive cross-platform structures.

Journalism, however, is not only challenged by transnational structural networked parameters that stretch *across* borders but also by the reciprocal implications of this enlarged discourse terrain *within* nation-states. Often overlooked is the transformation of the nation-state in the diverse contexts of globalization and the 'embeddedness of the global in the national' (Sassen, 2007: 82). Sassen has repeatedly argued that these globalization processes

> take place deep inside territories and institutional domains that have largely been constructed in national terms. What makes these processes part of globalization even though they are localized in national, indeed subnational, settings is that they involve transboundary networks and formations connecting or articulating multiple local or 'national' processes.
>
> (Sassen, 2007: 82)

Such a scaling of globalization to the subnational and even further to the subject has been the theme of Ulrich Beck's work in the paradigm of risk society for many years (Beck, 2009). The scaling of globalization has also recently been addressed by Bayart, who argues that subjects actively negotiate the narrative of memory in globalized discourses across various media forms. Despite these broadened discourses 'we also need to grasp how the nation-state, rather than the elusive dimension of global extent or the post-national points of reference, remains the political site of the practices of memory even though the latter are becoming globalized' (Bayart, 2007: 51).

We have not yet fully explored the consequences of this enlarged sphere on national journalism. Journalism is entangled in the politics of these scalar processes of globalization within nation-states, but is similarly entangled in national contexts. Thus, what is often labelled as national journalism is no longer national but accessible transnationally via networked communication. This reciprocal process of transnationalization – where a national narrative is contextualized in other public terrains – emerges as a new sphere of journalism practice in the context of normative memory politics. A recent study that addressed the way in which collective memory frames are used by journalists in the US and Serbia in the context of the Kosovo crisis considered how journalists from the *New York Times* and the Serbian *Politika* used similar memory frames through different 'semantic fields' of collective memory in order to frame a discourse of justice (Gajevic, 2012). The author argues that journalists should not understand collective memories as 'literally remembering' but rather through the 'constantly changing relationships between the past and the present, individuals and collectivities', thus actively opening up the normative frame of national remembering as public discourse practice (Gajevic, 2012: 13).

This opening of the frame of remembering is particularly relevant, for the multicultural dimensions of the semantic fields of memory of the other, as perceived by migrants and mobile communities, are rarely addressed in the national mainstream news media. This is the case, for example, in political conflicts, crises and moments of commemoration, particularly in the context of public remembering. Thus, the fall of the Berlin Wall was a key event, transforming the European geopolitical order, but it was also an important moment for the refinement of German national identity. Yet this event is rarely addressed in the German news media through the diverse transnational semantic fields of memory which, given the transnational relevance of this event, would allow journalists to incorporate a transnational scope of multi-sited sets of meaning. Similar phenomena emerge in the context of, for example, the memory of wars in the US and Australia, seen less as a transnational narrative of an increasingly transnational community than a very narrow national memory frame. Despite the transnationalization of various societal strata, then, the collective is often perceived through the traditional normative lens of the nation *despite* the otherwise cosmopolitan reality of modern nation-states and the increasing role of affluent mobile communities. These communities are no longer 'scapes' (Appadurai, 1996), often possessing multiple citizenships and – in the reality of contemporary mobility cultures – continuously meandering between multiple residences, living in several places at the same time. Such a new sense of multiple places – itself centered on continuous access to the same media and information spaces (via internet and satellite) as well as Twitter, Skype and Facebook – allows for a constant engagement in the same public spaces.

Within the communicative scope of a multi-directional prism – reflecting a spatial, 'mobile' (Urry, 2007), 'cosmopolitan' (Held, 2010) or 'reflexive' modernity (Beck, 2006) – the transformation of the national should set the stage for rethinking journalism in the context of ontological networked structures emerging around memories of events, trauma and crisis.

De-centering conceptions of collective memory

Reviewing studies of collective memory in the context of these scalar processes of transnationalization reveals that the field of collective memory seems to be conceptually centered in the framework of methodological nationalism. This, as Beck has argued, is a trap, because 'the sphere of experience can no longer be understood as nationally bound but is determined by global dynamics' (Beck and Beck-Gernsheim, 2009: 25). The national centering of memory studies relates in particular to the memories of traumatic events, such as wars and the Holocaust. Erll (2011) argues that 'only recently' has memory studies begun to address 'forms of remembering *across* nations and cultures' (Erll, 2011: 2; original emphasis). For example, generational memory has been identified in a transnational context, where a study of three generations in nine countries situated media biographical memory of childhood and youth beyond the national framework of the memory of events as generational 'entelechies' of particular world consciousness (Volkmer, 2006).

But despite these attempts to address the implications of transnational communication and identify non-national ontological structures of connectedness, the media-related research of collective memory is entrenched in the paradigm of the first modernity. This understanding, related to Halbwachs's conception of collective memory as intersubjectivity or a density of social and/or political identity (Halbwachs, 1925), laid the foundation for methodological approaches to the sphere of 'collective-ness' as adopted in media and journalism research and invoked as an approach to identify forms of collective memory across media representations. It is worth noting, however, that Halbwachs's approach situates collective memory in the larger construction of the 'self' vis-à-vis 'world' consciousness, reminiscent of the work of French social philosopher Henri Bergson (1963), who understood subjective inner time as 'durée', a linear subjective time perception, proceeding within the larger scope of 'universal time', of the 'flow of 'things.' While both Halbwachs's and Bergson's notions of memory considered it a dense and intersubjective sphere of consciousness, scholarship in media and communication research mainly uses this approach to assess collective memory not so much as an intersubjectively shared consciousness but as a collective construction vis-à-vis media forms that are often national in scope. Consequently, the identity sphere of collective-ness is related to a national centrality of (mass) media cultures and collective memory (see, for instance, Zelizer, 1992) but also to the cosmopolitanization of trauma and conflicts (Beck, Levy and Sznaider, 2009).

Only very recently have studies in media and journalism research begun to identify the sphere of mediated collective memory across digital space (Hoskins, 2009). For Hoskins the main distinct mediatization of memory in a digital context refers to the 'capacity of media to transcend and transform the relationships between media and the everyday negotiation of memories' (Hoskins, 2009: 31). More recently, Reading (2011) has situated memory studies within a 'globital memory field', a term that, through the combination of 'globalization' and the 'digital', identifies two extending conceptual axes of collective memory: the horizons of deliberately chosen connections, and the engagement in a communicative space.

It is relevant, however, to conceptually address journalism not only in the larger scope of multicultural societies but also in the density of multicultural publics as an identity space *within* one society. National multicultural publics not only engage with a broad cosmopolitan scope of information resources, including television, radio and newspapers via digital platforms, but also with increasingly 'authentic' fractured satellite television delivered to users on many continents. It is this ontological network which de-centers the day-to-day negotiation of news values and 'truth' and shapes collective memory as probed in a national public arena. Various studies have highlighted the ways in which migrants use diverse media forms for political information, which has also been the case in the context of national mass media. However, in today's context, satellite channels deliver thematically specific bundles of political information and historical documentaries, in particular targeting supranational migrant public spheres to actively negotiate between diverse media forms associated with a country of residence, country of origin and 'in-between' spaces (Morley and Robins, 1995; Slade and Volkmer, 2012).

These processes produce a multidirectional national public sphere and a multidirectional contextualization of memory in a new transnational scope of collectivity across societies, particularly relevant for journalism in today's network age. For example, Kellner described a negotiation of meaning in the context of spectacles as merging 'media texts and spectacles with the public' (Kellner, 2003: 29). We suggest addressing not so much the negotiation of text and public but rather the subjectively perceived link as communicative memory between diverse spheres of meaning of such a spectacle as a subjective positioning vis-à-vis normative forms of collective memory.

We argue there is a need to shift away from the centrality of mass media and the nation in order to articulate fine-lined intersections of new spheres of collective memory as links between transnational biographies, for example, those of mobile, migrant civic communities. Communities linking the memory of collective pasts, for example, with the country of origin, the collective present, the country of residence and, often invisible in mainstream journalism, moments of commemoration contribute important relativistic semantic fields to a national memory frame.

Intersections, communicative memory and journalism: a case study

To investigate the spheres of these intersections, we conducted in-depth semi-structured interviews with postgraduate students in the Faculty of Arts at the University of Melbourne (Volkmer and Lee, 2012). International respondents were chosen from diverse countries with quite different public cultures – Japan, Singapore and Botswana. The focus of the interviews was the subject's memory of 9/11, the construction of the memory mediated frame at the time of the event and processes of the event's mediatization since then. As all respondents now live in Australia, it is illuminating to see how different the associations are, depending on the locality during the time of the event. Interviews lasted about 20 minutes and were transcribed. We selected 9/11 as it is perceived as a globalized event which continually resurfaces in public contexts and is nationally framed through memory politics. Furthermore, the normative memory of the event is often used in journalism for the justification of military intervention, securitization, religious and ethnic stereotyping. Although 9/11 created a 'debounded' security environment, that is, debounded from nation-states (Hirst, 2007), national narratives highlight particular memory politics and associations in the mainstream media. In this sense, 9/11 is not merely an event but rather constitutes a geopolitical 'horizon' further specified through regional political angles.

Each respondent's memories were formed via national journalism in their country of origin – with the exception of the Botswanan interviewee who was in South Africa at the time of 9/11 – initially mediating the event in each location. This initial mediation constituted a common communicative moment, since it was certainly a macro event, in many cases shaping 'world experience' among an otherwise 'constant stream of content' (Volkmer and Deffner, 2010: 218). But importantly, because this common frame was experienced by all four respondents, at the time inhabiting different cultural contexts, this initial memory was inflected by local journalism before being subjectively appropriated in the particular lifeworlds of each of them. In this sense, each person's recollection of this particular mediated event can be understood 'as a performance of memory' (Smelik, 2010: 308). It thus can be subjected to 'microframe' analysis, which 'focuses on the subject in relation to particular globalization "micro" forces. … [an approach that] consider[s] the individual, the subject, as a central aspect of globalization' (Volkmer, 2006: 253).

The term 'intersection' is helpful here in drawing attention to a set of common elements – subjects at different locations all over the globe perceiving the same event through journalism, forming their own memories about the event and reflecting upon the trajectory of diverse paths veering away from each other. Given the globally ubiquitous nature of such a macro event as 9/11, it is to be expected that the memory flows will intersect repeatedly at irregular or regular intervals (for example, ten year commemoration), again through mediation and frequently via national journalism. The memories of individual transnational subjects will therefore be nationally and individually inflected, and will illuminate intersections in the context of communicative moments. In this way, subjects' memories and notions of inner time can form an important entry point for collective memory research that attempts to transcend analyses too often reduced to either national and/or mass media mediation. In thinking about subjects' inner times in the context of transnationalization, mobility and media use, we can see that subjects often find opposing meanings in their diverse intersections, always experienced from within their particular lifeworlds, that they then 'sort out' to make congruent with that lifeworld.

The four respondents were aged approximately 14–20 at the time of 9/11; thus there were some generational similarities of perception, although perhaps far less so than there would be today. Three of the respondents first obtained news of the event via television, the exception being the Singaporean respondent, who claimed not to remember whether she saw the media images as they were broadcast live, or 'if they were subsequently shown over the years.' But what was remembered was the image of the plane crashing and the towers falling as well as the image of 'someone jumping off and going down.' This respondent, fifteen at the time and at secondary school, 'had no media, and ... didn't watch the news or read the newspapers...' and had no strong memory of the event. Furthermore, she notes that her parents did not talk much about the event, and that she herself did not remember '9/11 being a big deal as an event.'

A possible explanation for this is that in Singapore, with its heavily restricted government-owned media, the images were very likely not shown repeatedly over several days, as they were in many other countries. The representation of the event may have been played down, due to the sizable Muslim population in Singapore and the explicit policy of the government to foster and preserve racial harmony, especially given the geographical proximity to and sensitive historical relations with Malaysia. With very little media available to this respondent at the time, such mediatization and the low-key framing of it played a significant role in the shaping of her memory, and bears out the fact that 'media technologies invariably shape our memories' (Smelik, 2010: 307). Indeed, this respondent's memory of the mediatized event was very much shaped in her sense of inner time. Once in Australia she contrasted her memory of 'then' through the lens of 'here-and-now' (Zelizer, 2008: 80), as framed in Australian media. This respondent also claims she reconstructed subjective remembering since living in Australia.

The three other respondents received news of the event via television and have distinct memories of where they were and what they were doing at the moment, a clear demonstration of marking specific moments of their inner time as 'then.'

The Japanese respondent, aged 18 at the time, and eating dinner in a boarding school canteen, initially thought that the repeated showing of the images of the 'twin towers and a plane going in' was a fiction film, as the sound was switched off. She asked for the television channel to be changed to 'news.' She was told that it *was already* on the news channel and 'people started coming in and ... we were looking... and the image was played again and again and ... it was a build-up of a storytelling or a movie.'

This sense of watching a disaster movie was very strong for this respondent, a feeling that may have been heightened by other viewers as she describes some (video) 'gamers' in the room who 'would repeat the sound of the blowing explosion as if they were referring to their own gaming life', and one of her core memories is the question 'is this real or is this staged?'

It is significant that this subject's memory of 9/11 begins with her thought that what she saw was 'storytelling or a movie', and that when she did accept that it was 'news', her acceptance quickly involved framing the event in alignment with gaming. This is arguably a logical frame in Japanese culture, and one that she remembers as emanating from others present in this first communicative moment. While it has been argued that the 'paradoxical effect of frequent repetitions is that they actually make the image unreal and present it as performed' (Smelik, 2010: 309), it is somewhat unusual, and certainly so among our four interviewees, to remember the event as unreal right from the start. Despite the unreality in the subject's memory, though, the event still cast aside other news at the time, for she cannot recall anything about other significant news events, saying that 9/11 '...sort of overshadowed my mind.' She relates this process of 'overshadowing' to the particular political relationship between Japan and the US:

> because it's very close and there are military bases around the country, and we are often referred to as the lapdog of the US... and I remember around that time there were a lot of debates of justifications of self-defence troops, and Japan would be ready if the US would call.

This respondent's memory of the event as framed in terms of Japanese/American identification is unsurprising. This was a common communicative frame in the beginning, reproduced in journalism and experienced by audiences in many countries, no matter how geographically distant from New York. In Europe, for example, the imagined community of the West was strong enough to establish 'a degree of proximity' (Chouliaraki, 2006), and it therefore helped to generate enormous empathy via transnational flows of journalism, of which one piece of evidence was the famous slogan in the French newspaper *Le Monde*, 'Nous sommes tous Americains' (Smelik, 2010: 320). It is significant that much European empathy diminished after the invasion of Afghanistan, whereas the Japanese respondent's memory of the first communicative moment right from the start involves thoughts of Japanese troops participating in military intervention. In her memory the 'mass media in Japan were debating about the legitimacy of the military....' She adds 'I remember [wondering]...if we would have an army because in our constitution in article 9 we can't have an army after World War II and I remember thinking that in the future we might.'

This is a significant observation, demonstrating the way in which the respondent sorts out the very complex intersections and their diverse meanings: the transnational frame of the historical US-imposed limitation to Japanese military activities intersects with the national frame of the military relationship between Japan and the US, which, during the mediation of 9/11, fed into (further mediated) debates about whether this close relationship might warrant an inversion of its earlier limitation.

In contrast to the unreality frame of this respondent's early memory, the Botswanan respondent, living in South Africa at the time, remembers the event through the 'sadness' of the television reporters. This respondent's memory is also heavily driven by emotions: 'Everyone [fellow students, probably] was excited and I remember seeing the reporter and he looked really sad' (this was her second mention of the reporter's sadness). The next emotion in her memory is fear: '...it was really scary for us.' This is unsurprising, given that the broadcasts have been described as 'the endless repetition of images from the scene, portrayals of rescue workers and interviews with victims, creating a new form of ritualized 24/7 conflict coverage' (Volkmer and Deffner, 2010: 219). As this Botswanan respondent says, '[the media in South Africa] covered [the event] really well because they had about five channels and on all ...channels...were covering the events in great depth so we got a lot of news....'

The endless daily repetition of images is remembered by all respondents except for the Singaporean, although only for one of the respondents did this repetition make the event actually seem unreal, as described above. For the Botswanan, the repetitions exacerbated both her fear and shock and heightened the identification, although she still needed time to get used to the fact that the event had happened at all. This suggests some sense of unreality, for she experienced the event as real on a visceral, emotional level: 'The next days we constantly got the news just like that, over and over, on a daily basis. We were still in shock and it took quite a while for us to get used to it....'

Her memory of fear remained fairly constant over the intervening years, despite being exposed to what would have been many differently-framed intersections. Significantly, this fear seems to have been generated in response to specific national frames. For example, her memory from the earliest days of the fear, delivered through the national media, was based on the fact that if the US was attacked, it implied 'no country was safe.' The respondent notes that 'most of the time we think of the USA as a safe country and for us to hear such a big thing (like it being attacked), it looked like there is no safe country... and it was really scary for us.'

In contrast to the memories of the Japanese and Australian respondents, this person's memory did not include identification with the US, but it did involve evidence of generational transnational proximity, exemplified by the sense that 'everyone is affected.' In addition, memories with specifically South African and Botswanan mediatizations of the events are addressed in broader terms: 'It wasn't really targeting the USA. It was targeting all the other countries, and so everyone feels that they also have to play a part in ensuring they curb this terrorist act. ... it's really all of us in it together.' This constant reference point in her memory – that the event was 'terrorists against the world' – revealed that she had spent the intervening years actively negotiating diverse media forms and had been aware of the 'Muslim terrorists versus the West' national frame in Australia. This can be seen as an active negotiation that results in resistance to the dominant Western Manichean discourse.

The memory of the Australian respondent also exhibited generational proximity, but it too includes strands of resistance to dominant nationally-framed Australian discourses. The event occurred when she was fourteen and is very much framed as 'then': she uses phrases such as 'looking back', 'back ten years ago', although her memory of the first communicative moment is clear: 'I was home from school that day so I saw it [on television]. I remember the awful news and the awful images of the planes. I felt really under threat for a good couple of years.' She attributes this feeling of threat to her memory of absorbing 'a lot of that fear and uncertainty of the terrorist attacks.' When she compares how she feels now to her memory of how she felt 'then', it is 'as though some of [the threat] has gone and maybe because we're over ten years past it now, I don't know if we've become more complacent about the risks involved or the uncertainty, or if I'm just older....'

Other contrasts appear between the 'then' of her memory and the 'now' of the present moment. These contrasts are no doubt informed by the ways in which she has sorted out the diverse mediatizations of the event in the intervening years, which are largely nationally-framed since this respondent has spent most of this period living in Australia. For her:

> the core message *back then* was that America was under attack. ... I don't remember feeling like Australia was under attack... *Now* I feel as though it's been talked about as the west versus Afghanistan/Iraq/ Muslim society, and I think it's taken on a different view ...that terrorism is something that the west has to deal with and that we're all in it. ...*ten years ago* I felt like it was really focused on America ... a direct hit on American [sic], similar to Pearl Harbour. But *now* I feel like that event has changed and become much more global *now*.
>
> (emphasis added)

She immediately demonstrates, however, how she actively negotiates between what is her perception of the nationally-framed Australian discourse of being involved in the 'global war on terror', and her own more subjective view developed more recently: 'I don't feel it in my everyday life, but I feel it permeates our media and it's everywhere. ... I don't feel it personally that there's us versus them, but I always view it in the media, and wish it wasn't so.' Here – in using the reflexive phrase 'us versus them' – she demonstrates that sorting out her perceptions with the multiplicity of mediatizations over the ensuing years also involves a certain resistance to the dominant Australian nationally-framed discourse.

The Singaporean respondent also recalls memories based on strong contrasts between the 'then' of the first communicative moment and the 'now' of her current lifeworld. She could not remember how she first apprehended the images and had little recollection of discussion of the event. When she moved to Australia three years later and engaged with Australian nationally-framed mediatizations, she remembered the event from reading newspapers and magazines in Australia or Singapore, especially at times of commemorations. Her way of actively negotiating these diverse memory spheres is by considering the impact on individuals, leading her to make sense of the event by subjectively constructing the new/innovative micro frame of 'healing.'

The entire progression of her memory – from first apprehending what could have been still images to reading articles over the subsequent decade – is illustrative of Bergson's concept of durée, because in the subject's inner time/consciousness she makes sense of her views of the event as proceeding from the larger flow of memories into a much more subjective and linear memory. Here the tight national frame permitted by Singapore, which de-emphasized the event, was to a certain extent fixed for the subject; but once she moved to Australia and read about it in Australian newspapers or saw documentaries on commemorations, she began to negotiate these diverse meanings into a much more nuanced memory that focused on humans – those killed or the partners and children who survived – rather than on the discourses about 'the US versus the Middle East', reflected in the national frames of the other three respondents.

Conclusion

Reviewing the processes of adjusting memory across diverse public sets of memory politics, from the country of origin to the country of residence, reveals at least four different types of intersections through which public frames are linked.

The first type could be described as 'intersection as mediation', capturing the shifting process of memory through a comparison of different forms of representation. These different forms are not merged but rather articulated as different, unassociated narratives.

The second type could be identified as 'intersection as negotiation.' This type proceeds from the national frame and extends to the subject's memory as it intersects with information from subsequent different national frames. Ultimately, it produces a synthesized memory which changes over a period of time through a process of reconciling later memories with earlier ones.

'Intersection as resistance' constitutes the third type. In this type of linking, the subject invokes the memory of a national frame in either a country of origin or in response to subsequent transnational mediatizations of the event, but reacts against it. The subject is thus critical of the national memory – for example, resisting the stereotyping of Muslims, the frame that 'everyone is affected', or the frame of normative inclusion of the country of origin with the US.

The fourth type could be defined as 'intersection as appropriation.' Here, subjects appropriate memory either from the first memory of the event or through a continuous engagement with its narrative. The subject's appropriation veers off into a completely new subjective frame or a highly subjective way of making sense of the event.

These complex layers of ontological density show how diverse forms of past and present in multicultural societies create new networks of public ontological connectivity. The articulation of these connected public discourse spheres, suggesting an ontological diversity of public memory layerings, underscore the negotiation with national memory politics and constitute an important aspect of journalistic reflexivity in a networked world.

In the context of national mass media, an event formed what Bergson might have described as a 'clock moment', where 'the simultaneity between two instants of two motions outside of us enables us to measure time; but it is the simultaneity of these moments with moments pricked by them along our inner duration that makes this measurement one of time' (Bergson, 1965 [1922]: 54). The diverse intersections in these interview responses reveal that such a simultaneity no longer exists. Although the event of 9/11 constitutes a simultaneous mediatized 'clock moment', the moments of 'inner duration' reveal quite different spheres.

Given the transnationalization of nation-states, it is clear that journalism should attempt to address these diverse ontological trajectories. At a time of advanced globalization and a new density of public space, it is important to remember that national collective memory constitutes only one form of remembering. Journalism operates in a globalized field which requires new forms of journalism practice. In this sense, the matrix of intersections suggested here could provide a framework for new journalistic fields of discursive engagement (for example, across content platforms) with diverse narratives. This framework could create links across a wide range of public spheres to open up the narrowly defined normative frameworks of public memory. It would thus help frame events, such as 9/11, not in the normative discourse of an event but rather as a diversity of communicative moments. This may be one of the most important lessons journalism has to learn from the contemporary workings of memory: the acknowledgement that journalists are performing their work in what is inevitably a transnational global public sphere, a situation that should necessitate a reflexivity about the wide range of frames in circulation that are generated by end-users' moments of inner duration, despite the initial mediatization of the same events at the same 'clock moments.' For this reason, as we have argued here, the role of collective memory can be conceptually fruitful when given a more central position in both journalism practice and research.

References

Appadurai, Arjun (1996) *Modernity at Large: Cultural Dimensions of Globalization.* Minneapolis: University of Minnesota Press.
Bayart, Jean-François (2007) *Global Subjects.* Cambridge: Polity.

Beck, Ulrich (2006) *Cosmopolitan Vision*. Cambridge and Malden, MA: Polity.

Beck, Ulrich (2009) *World at Risk*. Cambridge: Polity.

Beck, Ulrich and Beck-Gernsheim, Elisabeth (2009) 'Global Generations and the Trap of Methodological Nationalism. For a Cosmopolitan Turn in the Sociology of Youth and Generation,' *European Sociological Review*, 25(1), 25–36.

Beck, Ulrich, Levy, Daniel and Sznaider, Natan (2009) 'Cosmopolitanization of Memory: The Politics of Forgiveness and Restitution,' in Magdalena Nowicka and Maria Rovisco (eds) *Cosmopolitanism in Practice*. Farnham: Ashgate, pp. 111–21.

Bergson, Henri (1965 [1922]) *Duration and Simultaneity*. Indianapolis: Bobbs-Merrill.

Bergson, Henri (1963) *Oeuvres. Essai sur les donnees immediates de la conscience materiere et memoire*. Paris: Presses Universitaires de France.

Chouliaraki, Lilie (2006) *The Spectatorship of Suffering*. London and Thousand Oaks: Sage.

Erll, Astrid (2011) 'Traumatic Pasts, Literary Afterlives, and Transcultural Memory: New Directions of Literary and Media Memory Studies,' *Journal of Aesthetics & Culture*, 3, 1–5.

Gajevic, Slavko (2012) 'Beyond mediated conflict: journalism, justice and the transnational community,' PhD thesis, University of Melbourne, Australia.

Habermas, Jürgen (1988) 'Concerning the Public Use of History,' *New German Critique*, 44, 40–50.

Halbwachs, Maurice (1925) *Les cadres sociaux de la memoire*. Paris: F. Alcan

Hallin, Daniel and Mancini, Paolo (eds) (2012) *Comparing Media Systems beyond the Western World*. Cambridge and New York: Cambridge University Press.

Hanitzsch, Thomas and Mellado, Claudia (2011) 'What Shapes the News Around the World? How Journalists in Eighteen Countries Perceive Influences on Their Work,' *International Journal of Press/Politics*, 16(3), 404–26.

Heinrich, Ansgard (2011) *Network Journalism: Journalistic Practice in Interactive Spheres*. New York: Routledge.

Held, David (2010) *Cosmopolitanism*. Cambridge and Malden, MA: Polity.

Hirst, Christian (2007) 'The Paradigm Shift: 11 September and Australia's Strategic Reformation,' *Australian Journal of International Affairs*, 61(2), 175–92.

Hoskins, Andrew (2009) 'The Mediatisation of Memory,' in Joanne Garde-Hansen, Andrew Hoskins and Anna Reading (eds) *Save as ... Digital Memories*. New York: Palgrave Macmillan, pp. 27–43.

Jones, Janet (2012) *Digital Journalism*. Thousand Oaks, CA: Sage.

Kellner, Douglas (2003) *Media Spectacle*. New York: Routledge.

McNair, Brian (2006) *Cultural Chaos: Journalism, News and Power in a Globalised World*. London and New York: Routledge.

Meyers, Oren (2007) 'Media in Journalism and the Memory of Journalism: Israeli Journalists and the Constructed Legacy of Haolam Hazeh,' *Journal of Communication*, 57(4), 719–38.

Morley, David and Robins, Kevin (1995) *Spaces of Identity: Global Media, Electronic Landscapes, and Cultural Boundaries*. London and New York: Routledge.

Reading, Anna (2011) 'Memory and Digital Media: Six Dynamics of the Globital Memory Field,' in Motti Neiger, Oren Meyers and Eyal Zandberg (eds) *On Media Memory: Collective Memory in the New Media Age*. New York: Palgrave Macmillan, pp. 241–52.

Robinson, Sue (2011) 'Convergence Crises: News Work and News Space in the Digitally Transforming Newsroom,' *Journal of Communication*, 61(6), 1122–41.

Sassen, Saskia (2007) 'The Places and Spaces of the Global: An Expanded Analytic Terrain,' in David Held and Anthony McGrew (eds) *Globalization Theory.* Cambridge: Polity, pp. 79–105.

Slade, Christina and Volkmer, Ingrid (2012) 'Media Research and Satellite Cultures: Comparative Research among Arab Communities in Europe,' in Ingrid Volkmer (ed.) *Handbook of Global Media Research.* Malden, MA: Wiley Blackwell, pp. 397–410.

Smelik, Anneke (2010) 'Mediating Memories: The Ethics of Post 9/11 Spectatorship,' *Arcadia International Journal for Literary Studies*, 45(2), 307–25.

Urry, John (2007) *Mobilities.* Cambridge and Malden, MA: Polity.

Volkmer, Ingrid (2006) 'Globalization, Generational Entelechies and the Global Public Space,' in Ingrid Volkmer (ed.) *News in Public Memory.* New York: Peter Lang, pp. 251–68.

Volkmer, Ingrid and Deffner, Florian (2010) 'Eventspheres as Discursive Forms: (Re-)Negotiating the "Mediated Center" in New Network Cultures,' in Nick Couldry, Andreas Hepp and Friedrich Krotz (eds) *Media Events in a Global Age.* London and New York: Routledge, pp. 217–30.

Volkmer, Ingrid and Lee, Carolyne (2012) 'Memory across public spaces: a pilot study,' University of Melbourne.

Zelizer, Barbie (2008) 'Why Memory's Work on Journalism does not Reflect Journalism's Work on Memory', *Memory Studies*, 1, 79–87.

Zelizer, Barbie (1992) *Covering the Body: The Kennedy Assassination, the Media, and the Shaping of Collective Memory.* Chicago: University of Chicago Press.

4
Collective Memory in a Post-Broadcast World

Jill A. Edy

If journalism plays an important role in the generation and maintenance of social memory, then the current transformation of journalism has important implications for the ways in which society remembers. Earlier research has described journalism's role in the creation and maintenance of shared memory (for example, Edy, 1999; Edy, 2006; Lang and Lang, 1989; Zandberg, Meyers and Neiger, 2012; Zelizer, 1992). Other works have described the role of mass media more generally in shared memory processes (for example, Edgerton and Rollins, 2001; Kammen, 1978; Meyers, Zandberg and Neiger, 2009). However, recent scholarship has also documented a media environment, and particularly a journalism environment, that is rapidly changing. The mass media audience of the twentieth century has transmuted into the fragmented media audiences of the twenty-first (Turow, 1997). The commercial model of news production, predominant for over a century, is said to be rapidly collapsing (McChesney and Nichols, 2010; McChesney and Pickard, 2011), and the primacy of journalism as a source of political information is increasingly challenged by alternative information sources (Williams and Delli Carpini, 2011). As journalism's role in society changes, its role in shared memory processes may be changing as well.

This chapter explores the theoretical implications of this transformed media and journalism environment for collective memory research. The new media environment will necessitate more sophisticated conceptual and operational definitions of what constitutes *collective* memory, as well as of what 'dominant', 'mainstream' and 'alternative' memories are. It will require a re-examination of the causes and consequences of historical ignorance. Perhaps most importantly, the new media environment may restructure shared memory in ways that have political and social consequences, raising new and important questions for collective memory scholars to address.

The changed assumptions of the post-broadcast world

Early studies of mediated collective memory relied implicitly on the logic of commercial mass media or the relationships between democratic governments and national broadcast media generated by public service media systems such as those in European countries. In the case of commercial media, the assumption is that mediated messages reach a mass audience or at least are intended to appeal to a mass audience in order to maximize profit and influence. The implied presence of or desire to reach a mass audience meant that the representations of the past could be understood to represent broadly shared social understandings and values. Public service media similarly could be assumed to represent broadly shared social values and understandings, albeit potentially somewhat more elite driven than in commercial systems, and to seek a mass audience as a requirement of their funding with taxpayer or ratepayer support. Some media scholars have pointed out that content across available channels was remarkably similar (for example, Neuman, 1991; Tunstall, 1977), further supporting such assumptions.

In such an environment, it seemed highly plausible that mass media created a shared public understanding of the social world and would therefore be instrumental in creating shared public memory. Some studies suggested an audience so large that these representations of the past were essentially unavoidable. Moreover, the implied presence of a relatively undifferentiated mass audience rendered the notion of 'collective' memory largely unproblematic. One might find small groups of non-believers, but in general, mediated collective memory scholars could conceptualize a community that was roughly coterminous with the boundaries of a particular mass media system. Indeed, Benedict Anderson's (1983) influential theory on the development of national identity explained the role of mass media in creating a sense of community and nationhood among previously disparate groups bound together by colonial powers. Other scholars explicitly recognized the role of shared memory in fostering national bonds via the media. Henry Steele Commager (1965) reflected on how developing a shared past as articulated in nineteenth-century popular culture and literature helped to create a sense of community in an immigrant nation, the United States. Meyers, Zandberg and Neiger et al. (2009) described how the Israeli media commemorate the Holocaust for that relatively new nation's public. Michael Kammen (1978) documented the way in which national division interfered with mediated collective remembering. He described the reluctance of the American commercial media to commemorate the centenary of the American Civil War in the 1960s, fearing lingering regional animosities would preclude a commemoration that would appeal to a mass national audience. Any number of studies have examined and critiqued the portrayal of the past on television in terms of its role in creating and disseminating collective memories (see Edgerton and Rollins, 2001).

The logic of commercial mass media could also be effectively applied to journalistic representations of the past. News organizations, too, sought the money and influence generated by mass audiences. From at least the 1970s until the end of the century, news audiences in the United States were becoming even more concentrated as the number of towns and cities that supported more than one newspaper fell. Moreover, a growing number of scholars were finding the news looked essentially the same, regardless of the specific outlet. From the late 1980s until the new millennium, a number of prominent US scholars of media and politics repeatedly documented the hegemonic nature of journalism. They pointed out that no matter which specific news source one chose, the news generally served as an amplifier of the government (for example, Bennett, 1990; Bennett, Lawrence and Livingston, 2007; Entman, 1989, 1991; Zaller and Chiu, 1996). Thus, once research documented journalism's frequent use of the past (for example, Barnhurst and Mutz, 1997; Edy 2006), scholars studying its role in collective memory processes could assume that narratives and images of the past in the news reached an audience roughly coterminous with the geographic coverage of the news outlet. Representations of the past in national television news reached a national audience; representations in local news reached the local media market that news organization served (for example, Edy, 2006). Perhaps not every person would see every mediated representation, but these few media sources would provide the vast majority of information and interpretation available to a community to make sense of its past. The repeated, mass distributed representations of the past would be hard to resist in much the same way as is George Orwell's all-encompassing State's constant rewriting of history in the novel *1984*: 'The only evidence to the contrary was the mute protest in your own bones' (1949, 73).

Yet even as studies of mediated and journalistic collective memory were getting off the ground in the 1990s, the media environment was rapidly changing in ways that challenged some underlying assumptions of these studies. By 2008, Nielsen estimated that nearly 90 percent of US homes had either cable or direct broadcast satellite service (Household TV, 2009) and received an average of 118 channels (US Homes, 2008). Even more entertainment and information sources were available via the internet, and a 2012 report estimated 75percent of US households with televisions also had broadband internet access (Perez, 2012), allowing them to stream internet video. The advent of what Marcus Prior (2007) has termed a 'high choice media environment' changed both what was available to media consumers and how they engaged with media.

One kind of choice offered to consumers was a choice in news programming. The first all-news network in the US, Cable News Network (CNN), attracted audiences by offering a 24-hour alternative to traditional half-hour broadcast network news, but newer networks created a niche for themselves by appealing to political partisans – Fox News to conservatives and MSNBC to liberals. Audiences could now select news sources they found ideologically congenial, and in recent years, interest in the theory of selective exposure has come roaring back as scholars have begun to consider the social consequences of the high choice media environment (for example, Bennett and Iyengar 2008; Stroud 2011; Sunstein 2007). Virtually all of this literature suggests that selective exposure to media content, particularly news content, leads to a public that has less common ground than it did in the broadcast era and brings into question previous assumptions about the mass audience and about mediated collective memory.

Defining collective memory in a post-broadcast world

Recent transformations in media and journalism will require collective memory scholars to reconsider how they define a 'collective' that 'shares' a memory. Scholars studying collective memory in the era of mass media audiences were not immune to the notion that collective memory was not necessarily shared across an entire community. In 1923, Karl Mannheim (1952 [1923]) proposed the idea that shared memory was a generational phenomenon. Each generation's worldview was especially influenced by public events that occurred in their early adulthood, and thus each generation's worldview was different, creating generation gaps. In a more recent example, Emily Robinson (2003) pointed out that Japanese Americans remember Pearl Harbor quite differently from most other Americans.

Yet the contribution of selective exposure to these differences has not been explored. Indeed, some who studied contested collective memories constructed them as social problems awaiting a resolution that takes the form of an agreement about the meaning of the past. Edy (2006), for example, described how controversial memories are transformed into consensual ones in a social process mediated by journalism. More recently, the ongoing conflict in Japan over World War II memory enacted in a debate over the meaning of the Yasukuni shrine to Japanese war dead (see, for example, Breen 2008) has largely been represented as a struggle whose resolution will have political consequences. Studies of truth and reconciliation commissions and other techniques for coming to terms with traumatic and divisive public pasts also follow this model. Even scholars who studied the survival of alternative memories embraced a mass audience perspective, constructing memory differences within a community as a struggle between a socially powerful mainstream memory and a threatened alternative. Edy (2006) addresses this issue somewhat obliquely, considering how a local memory of the 1968 Democratic National Convention was preserved in a Chicago newspaper and was challenged by national press attention to 1968 convention memories during the 1996 Democratic Convention. Although he focused on non-mediated aspects of commemoration, John Bodnar (1992) described how vernacular activism subverted the goals of state-sponsored memory.

These studies, both of negotiating a meaning for the past and of preserving alternative memories, typically imply a mutually aware community conscious of what the dominant memory (Popular Memory Group, 1982; Bommes and Wright, 1982) is, even if it does not subscribe to that memory. Where pockets of alternative memory exist, it is their interaction with dominant memory that is the focus of research. In contrast, effective selective exposure could create pockets of memory that never interact at all, raising questions not about the survival of alternative memories but about whether and under what conditions memory might be called 'collective.' In a post-broadcast world, the idea of a mainstream or dominant memory begins to seem problematic. Thus, collective memory scholars are faced with fundamental questions about how to operationally define their phenomenon of interest.

Previous scholarship has wrestled with this issue to some extent. Some define collective memory as individual memories of public events (for example, Lang and Lang, 1989; Johnson, 1995; Mannheim, 1952 [1923]; Schuman and Corning, 2006). Others locate collective memory in artifacts constructed and rituals performed by a community (for example, Balthorp, Blair and Michel, 2010; Connerton, 1989; Wagner-Pacifici and Schwartz, 1991). Still others have located it in stories shared within a community (Edy, 2006; Orenstein, 2002; Zelizer, 1992). All have skated around the issue of defining the boundaries of the collective. Are individual memories of public events collective if not every individual shares them or if different groups remember the same event differently? Are artifacts and rituals signifiers of collective memory if the passage of time has rendered them objects and activities without meaning or if their meaning is subverted by those required to revere or practice them (see Bodnar, 1992)? In the case of shared stories, during the mass media era one could define the 'collective' as the potential audience reached by a particular media organization and assume the values expressed by media texts were congruent with mainstream social values within the audience that media source sought to reach. In a post-broadcast world, virtually none of these assumptions may hold true.

Some collective memory research may not be much affected by this transformation. For example, Barbie Zelizer's (1992) study of media representations of John F. Kennedy's assassination examines how journalism's attempts to retain its authority during an important national event affected national memories of that event, a motivation likely unchanged by recent media transformations. Oren Meyers's (2007) study of journalists' recollections of a defunct Israeli newspaper examines the memories of a well-defined professional community. His and similar studies of collective memory within small, well-defined groups (especially studies of what have been called 'alternative' memories of minority groups) may be relatively unaffected. However, those interested in the role journalism and media play in maintaining and disseminating stories and images of the past to general audiences will need to better explicate the media/audience relationship under study. Moreover, scholars studying 'alternative' memory may not be able to assume a 'mainstream' or 'dominant' memory to which that alternative is opposed.

Some tools for understanding this changed social environment and for effectively defining community and shared memory in the new environment may come from other fields. Sociologist Robert Bellah and his associates (1996) offer a useful tool for describing the contours of community, distinguishing two types of communities: communities of place and communities of interest. The former consist of individuals who live in physical proximity to one another. They are neighbors, even if they do not know one another, bonded together by their shared physical environment. The latter are self-created communities that come together because they share an interest, a concern, a point of view and so on. In some respects, the move from a broadcast to a post-broadcast world is one from a media world dominated by communities of place to one dominated by communities of interest. It is relatively easy to imagine (and to imagine studying) collective memories emerging within well-defined communities of interest. Yet the enhanced opportunities to create communities of interest have not wiped out communities of place, and the hard work of community decision-making occurs in communities of place. People who dislike group decisions made within a community of interest can abandon the community with little effort, but the decisions reached within a community of place tend to have lasting repercussions for members. This raises questions about what happens when people share memories within communities of interest but not within communities of place. What happens if a community of place lacks the sense of shared history Commager (1965) and Anderson (1983) suggest is key to perceiving oneself as part of that community? How do we study these communities of place, particularly when the relevant community is the size of a state or a nation?

Historical ignorance in a post-broadcast world

Another aspect of selective exposure in a high choice media environment documented by media scholars but not yet explored by collective memory scholars is the possibility of avoiding a particular type of media content altogether. Prior (2007) points out that in the broadcast era, US news was virtually unavoidable. If one wanted to watch television at the dinner hour, one watched news because there was nothing else on the air, which meant that even people who were not especially interested in public affairs had some limited knowledge of them (Prior, 2007). In the post-broadcast media environment, however, those uninterested in government and politics can effectively avoid gathering any information about them (Prior, 2007). Indeed, this strategy of avoiding political information altogether seems to be more commonplace than partisan selective exposure (Stroud, 2011).

Similar selection processes might affect collective memory. First, collective memories often have their origins in news events, such as the Kennedy assassination (Zelizer, 1992), Hurricane Katrina (Robinson, 2009), or 9/11. If some substantial proportion of a community effectively avoids exposure to news (perhaps not of overwhelming events such as 9/11, but of more complex trends such as the financial crisis of 2008), then a view of collective memory derived from Mannheim's (1923) concept of generations becomes problematic. Those who avoid the news may have a fundamentally different sense of lived history, for they would not have shared news narratives about important community events as they unfolded nor the uncertainty and emotion that accompanies such moments. For example, having missed the early news coverage of Hurricane Katrina because I was traveling, I find that I cannot summon the same sense of shock and outrage that shapes the memories of colleagues and friends who watched the events live. I did not share the experience, so even though I know about the event, in some key ways, I do not share the memory. If this sort of selectivity becomes commonplace, could one speak of a generational worldview among people who did not experience the events of their formative years collectively?

Second, critics who once denigrated media for failing to represent the past adequately (or at all) will now need to contend with the fact that many citizens, given the choice, may opt out of learning about the history they share as members of a particular community. More attention may need to be paid to the incidental learning phenomenon, the idea that people who use media content to obtain a particular gratification may get more than they bargained for. More representations of the past may be encountered accidentally in pop culture than are encountered through formal mediated commemoration processes like those documented by Meyers and his colleagues (2009). This raises anew the question of whether depictions of the past in fictional television should be historically correct, modeling the way things 'really' were, or should be politically correct, modeling advances in social equality that have been made over time. It also raises the question of whether those who use different kinds of pop culture materials may form distinct memory enclaves. Collective memories of the Vietnam War grounded in the videogame *Call of Duty: Black Ops* may not share much in common with those grounded in journalistic retrospectives.

Memory silos in a post-broadcast world

While some citizens may avoid their shared past altogether, it is also possible that a high choice media environment could facilitate the development of distinctive communities of memory within geographic or political boundaries. Thus, another conceptual tool for understanding the new collective memory environment comes from information systems and organization management literature. Selective exposure may result in *memory silos* similar to the information silos that occur when a specific unit within a company (or computer system) is incapable of interacting with other units either because it refuses to share information or because its goals and practices do not align with those of other units or the organization as a whole (Cromity and de Stricker, 2011). A memory silo may emerge if distinct groups of people within a social system come to share a collective memory unique to them and are unaware that this memory is not typical beyond the boundaries of their group.

One model of what this might look like can be derived from scholarship examining national differences in public memory. For example, Michael Hogan's (1996) edited volume explored how differently the Americans and the Japanese understand the atomic bombing of Hiroshima and Nagasaki. American memory views the bombing as necessary to end the war: facing an enemy determined to defend its homeland to the death and to the last man, using nuclear weapons was the best available option to save both American and Japanese lives. It is unlikely that many Americans are aware the Japanese memory is one of victimhood: as their military prepared to defend their homeland against invasion, their civilians were devastated by a weapon unleashed by white people against non-white people (Hein and Selden, 1997). Here, two memory communities exist side by side, largely unaware of each other – at least in part because they share almost no media in common. Anderson (1983) showed how having media in common helps create a bond between disparate villages and tribes, making invisible and arbitrary national borders real by giving those within them a sense of shared fate. Yet the incompatible memories of Americans and Japanese about the end of World War II show that boundaries may also be made real by incompatible worldviews that are the result of non-contact, which may in turn be fostered by social groups using rival media sources.

There could be benefits to a media system that facilitates the development of such memory silos. One positive effect might be greater viability of collective memory alternatives silenced in a mass media environment. In a post-broadcast media environment, feminist, ethnic minority, language minority, or other forms of alternative collective memory might be more easily shared both within the relevant group and with interested outsiders. Moreover, alternative memory narratives could be shaped and expressed without having to conform to the communication principles of the majority. However, management and information systems scholarship suggests that information silos hinder the effective functioning of an organization or system since important information or perspectives are missing from decision-making processes. Similarly, memory silos may have deleterious effects on social processes, and indeed one type of harmful effect has already been suggested by critical scholarship on alternative memories. This work typically proceeds from a social justice perspective, emphasizing the right of minority memory to exist and be acknowledged by the mainstream (for example, Robinson, 2003), and sometimes couched in terms of an admonition not to forget (for example, Hoerl, 2012). In asserting the value of minority voices, the studies suggest that the mainstream generates a memory silo, unaware and surprised to learn of minority perspectives, and the harmful effects of the silo include impeding the path of genuine human equality. Thus, the potential social justice benefits of a high choice media environment that enables the expression and dissemination of alternatives to dominant memories might never be realized because the mainstream could so thoroughly isolate itself from those alternatives.

Memory silos might also have negative effects on collective decision-making within a political community. A good deal of scholarship reveals the links between shared memory and the political life of a community. Both Commager (1965) and Anderson (1983) suggest a sense of shared history and shared fate are necessary components of establishing nationhood. Smith (1985) and Edy (2006) point out that memory can serve as the basis of political action, for using the lessons of the past makes the outcomes of policy action seem more predictable and thus less risky. Bodnar (1992) argues that state-sponsored appeals to shared memory teach citizens patriotic lessons about sacrificing personal comforts (or even their lives) for the good of the nation. What if memory silos emerge that align with particular political interests? For example, most Americans living today have no personal memories of the Vietnam War, and when the past is beyond personal memory, the media's power over collective memory likely expands (Edy, 2006), increasing the likelihood that selective exposure will affect collective memory. When queried, most agree that the war was a mistake (Edy, 2005), but there are two major threads of reasoning about why it was a mistake. One says the United States erred in not committing enough resources to the war effort to achieve decisive victory. The other says the United States erred in becoming involved in the internal affairs of another country. What if political conservatives selected media that only offered one version of the story while political liberals selected media that only told the other? And what if analogies to Vietnam continue to be used to make sense of military conflicts, as they have been for US military undertakings from the 1980s until now (Edy, 2005)? Could such memory silos undermine the potential for political compromise?

This scenario is perhaps the least troubling of many, for it involves a historical analogy in which the past is compared to the present

(Edy, 1999; Lang and Lang, 1989). More problematic for political deci-sion-making are cases where political adversaries fail to share a sense of historical context. Trying to reach policy decisions when the meaning of the past upon which they are based is in dispute generates profound political conflict that is ideological (grounded in differences over goals) rather than pragmatic (grounded in differences over means). Thus, for those who saw 9/11 as the beginning of a war on terrorism, any scaling back of national security or military operations said to thwart potential acts of terrorism amounts to 'forgetting' the thousands lost on that day. For others who saw 9/11 as a national tragedy grounded in a particular historical and political moment that has now passed, the cost of anti-terrorism measures needs to be weighed against other national values. Where such communities are insulated in memory silos generated by selective exposure, the lack of a shared past creates an environment where the need to make shared decisions strains the political community.

Such problems could resonate both forward and backward in time, for the news media not only generate analogies and contexts; they also play an important role in commemoration (Meyers et al., 2009). What if politically distinctive patterns of mediated commemoration emerged, with conservative media recalling events like VJ Day and the fall of the Berlin Wall, while liberal media recall events like school desegregation and the *Roe v. Wade* abortion decision? Could such patterns of mediated remembering produce a community that shares geographic bounda-ries and political institutions but lacks a sense of national identity (Commager, 1965; Anderson, 1983)? How would such a community engage in collective decision-making?

Conclusion

Scholars of journalism and memory and of mediated memory more generally need to begin to incorporate recent profound changes in the media system into their scholarship. Where scholarship from the mass media era highlighted the dominance of mainstream public memories (often generated or facilitated by the state) and the survival of alterna-tive memories, in a post- broadcast environment even these categories may be outdated. In a world of networked, rather than broadcast audiences, media scholars need to consider the possibility of partisan memories and memory silos and the kinds of collectivity they facili-tate and impede. The fast-growing literature on the psychological and social processes influencing selective exposure, as well as the evolving literature on the social consequences of media choice, can help us appreciate the impacts of this changed media environment. It is still not clear just how selective people are or can be. However, in a mass media world, scholars worried about the survival of what was different. In a networked world, we may need to turn our concern to the survival of what is communal.

References

Anderson, B. (1983) *Imagined Communities: Reflections on the Origin and Spread of Nationalism.* New York: Verso.

Balthrop, V., Blair, C. and Michel, N. (2010) 'The Presence of the Present: Hijacking "The Good War"?' *Western Journal of Communication*, 74(2), 170–207.

Barnhurst, K.G. and Mutz, D. (1997) 'American Journalism and the Decline of Event-Centered Reporting,' *Journal of Communication*, 47(4), 27–53.

Bellah, R.N., Madsen, R., Sullivan, W.M., Swidler, A. and Tipton, S.M. (1996) *Habits of the Heart: Individualism and Commitment in American Life.* Berkeley: University of California Press.

Bennett, W.L. (1990) 'Toward a Theory of Press–State Relations,' *Journal of Communication*, 40(2), 103–25.

Bennett, W. L. and Iyengar, S. (2008) 'A New Era of Minimal Effects? The Changing Foundations of Political Communication,' *Journal of Communication*, 58(4), 707–31.

Bennett, W.L., Lawrence, R.G. and Livingston, S. (2007) *When the Press Fails: Political Power and the News Media from Iraq to Katrina.* Chicago: University of Chicago Press.

Bodnar, J. (1992) *Remaking America: Public Memory, Commemoration and Patriotism in the Twentieth Century.* Princeton, NJ: Princeton University Press.

Bommes, M. and Wright, P. (1982) 'Charms of Residence: The Public and the Past,' in R. Johnson, G. McLennan, B. Schwarz and D. Sutton (eds) *Making Histories: Studies in History-Writing and Politics.* Minneapolis, MN: University of Minnesota Press, pp. 253–302.

Breen, J. (2008) *Yasukuni, the War Dead, and the Struggle for Japan's Past.* New York: Columbia University Press.

Commager, H.S. (1965) 'The Search for a Usable Past,' *American Heritage*, 16(2), 4–9.

Connerton, P. (1989) *How Societies Remember.* Cambridge, MA: Cambridge University Press.

Cromity, J. and de Stricker, U. (2011) 'Silo Persistence: It's not the Technology, it's the Culture!,' *New Review of Information Networking*, 16(2), 167–84.

Edgerton, G.R. and Rollins, P.C. (2001) *Television Histories: Shaping Collective Memory in the Media Age.* Lexington: University of Kentucky Press.

Edy, J.A. (1999) 'Journalistic Uses of Collective Memory,' *Journal of Communication*, 49(2), 71–85.

Edy, J.A. (2005) 'Trends in Collective Memory: The Lessons of Vietnam.' Paper presented at the International Communication Association Annual Meeting, New York, May.

Edy, J.A. (2006) *Troubled Pasts: News and the Collective Memory of Social Unrest.* Philadelphia, PA: Temple University Press.

Entman, R.M. (1989) *Democracy without Citizens.* New York: Oxford University Press.

Entman, R.M. (1991) 'Framing U.S. Coverage of International News: Contrasts in Narratives of the KAL and Iran Air Incidents,' *Journal of Communication,* 41(4), 6–27.

Hein, L. and Selden, M. (1997) *Living with the Bomb: American and Japanese Cultural Conflicts in the Nuclear Age.* Armonk, NY: M.E. Sharpe.

Hoerl, K. (2012) 'Selective Amnesia and Racial Transcendence in News Coverage of President Obama's Inauguration,' *Quarterly Journal of Speech,* 98(2), 178–202.

Hogan, M.J. (1996) *Hiroshima in History and Memory.* Cambridge: Cambridge University Press.

'Household TV Trends Holding Steady: Nielsen Economic Study 2008' (2009), available at http://www.nielsen.com/us/en/newswire/2009/household-tv-trends-holding-steady-nielsen%C3%A2%C2%80%C2%99s-economic-study-2008.html (accessed 13 October 2013).

Johnson, T.J. (1995) *The Rehabilitation of Richard Nixon: The Media's Effect on Collective Memory.* New York: Garland.

Kammen, M. (1978) *A Season of Youth: The American Revolution and the Historical Imagination.* New York: Alfred A. Knopf.

Lang, K. and Lang, G.E. (1989) 'Collective Memory and the News,' *Communication,* 11, 123–29.

Mannheim, Karl (1952 [1923]) 'The Problem of Generations,' in Paul Kecskemeti (ed.) *Essays on the Sociology of Knowledge.* London: Routledge, pp. 276–320.

McChesney, R.W. and Nichols, J. (2010) *The Death and Life of American Journalism: The Media Revolution that Will Begin the World Again.* Philadelphia: Nation Books.

McChesney, R.W. and Pickard, V. (2011) *Will the last Reporter Please Turn out the Lights: The Collapse of Journalism and What Can be Done to Fix it.* New York: New Press.

Meyers, O. (2007) 'Memory in Journalism and the Memory of Journalism: Israeli Journalists and the Constructed Legacy of Haolam Hazeh,' *Journal of Communication,* 57(4), 719–38.

Meyers, O., Zandberg, E. and Neiger, M. (2009) 'Prime Time Commemoration: An Analysis of Television Broadcasts on Israel's Memorial Day for the Holocaust and the Heroism,' *Journal of Communication,* 59(3), 456–80.

Neuman, W.R. (1991) *The Future of the Mass Audience.* Cambridge: Cambridge University Press.

Orenstein, C. (2002) *Little Red Riding Hood Uncloaked: Sex, Morality and the Evolution of a Fairy Tale.* New York: Basic Books.

Orwell, G. (1949) *Nineteen Eighty-Four.* New York: Harcourt, Brace and World.

Perez, S. (2012) 'Nielsen: Cord Cutting and Internet TV Viewing on the Rise,' *Techcrunch,* 9 February, available at http://techcrunch.com/2012/02/09/nielsen-cord-cutting-and-internet-tv-viewing-on-the-rise, accessed 18 September 2013.

Popular Memory Group (1982) 'Popular Memory: Theory, Politics, Method,' in R. Johnson, G. McLennan, B. Schwarz and D. Sutton (eds) *Making Histories: Studies in History-Writing and Politics.* Minneapolis, MN: University of Minnesota Press, pp. 205–52.

Prior, M. (2007) *Post Broadcast Democracy: How Media Choice Increases Inequality in Political Involvement and Polarizes Elections*. Cambridge: Cambridge University Press.

Robinson, E.S. (2003) *A Date Which Will Live: Pearl Harbor in American Memory*. Durham, NC: Duke University Press.

Robinson, S. (2009) '"If You Had Been With Us": Mainstream Press and Citizen Journalists Jockey for Authority over Memory of Hurricane Katrina,' *New Media & Society*, 11(5), 795–814.

Schuman, H. and Corning, A.D. (2006) 'Comparing Iraq to Vietnam: Recognition, Recall, and the Nature of Cohort Effects,' *Public Opinion Quarterly*, 70(1), 78–87.

Smith, B.J. (1985) *Politics and Remembrance*. Princeton, NJ: Princeton University Press.

Stroud, N.J. (2011) *Niche News: The Politics of News Choice*. New York: Oxford University Press.

Sunstein, C. (2007) *Republic 2.0*. Princeton, NJ: Princeton University Press.

Tunstall, J. (1977) *The Media are American*. New York: Columbia University Press.

Turow, J. (1997) *Breaking Up America: Advertisers and the New Media World*. Chicago: University of Chicago Press.

US Homes Receive a Record 118.6 TV Channels on Average (2008) *Marketing Charts*, available at http://www.marketingcharts.com/television/us-homes-receive-a-record-1186-tv-channels-on-average-4929, accessed 18 September 2013.

Wagner-Pacifici, R. and Schwartz, B. (1991) 'The Vietnam Veterans Memorial: Commemorating a Difficult Past,' *American Journal of Sociology*, 97(2), 376–420.

Williams, B.A. and Delli-Carpini, M.X. (2011) *After Broadcast News: Media Regimes, Democracy, and the New Information Environment*. New York: Cambridge University Press.

Zaller, J. and Chiu, D. (1996) 'Government's Little Helper: U.S. News Coverage of Foreign Policy Crises, 1945–1991,' *Political Communication*, 13(4), 385–405.

Zandberg, E., Meyers, O. and Neiger, M. (2012) 'Past Continuous: Newsworthiness and the Shaping of Collective Memory,' *Critical Studies in Media Communication*, 29(1), 65–79.

Zelizer, B. (1992) *Covering the Body: The Kennedy Assassination, the Media, and the Shaping of Collective Memory*. Chicago: University of Chicago Press.

Part II
Domains of Journalism and Memory

Journalism and Narrative Memory

5
Journalism as a Vehicle of Non-Commemorative Cultural Memory

Michael Schudson

Memory is not only an individual but a collective process and journalism has been our most public, widely distributed, easily accessible and thinly stretched membrane of social memory. (I will use the terms social memory, collective memory, cultural memory and public memory interchangeably.) But just how do the news media contribute to memory?

It is well recognized that the news media act as institutions of commemoration (Edy, 1999). Journalists cover holidays, anniversaries of famous events, sometimes the birthdays and invariably the deaths of notable people, and they also write about public conflicts over memorials, museums, controversial books and films about historical figures, and more.

All of these journalistic ventures into memory-keeping are influential in shaping, reinforcing, or renewing cultural memory. Even so, it may be that commemorative news or news about commemoration are not the most important ways in which news contributes to memory. In this chapter, I want to focus on what journalism does as a keeper of *non-commemorative* memory. Not all of what societies remember is recalled through or in relation to self-conscious or dedicated memory projects. Instead, the past is often incorporated into the present in ways that do not aim at commemoration (Schudson, 1997). People learn lessons, generals fight the last war, traumatic experiences live on in bodily or psychological scar tissue, and social traumas affect social collectivities and maintain their place through the ways in which they are consciously or not so consciously kept in view. All people act in relation to memories and usually without commemoration as an objective. So do organizations. So do societies. So does journalism. Every time a news story covers some event or action of a person, group, organization, or society where the consciousness of time past or time passing is a factor, the media collaborate with larger social processes of cultural memory.

They ordinarily do so, I will argue, in an effort not to commemorate but to serve internal journalistic incentives; the media seek to capitalize on human drama or to connect to historical shifts, coincidences, or trends that might give their stories a distinctive importance.

We are drenched in Memory with a capital 'M' as never before. We have 'The History Channel' and hot and cold running video faucets of old television shows and old movies. We have historical consciousness as a real estate development strategy for saving historic districts or as a marketing tool for 'The American Girl' dolls, clothing, books and accessories. We have the past mobilized as a force for group identity in the way women, blacks, gays, lesbians and many other groups reconstruct and reconstitute group identity. We use monuments and museums to boost local pride and snag tourists. Memory is a set of industries, strategies, mobilized identities and much more.

The flourishing academic study of public memory has accordingly focused on the study of commemorative practices – biographies, histories, textbooks, holidays, anniversaries, funerals, eulogies, obituaries, commencement ceremonies and addresses, high school and college reunions, statues, images on stamps and currency, street names and school names and park names. Yet there are many other ways in which people's awareness of the past shapes the present. Non-commemorative memory is pervasive in human affairs – for instance, in the everyday operation of economics (the ways that the past endures in relationships of credit and debt and mortgage), of legislation (laws often intend to prevent some future injury by closing options that in the recent past caused such injuries), or extrapolations, plans and projections. Think of concepts and activities such as exercise, practice, rehearsal, revenge, restitution, reform, restoration and almost any other noun that begins 're-.' Think of the experience of a sense of the past slipping away – nostalgia, loss, mourning, regret, 'biological clock.' People's orientation to the future – goal, hope, despair, plan, anticipation, expectation, destiny, fate, apocalypse, millennium, schedule, deadline, clock-watching – imagines the present as the past. A person's sense of continuity over the life span – identity, character, reputation, track record – or beyond the life span – is also a form of memory. Some concepts emphasize a moral continuity over time – debt, loyalty, commitment, promise, guilt, shame, pride, punishment, justice, and the economist's notion of 'sunk costs' or investment. Any concept regarding learning invokes a special tie to the past – model, demonstration effect, role model, mentor, backlash, horror stories. The study of social memory need not wait for societies to encase the past in various memorial ambers but can and should tease out relationships to the past to be found in a wide variety of practices, attitudes and experiences in everyday life.

One prefatory remark remains before turning directly to the role of news in non-commemorative memory: attention to history varies across times and places. The British historian Peter Burke has offered a minimal definition of a 'true' sense of the past – that a sense of the past must include a sense of anachronism, that is, a sense that things truly change, that the past really is different. It must include also some awareness of evidence: that some things are more believable than others, and that there are standards for making judgments about types of evidence. And it must include an interest in causation. Even by this broad definition, Burke writes, a sense of the past has been relatively rare in human experience. It includes the Romans, he argues, but not the ancient Greeks or the biblical Jews or medieval Europeans or most primitive societies. In Burke's view, a society is unlikely to supply historical awareness without both literacy and relatively rapid social change. The ancient Greeks had relatively rapid social change but no widespread literacy and the Chinese for centuries had literacy but no rapid social change and so neither had a sense of the past as we understand it (Burke, 1969: 1, 18, 141, 149).

The successful establishment of modern historical consciousness has also to do with the secure establishment of the nation-state as the primary political organization of the past two centuries and the worldwide spread of compulsory formal schooling that includes required instruction in the history of the nation-state providing the education. This is a major source of the triumph of historical consciousness in our own day and it is a very good reason to take historical consciousness not as a self-evidently good thing but as a self-evidently social thing, a self-evidently historical phenomenon in itself, richly deserving of academic attention, criticism and research.

Burke paints in very large strokes and speaks of history as professional historians understand it. In a less encompassing study – a study of references to time in American newspapers over the past 100 years – Kevin Barnhurst has identified a changing journalistic awareness of the past that is notable and measurable but responds to causes much more proximate than, say, 'rapid social change.' In looking at the *New York Times*, the *Oregonian* and the *Chicago Tribune*, sampling each paper every twenty years from 1894 to 1994 for news stories about accidents, crimes and employment, he found a fairly steady increase in the percentage of articles that made some reference to past and future time periods. References to the past grew from about 25 percent of stories in 1894 to nearly 50 percent by 1994 (Barnhurst, 2011: 101).

An earlier study by Christine Ogan and colleagues found comparable changes. In 1900–05, Ogan's study of the *New York Times* front page found 87 percent of stories had a 'time orientation' that assumed the story was of only immediate interest rather than potentially of 'long-range' interest; this figure dropped to 72 percent in 1920–25, 67 percent in 1930–35, 61 percent in 1940–45 and 57 percent in 1970 (Ogan et al., 1975). The growing attention to historical context over the past century of US journalism surely reflects, among other things, the sense among journalists, often articulated from at least the 1930s (Schudson, 1978), that the world is complex beyond measure and that part of the journalist's job is not just to report the latest happenings but to fit them into some kind of coherent framework for the audience. It is in the quest for coherent understanding, not in the service of commemoration, that journalists may make their most vital contribution to social memory.

How does the past endure in the present through non-commemorative practices that keep the past alive without necessarily intending to do so? In the case of the news media, I think journalists use the past non-commemoratively in three ways. First, they may use history to heighten or intensify the news value of a story – showing that the event they are covering is relatively rare and relatively unprecedented. Second, they draw the past into their story of an event to help make it comprehensible. The first reason – heightening news value – calls the reader or viewer's attention to a story – 'look at me!' The second reason – explaining what an event means – helps the audience understand the story – 'let me explain.' Both of these modes of non-commemorative memory influence a great many news stories. The third journalistic use of non-commemorative awareness of the past occurs primarily when news comments directly on human behaviors that are themselves non-commemorative uses of the past. In what follows, I illustrate all three types of journalistic participation in non-commemorative memory. My approach is methodologically informal – I simply observe, and interpret, stories in the *New York Times*, almost all of them on the front page, and almost all of them from 2012, each of which illustrates one of my categories. Although I cannot claim that most other news organizations – or any other news organizations, for that matter – do something similar, Ogan's and Barnhurst's research encourages me to think that further study would show that they do.

'Look at me!' Uses of the past: heralding the newsworthy

If historical evidence can show that an event a reporter is covering is very unusual, this can intensify the importance of the story and so promote it from unpublishable to publishable, from a back page to the front page, or from a subordinate to a lead position on the front page. This is a claim on editors to give the piece prominent play and it acts as a prod to audiences to pay attention.

On the front page on 17 June 2012 (a day on which the *New York Times* chose not to run anything on the fortieth anniversary of the Watergate break-in), a story took up the practice of professional photographers hired by couples to photograph childbirth. The story provided the barest minimum of a historical context – 'Birth was once considered a behind-closed-doors affair' and 'Then, expectant fathers entered the picture, snapping photos or taking videos with shaky hands' (Gootman, 2012). 'Once...then' is all the legitimation the reporter offers for why the story is worthy of journalistic attention, why the subject is 'new' and therefore news. This is as minimalist – indeed, as lame – as historical consciousness can get. It is a mere wave of the hand toward situating the story in time, but it probably seemed sufficiently in accord with personal knowledge of editors in the newsroom or presumed readers of the paper to suffice.

Also on the front page that day, the *Times* ran a story on the election in Egypt for President Hosni Mubarak's successor that began, 'Voters cast ballots on Saturday for the first competitively elected leader in Egypt's history....' (Kirkpatrick and Fahim, 2012). Readers know without being reminded that Egypt is an important country with great influence in Middle East politics and a very long history, and so this 'first' is a powerful authorization of why the reader should take note. 'Once... then' pales by comparison. Similarly, three weeks later, a front-page story is headlined, 'Libya Holds Vote After 40 Years of Dictatorship' (Kirkpatrick, 2012). 'Libya Holds Vote' is the event that happened but that event out of historical context does not herald its weight in the world. The lead therefore offers readers some history: 'Defying expectations and, in some places, bullets, Libyans across most of the country voted Saturday in the first election after more than four decades of isolation and totalitarianism under Col. Muammar el-Qaddafi.' This does not 'explain' anything about the election but calls attention to the importance of the event by asserting its unprecedented status.

When Israel's prime minister, Benjamin Netanyahu, made a deal on 8 May 2012 with the opposition in the Knesset, securing greater power for himself, this was more than enough for a news story – a change in the power structure of a national government, a change in a key foreign government with inevitable consequence for US national interests. But political change happens all the time – what brought this change to the front page? Reporter Jodi Rudoren wrote in her opening sentence that this change created 'the largest and broadest coalition government in recent memory' in Israel (Rudoren, 2012). 'In recent memory' is nearly as vague as 'once...then' but it suggests that the change was large, potentially epochal, a once-in-several-decades event. Rudoren's judgment offers editors a justification for front-page placement and provides readers with a sense of proportion and an incentive to read on.

President Barack Obama's endorsement of same-sex marriage on 9 May 2012 was obviously news – this was a controversial political issue on which Obama changed his position. In this case proof of newsworthiness does not need 'history', apart from Obama's own history from his 2008 campaign forward through 8 May 2012, when he had not been prepared to endorse same-sex marriage, up until 9 May, when he took the plunge. This is the simple 'once...then' formula so well known it did not even have to be stated. But what made journalists see this as a breakout story? The *New York Times* on 10 May ran two front-page pieces below a four-column headline. One of the stories was a 'news analysis' with the headline, 'A Watershed Move, Both Risky and Inevitable.' Adam Nagourney's lead says that Obama's move was 'by any measure a watershed.' He added that in endorsing same-sex marriage Obama took sides 'in what many people consider the last civil rights movement.' This invokes 'the civil rights movement' of American history, which in the American idiom means the century-long African-American movement that culminated in the equal rights legislation of the 1960s, and specifically recalls the conflicts over rights for African-Americans which erupted in the 1950s and 1960s. It also implicitly invokes the succession of liberation struggles that followed, notably the women's movement, which learned so much from the African-Americans' battles and transformed American life so profoundly. Nagourney's adaptation of this unattributed phrase, 'the last civil rights movement,' declares of Obama's action that 'This is not just politics' or 'This is the kind of moment when politics transcends itself and transfigures a nation.' It is a 'watershed.' It is what we often call 'historic.'[1]

'Let me explain.' Uses of the past: explaining complexity

The second journalistic use of non-commemorative memory offers explanation. Journalists try to give their audience some appreciation of the context – often but not always locating the event they cover in time – to help people comprehend a current event, why it happened and what its weight in the world might be. Jenny Kitzinger has called attention to the use of what she calls 'media templates,' past media stories that have attained 'a single primary meaning' and that 'are used to explain current events' (Kitzinger, 2000: 76). Explaining is a vital way in which the past may be used non-commemoratively.

A front-page story on 5 May 2012 focused on Chinese dissident Chen Guangcheng who had taken refuge in the US Embassy in Beijing while Secretary of State Hillary Clinton was in the city on a high-level visit to confer with Chinese leaders (Perlez and Wines, 2012). In a related 'let me explain' story adjacent to the page twelve continuation of the front page story, Andrew Jacobs (2012) set the incident in the context of how China has dealt with other dissidents ('For China, a Dissident in Exile Is One Less Headache Back Home'). The lead paragraph recounts the top news of the day – that after a week of feverish diplomacy, China made a concession to allow Mr Chen to go to the United States. The second paragraph is one brief sentence: 'The bigger concession would have been allowing him to stay.' Why does Jacobs say that? The next paragraph introduces the rest of the story: 'Based on past experience, China is often all too pleased to see its most nettlesome dissidents go into exile, where they almost invariably lose their ability to grab headlines in the West and to command widespread sympathy both in China and abroad.'

Here Jacobs, with that very general 'based on past experience' phrase, launches into a discussion (the full story runs twenty-three paragraphs) about a set of other dissidents in exile, going back to the years immediately after Tiananmen Square in 1989. Jacobs then predicts the future based on the historical record he has assembled: 'And if history is any guide, the Chinese authorities are unlikely to allow Mr. Chen, a self-taught legal advocate who had been silenced by seven years of prison and house arrest, to return home after his studies, especially if he continues his full-throated criticisms of the country's authoritarian political system.' The *New York Times* thus offers readers an analysis of a current event that goes back two decades and calls to mind a traumatic event that the Chinese government not only fails to commemorate but actively seeks to erase.

Consider the same day's lead story concerning the sluggish US economic recovery, Catherine Rampell's 'Rate of Growth in Jobs Slowed for U.S. in April.' The lead is as follows: 'The nation's employers are creating jobs at less than half the pace they were when this year began, according to a government report released Friday.' However, this is not what the press release from the Bureau of Labor Statistics said. To arrive at this lead, Rampell (2012) did much more than just paraphrase the report. The report contended that employment rose by 115,000 jobs and the unemployment rate was unchanged. It did not say, as Rampell does in her second paragraph, 'The addition of just 115,000 jobs in April was disappointing, but economists urged no panic just yet.' The Bureau of Labor Statistics did not mention that job creation for April was less than half of what it had been 'when the year began.' In other words, the news organization – not the government – made sense of the new data by comparing it to past data. Rampell takes readers still further back – the proportion of working-age Americans who are working or looking for work is 'at its lowest level since 1981.' And the proportion of men in the labor force fell to 70 percent in April, 'the lowest figure since the Labor Department began collecting these data in 1948.' Comparisons to five months earlier, thirty-one years earlier and sixty-four years earlier underscore how dismal the economic situation is and give the story front-page standing which the Bureau's press release did not provide (and which the administration did not wish for).

Did Jacobs present a sufficient account of the cases of past Chinese dissidents? Did Rampell consult the right assortment of economists? It is possible to raise objections to the ways these reporters constructed a historical framework for their reporting. Journalists are better protected from criticism if they omit context and just declare what is right before their eyes. But, as critics of a minimalist 'he said, she said' journalism have long noted, this creates distortions of its own. Facts without a context leave much to be desired and the move toward a more 'explanatory' or 'analytical' or 'contextual' journalism seems to me a salutary, if risky, shift.

By no means do journalists always repair to history to offer an explanatory context for the news. In this regard, a story in the *Times* (12 November 2011) concerning the Penn State University scandal over child sexual abuse committed by an assistant coach in the school's famous football program struck me by its rarity, not its familiarity. Reporter Nina Bernstein (2011) wrote a front-page story in the wake of the scandal reviewing a set of cases of serious crimes on college and university campuses where very often law enforcement is in the hands of police officers who report to their universities and not to state or municipal police authorities. University police may choose not to refer cases to the district attorney but to try to manage them quietly and internally. It was only in 1986, Bernstein informs readers, that the murder of a student on campus at Lehigh University led to the Clery Act of 1990 (named after the victim) that required colleges and universities to report campus crimes to government law enforcement. The story discusses five prior cases at five other colleges and universities where questions have been raised about whether campus police put the interests of the victims or the interests of an unruffled school reputation first. This story was rare in following an institutional thread from the Penn State case back into the past and across the country to other universities with comparable law enforcement arrangements to those at Penn State. Bernstein thus turned a scandal about a single person at a single institution into a query about a national shortcoming in public policy and enforcement of criminal law. Here history is not used to explain Penn State; Penn State is used to point to a larger pattern in history.

Any story about a 'trend' must invoke the past to make any sense at all. 'Trend' stories beg for explanation. In a 29 June 2012 story in the *Times* (on A13), Erica Goode plays off social science data that document a 60 percent decline in child sexual abuse from 1992 to 2010 against the headlines of the past week, including juries finding guilty verdicts against Penn State assistant football coach Jerry Sandusky for child sexual abuse and against Monsignor William J. Lynn of Philadelphia's Archdiocese for protecting pedophile priests (Goode, 2012). Relying on several experts to try to explain the trends, Goode also cites two experts on why organizations in the area of child abuse are reluctant to accept what should be very good news. These organizations depend on a rhetoric that the problem that defines their mission is 'getting worse every year, it's an epidemic.' Is it? Well, says one of the experts: 'It is very risky to suggest that the problem you're involved with has gotten smaller' (Goode, 2012). Organizers who must raise funds for their work find that bad news about the growth of the problem before them is good news for fundraising efforts.

Covering non-commemorative experiences of time

The third way journalists make use of non-commemorative memory is when they cover some moment of human drama in which individuals or groups themselves employ non-commemorative practices that have some news interest. Consider the front page story by Michael M. Grynbaum (*New York Times*, 4 May 2012) headlined, 'Broken Leg Adds Hurdle to Her Quest, at 82, for 14th House Term.' The story is about a 13-term Democrat in the Congress from Rochester, New York, Louise Slaughter, pictured with her leg in a cast. Suggesting her spunk, Grynbaum (2012) writes that she has joked about trying out a new campaign slogan, 'Vote Louise. She has a leg up.' But the story also relates that in a recent press conference Slaughter was pushed 'to redeclare her intention not only to run for Congress, but also to live long enough to serve out her term.' At that news conference she said, 'I wouldn't be running for office if I was about to die.' If Rep. Slaughter had been sixty or even seventy and seeking her fourteenth term, it is very unlikely that there would have been a story at all. But at eighty-two, she was well past an expected retirement age and coming close to the upper bound of the normal productive life span. The question of 'living long enough to serve out her term' brings to the story a drama that many readers have considered in their own experience personally or with close friends and family. We might think of this as an anticipatory commemoration, looking ahead to Rep. Slaughter's obituary. It invokes – as did Rep. Slaughter and her critics – knowledge about the normal human life span, the normal human working career, the normal political career. The normal human lifetime makes this theater-piece journalism worthy of the front page. (Incidentally, Rep. Slaughter won re-election.)

Similarly, there is a human drama in the story science writer Gina Kolata wrote concerning Dr Lukas Wartman, 'a young, talented and beloved colleague' at a genetics research center at Washington University in St Louis who contracted adult acute lymphoblastic leukemia, 'the very cancer he had devoted his career to studying' (Kolata, 2012). Or in a long front-page story a few days earlier about Lonnie G. Thompson, a climate scientist at Ohio State whose work takes him on difficult field trips to mountaintops around the world to recover cylindrical cores of ice as much as 25,000 years old. With some of these glacial ice sites melting, Thompson felt he was fighting against time; when in 2009 he learned he had serious heart disease, this became personal, more so in fall 2011 when doctors told him only a heart transplant might save him. When the *Times* wrote about him (3 July 2012), he had recently had a successful heart transplant operation and was already looking toward going to an ice cap in China. Reporter Justin Gillis portrays him in the context of other key climate scientists working into their seventies and eighties in what they saw as both a personal race against time and a world race against disaster (Gillis, 2012). Versions of peering over the shoulder of someone whose life is nearing its end or balances on the precipice of fatal disease in a particularly dramatic fashion engages the audience for news as it does for film or theater or a novel. In these cases, there is not a specific past that is invoked but a generalized understanding of the human lifetime and its brevity.

On 18 June 2012, the *New York Times* ran a front-page obituary for Rodney G. King, whom Los Angeles police brutally beat when he appeared to be resisting arrest in 1991. The next year, when the police officers were acquitted and a bloody race riot erupted, King pleaded with his fellow citizens to get along. What's interesting in this sad story of a sad life is how much King's accidental moment in the sun – his moment in history – meant to him. This piece of commemorative-memory journalism is not just about the events of King's life which brought him to national attention but how he himself responded to his surprising celebrity. This extensive piece – a thirty paragraph story with five photos, focuses on a complex interplay of commemorative and non-commemorative practices. With the $3.8 million King was ultimately awarded in damages from the city of Los Angeles, he bought the modest house where he died. He was found, drowned, in the backyard pool he had built and where he had inscribed in two tiles the dates of his beating and of the outbreak of the riots. A cop at the jail where he was once held told him, 'People are going to know who you are when you're dead and gone. A hundred years from now, people still going to be talking about you.' And King, accepting this, commented on it in an interview the obituary cites from some months before King died: 'It's scary, but at the same time it's a blessing.' Not only would Rodney King's life be commemorated but he knew it. He said, 'I realize I will always be the poster child for police brutality, but I can try to use that as a positive force for healing and restraint' (Medina, 2012). King recognized that, as a poster child, he had become a symbol in which larger cultural forces were condensed and he could use that fact to help make a better world. As a person, King lived in a way to anticipate his own commemoration.

In these three ways – referencing the past to bid for editorial prominence, using the past as a context to help explain a news event, and showing how people act in their everyday lives, sometimes very dramatically, in ways that incorporate a sense of past or future – journalism makes itself a vehicle or agent of cultural memory without the intention of commemorating.

Note

1. 'The last civil rights movement' has referred to the rights of the disabled since at least 1989, see John Hole, 'The Last Civil Rights Movement,' *British Medical Journal*, 22 April, 1121–3 and, also referring to the rights of people with disabilities, Diane Driedger (1989), *The Last Civil Rights Movement*. London: Hurst & Company.

References

Barnhurst, K.G. (2011) 'The Problem of Modern Time in American Journalism,' *KronoScope*, 11(1–2), 98–123.

Bernstein, N. (2011) 'On Campus, a Law Enforcement System to Itself,' *New York Times*, 12 November, A1.

Burke, P. (1969) *The Renaissance Sense of the Past*. London: Edward Arnold.

Edy, J. (1999) 'Journalistic Uses of Collective Memory,' *Journal of Communication*, 49(2), 71–85.

Gillis, J. (2012) 'A Climate Scientist Battles Time and Mortality,' *New York Times*, 3 July, A1.

Goode, E. (2012) 'Researchers See Decline in Child Sex Abuse Rate,' *New York Times*, 29 June, A13.

Gootman, E. (2012) 'Honey, the Baby is Coming; Quick, Call the Photographer,' *New York Times*, 17 June, A1.

Grynbaum, M. (2012) 'Broken Leg Adds Hurdle to Her Quest, at 82, for 14th House Term,' *New York Times*, 4 May, A1.

Jacobs, A. (2012) 'For China, a Dissident in Exile is One Less Headache Back Home,' *New York Times*, 5 May, A12.

Kirkpatrick, D. (2012) 'Libya Holds Vote After 40 Years of Dictatorship,' *New York Times*, 8 July, A1.

Kirkpatrick, D. and Fahim, K. (2012) 'With Fate of Revolution at Stake, Egypt Holds Presidential Runoff,' *New York Times*, 17 June, A1.

Kitzinger, J. (2000) 'Media Templates: Patterns of Association and the (Re)construction of Meaning Over Time,' *Media, Culture & Society*, 22(1), 61–84.

Kolata, G. (2012) 'In Leukemia Treatment, Glimpses of the Future,' *New York Times*, 8 July, A1.

Medina, J. (2012) 'Police Beating Victim Who Asked "Can We All Get Along?"' *New York Times*, 18 June, A1, B8.

Ogan, C., Plymale, I., Smith, D.L., Turpin, W.H. and Shaw, D.L. (1975) 'The Changing Front Page of the New York Times,' *Journalism Quarterly*, 51, 340–4.

Perlez, J. and Wines, M. (2012) 'Deal Would Let China Dissident and Family in U.S.,' *New York Times*, 5 May, A1.

Rampell, C. (2012) 'Rate of Growth in Jobs Slowed for U.S. in April,' *New York Times*, 5 May, A1.

Rudoren, J. (2012) 'Master Tactician in Israel Adds Power in a Deal,' *New York Times*, 9 May, A1.

Schudson, M. (1978) *Discovering the News*. New York: Basic Books.

Schudson, M. (1997) 'Lives, Laws, and Language: Commemorative versus Non-Commemorative Forms of Effective Public Memory,' *Communication Review*, 2(1), 3–18.

6
Counting Time: Journalism and the Temporal Resource

Keren Tenenboim-Weinblatt

'Time affects the work of every institution, but few so substantially as the news media.' This statement by political scientist Thomas Patterson (1998: 56) underscores the significance of time for understanding journalism and its challenges (see also Barnhurst, 2011). Concurrently, it exposes the prevailing view about the direction of the relationship between time and journalism. In scholarly, journalistic and popular discourse, time is commonly viewed as a factor that influences, shapes and constrains journalistic practice. From this perspective, journalists increasingly struggle to meet the demands of accelerating news cycles (Boyer, 2010; Klinenberg, 2005), while having to produce more news in less time (Boczkowski, 2010) and compete with online actors who have temporal advantages over traditional journalism. This news culture of immediacy and speed is situated within the broader temporal conditions of contemporary society, including the accelerated compression of time in post/late modernity (Harvey, 1989; Virilio, 2000), or what Douglas Rushkoff (2013) calls 'Present Shock.' Time pressures are also seen as undermining the ability of journalists to fulfill their societal roles (Patterson, 1998; Plasser, 2005; Rosenberg and Feldman, 2008). According to this view, the focus on an ever-more fleeting present and the need to produce news that meets the demands of accelerating news cycles lead to the production of news stories that are shortsighted, shallow and inadequately verified, and that reflect sudden events rather than enduring problems.

But can we think of time not only as shaping and constraining the news, but also as a resource for journalists? Scholarship on journalism and collective memory has started to demonstrate the various uses of the past by journalists, from making sense of current events and enhancing their news value (for example, Berkowitz, 2011; Edy, 1999;

Schudson, Chapter 5 above) to establishing journalists' own authority, boundaries and identity (for example, Carlson and Berkowitz in
Chapter 12 below; Kitch, 2002, and Chapter 14; Meyers, 2007; Zelizer,
1992). A less developed strand of scholarship has focused on future references in the news and their uses, from prediction (Neiger, 2007) and
precontextualization (Oddo, 2013) to shock avoidance (Grusin, 2010).

This chapter shifts the focus to a more direct engagement with the
question of what it is that journalists do with time in the telling of news
stories. It seeks to develop the idea of time as a discursive and narrative
resource for journalists by focusing on time itself as an object of representation and a narrative theme in its own right, by looking at news as
consisting of serial narratives and layers of speech acts, and by combining the backward- and forward-looking in news within the framework
of journalism and memory. For these purposes, I draw on the strategic
example of the media coverage of cases of kidnapping and captivity,
focusing in particular on the rich mnemonic practice of counting time
in the news.

Three related characteristics make kidnapping and captivity stories
particularly valuable for exploring the multi-layered functioning of
time as a discursive and narrative resource for journalists: first, these are
dramatic stories that stretch across time, thereby creating a narrative
space that needs to be filled and managed by the news media. As will be
shown below, representations of time were used to fill this space. Second,
kidnapping and captivity stories are deeply tied to memory, in both its
retrospective and prospective dimensions (see Tenenboim-Weinblatt,
2013a). On the one hand, they look back to cultural myths as well as
to the constituting event of the kidnapping; on the other, they require
future action to be resolved and involve public reminders of what is
yet to be done. Finally, while the passage of time is one of the most
fundamental conditions of human existence, captivity stories bring the
experience of time to the forefront, as vividly described in memoirs
by captives and their family members (for example, Betancourt, 2010;
Gonsalves, Howes and Stansell, 2009; Rohde and Mulvihill, 2010). The
questions of how much time has passed, how much is still left, and
what needs to be done both to pass the time in captivity and to shorten
it become central concerns and sources of agony, hope and creativity for
the captives and their families. As will be demonstrated below, occasionally this also extends to their larger communities and the news media.

The study discussed in this chapter focused on seven cases of political
kidnapping, including stories of Colombian, French, Israeli and US citizens who were taken captive between 2002 and 2008 during conflicts

in Colombia, Iraq, Afghanistan and Gaza. In three of the cases – those of the Israeli soldier Gilad Shalit, Colombian-French politician Ingrid Betancourt, and three US military contractors taken captive in Colombia (Marc Gonsalves, Tom Howes and Keith Stansell) – the captivity period lasted over five years. In the four other cases, including two involving French journalists (Florence Aubenas and Christian Chesnot and Georges Malbrunot), and two involving US journalists (Jill Carroll and David Rohde), the captivity period lasted between three and seven months. Coverage of the seven cases was examined in eleven leading newspapers in Colombia, France, Israel and the US,[1] focusing in particular on front page coverage.

One of the prevailing trends in the front page coverage of these cases was the practice of counting the time that had elapsed between the abduction and other key events. The subsequent analysis demonstrates how such time-focused practices allow journalists, on the one hand, to sustain continuous stories in the news, and, on the other, to discursively enact a wide spectrum of identities and roles, linked to retrospective and prospective remembrance, information and ritual, representation and intervention. Time emerges from this analysis as a unique and valuable resource for exploring and negotiating journalistic practices and roles in the contemporary media environment.

Sustaining news stories: time as narrative filler and a dramatic resource

The role of time as a constituent element and major theme in fictional narratives has been widely studied by literary scholars and narrative theorists (see useful reviews in Rimmon-Kenan, 2002; Richardson, 2006). News, as a form of nonfiction storytelling, also heavily relies on temporal strategies and themes, although the topic has received relatively little attention in journalism studies. Available research in this area has focused primarily on the individual news item as the narrative unit, examining issues of temporal sequencing in news narratives (Barnhurst, 2011; Bell, 1991, 1995), as well as uses of the collective past and collective future in crafting stories on current events (for example, Berkowitz, 2011; Edy, 1999; Neiger, 2007; Schudson, in the previous chapter).

A wider spectrum of the uses of time in news narratives is revealed when we look at news items not only as autonomous short stories but also as episodes or chapters in serial narratives (Tenenboim-Weinblatt, 2008). One example is the use of time in sustaining ongoing stories in the news. How do journalists engage readers in the unfolding narrative and how is narrative continuity maintained over long periods of time? In particular, what happens when there are not enough new developments to sustain these stories as news? Such is often the case in stories of kidnapping and captivity. The mythic resonance and dramatic value of captivity narratives, particularly when combined with pressures to keep the stories high on the media agenda so as to exert pressure on decision-makers and not let the captives be forgotten, demand that the news media maintain their high profile. However, as stories in which the main protagonist is absent and in which actual developments are either scarce or take place under a veil of secrecy, kidnapping and captivity cases present a narrative challenge for journalists.

Unlike literary authors or screenwriters, journalists cannot simply invent plot twists to generate interest and fill the weekly/daily episodes or the book chapters. My research suggests that in the absence of standard newsworthy developments, journalists often draw on time-related themes and discursive resources to maintain narrative continuity, readers' engagement and a certain level of visibility for news stories over time (Tenenboim-Weinblatt, 2008, 2013b). Some of these narrative strategies involve the creation of either past- or future-oriented suspense (Tenenboim-Weinblatt, 2008). Looking back, the hostages' stories are built as a mystery (raising questions such as what happened to the captives? Who holds them?). Looking forward, the stories raise questions regarding the unfolding of the narrative, construct future expectations regarding its closure, and sustain waves of coverage using narrative structures such as 'a race against the clock' (to save the captives). Other strategies, on which I focus here, involve a more direct engagement with time itself as a theme for the coverage.

Among the most frequently recurring aspects of the media discourse surrounding kidnapping and captivity cases are practices that involve counting the time spent in captivity. The prevalence of counting practices can be seen in the sheer number of front pages that included references to the time spent in captivity. Of the 809 front pages covering the seven cases of kidnapping and captivity examined in this study, 364 (45 percent) included one or more references to the amount of time that had passed since the abduction or the total amount of time spent in captivity. In 232 front pages (29 percent of all front pages), marking the time that had passed since the abduction was the main topic of the front-page story.

The use of time-counting as a major component of coverage was associated with the density of front page coverage during the period of captivity: the more frequent the coverage, the greater was the use of time-counting as the main topic of the story. This practice was most prevalent in the treatment of the stories of the kidnapped French journalists by their home newspapers – *Libération* and *Le Figaro* – who led forceful campaigns to bring their journalists home. This involved near daily front page coverage of the cases – of Florence Aubenas in *Libération* and of Chesnot and Malbrunot in *Le Figaro* – throughout their captivity period (157 days for Aubenas and 124 days for Chesnot and Malbrunot). When there were no major events associated with these stories, the front page coverage focused on counting the number of days that had passed since the abduction. In *Libération*, for example, pictures of Florence Aubenas and her guide were accompanied by the headline '*Disappeared XX days ago*' (55 days ago, 56 days ago, and so on), and later (following a video of Aubenas released by the captors): '*Abducted XX days ago*' (106 days ago, 107 days ago, and so on). The repeated main text on the front page read: 'Yesterday evening there was no new information on the fate of our reporter Florence Aubenas and her guide Hussein Hanoun al-Saadi, who disappeared in Iraq on January 5th'; and later: 'A video which shows Florence Aubenas calling for help was broadcast on March 1st. Our special correspondent was kidnapped in Iraq on January 5th with her guide Hussein Hanoun al-Saadi, of whom we remain without news.'

These ostensibly simple daily countings constitute a multi-layered discursive work, to be discussed in detail below, but on one level, we can consider them 'narrative fillers,' or what Barthes (1977: 93) called 'catalysers' (as opposed to 'nuclei'). These are episodes that do not advance the plot, but sustain the story and fill in the spaces between its main nodes. In this context, these fillers maintain narrative continuity in order to keep the issue on the public agenda. The question is what makes these texts front page news. In the case of Florence Aubenas neither of the two events to which the newspaper keeps returning – the disappearance/abduction and the release of the video – constitutes new information, and the 'no news news' frame fails to meet the requirement that news depicts a change in the world's state of affairs. In this case, the only change from one day to another is the amount of time that has passed since the abduction. In a sense, then, what we have here is the minimal development that can be reported as news – the passing of time. Even if nothing else happens, time passes, and in this context, it becomes a news fact in and of itself. This can be viewed as a practice of 'elastic newsworthiness,' referring to the flexible definition of what constitutes news, based on the need to maintain a certain level of visibility for the story at a given point in time (Tenenboim-Weinblatt, 2013b). Time, as in other cases, serves here as a resource for molding and refashioning news criteria.

The use of time-counting in sustaining front page coverage was also apparent in the cases of Gilad Shalit and Ingrid Betancourt, both of which constituted culturally-resonant stories that successfully mobilized collective solidarities and sentiments in national and transnational communities. In these two long drawn out cases, the longer the captivity lasted, the more creative the time markings became. For example, the main front page headline in *Yedioth Ahronoth* on the one thousandth day in captivity for Gilad Shalit was the number '1000' composed of dozens of small pictures of Shalit (see Figure 6.1). On the fourth anniversary of Shalit's captivity, the newspaper featured a front page picture of Tami and Yuval Arad, wife and daughter of the

Figure 6.1   Marking 1000 days in captivity for Gilad Shalit (*Yedioth Ahronoth*, 20 March 2009, front page; top headline: 'How much we would have wanted to see him home; Gilad Shalit's one thousandth day in captivity will be marked on Saturday')

missing soldier Ron Arad (who was captured in 1986 and later disappeared without a trace). The arms of Tami and Yuval are tied together in a configuration creating the number four and the picture is juxtaposed with a logo in the shape of '4' filled with the picture of Shalit. *Le Monde*, on the sixth anniversary of Ingrid Betancourt's captivity, under the headline 'Ingrid Betancourt: Held Hostage for Six Years' (15 February 2008), featured a front-page montage composed of Betancourt's picture and drawings of various elements and symbols associated with her captivity.

These creative visualizations expose not only the challenge of maintaining readers' engagement with repetitive stories over a long period of time, but also the use of time as a dramatic-affective resource. Roeh and Feldman (1984) argued that while the common use of numbers in the news supports journalists' rhetoric of objectivity, it is often used for melodramatic purposes. Counting time can be viewed as a subcategory of this general phenomenon, analogous to counting the dead in an accident, terrorist attack, or natural disaster. However, as an object of counting, time is distinct in being a dramatic resource that is intrinsic to reality, and as such can be readily drawn upon (irrespective of external events). In addition, as will be further discussed below, it is a dramatic resource that deepens the complex relationship between news and social ritual (see Carey, 1989).

Enacting journalistic roles: representational, ritual and directive uses of time

In addition to filling voids in coverage and maintaining visibility for the stories, the practice of counting time reflects the different roles that the news media in different countries undertake in relation to these cases. These range from reporting on the events and telling the stories of the captives, to ritual and mnemonic roles tied to future political action. Viewed from this perspective, counting practices exhibit at least three different journalistic acts in relation to collective time: conveying facts about temporal dimensions of reality, organizing and ritualizing collective time, and reminding the public and decision-makers that the time has come to resolve the issue.

These different uses of time-counting in the news can be understood in terms of different types and layers of speech acts, or what Zohar Kampf calls 'mediated speech acts' (Kampf, 2013).[2] Drawing on Austin's (1962) and Searle's (1979) classifications, time-countings can be viewed as belonging to at least three categories of speech acts: representatives/ assertives, performatives and directives. In summarizing and giving information about the amount of time spent in captivity, they are repre-sentatives/assertives; in organizing and ritualizing collective time, they are performatives; and in providing reminders of what needs to be done and trying to bring about a future state of affairs, they are directives.[3]

Time counting as representational discourse

Representatives/assertives reflect the state of affairs in the world (Searle, 1979). While the representational-assertive discursive layer was present in all news references to the time spent in captivity, it was not neces-sarily the sole or dominant category. However, it was the dominant dis-cursive category in cases where the examined stories received relatively low media coverage (in particular the cases of US captives and media coverage outside the captives' home countries). In these cases, counting usually took the form of post-captivity summaries of the total amount of time the hostages had spent in captivity. A typical example is the *New York Times* headline following Jill Carroll's release: 'Reporter Freed in Iraq 3 Months after Abduction' (31 March 2006: A1), or its equiva-lent headline following David Rohde's escape: 'Times Reporter Escapes Taliban after 7 Months' (21 June 2009: A1).

Such summaries provide factual information on what is perceived as one of the most significant facts of these stories – the total amount of time spent in captivity – and as such they fit the widely-accepted view of journalists as conveyors of information. At the same time, these headlines can be viewed as reproductions of a common formula of the mythic genre of captivity narratives (see Sayre, 2000). This formula is apparent in the titles of many contemporary captives' memoirs, such as that of the three US military contractors, *Out of Captivity: Surviving 1967 Days in the Colombian Jungle* (Gonsalves, Howes and Stansell, 2009), or Ingrid Betancourt's memoir, *Even Silence Has an End: My Six Years of Captivity in the Colombian Jungle* (Betancourt, 2010). Indeed, this formula can be traced back to the most famous work in the popu-lar genre of captivity narratives in early American literature: the story of Mary Rowlandson, who was captured in 1675 by Native Americans. One of the major editions of her book (published in London in 1682) was entitled *A True History of the Captivity and Restoration of Mrs. Mary Rowlandson, A Minister's Wife in New-England: Wherein is set forth, The Cruel and Inhumane Usage she underwent amongst the Heathens for Eleven Weeks time: And her Deliverance from them* (in Andrews, 2003: 20).

Assertive summaries of the time spent in captivity are therefore more than conveyors of information. They are part of the cultural-symbolic system 'within which and in relation to which reporters and officials go about their duties' (Schudson, 2005: 187), and they participate in news stories' reproduction of the culture's narrative formats and myths (Bird and Dardenne, 1988; Carey, 1989). However, they lack the performative and directive characteristics of the other categories of counting.

Time counting as ritual-performative discourse

The most famous example of Austin's (1962) notion of 'performatives' and Searle's (1979) narrower category of 'declarations' is the utterance 'I now pronounce you husband and wife,' which brings about a change in the condition or state of things in the world. Other examples include the declaration of public holidays and observances. While the news media often participate in marking official holidays and observances (such as Memorial Day, Martin Luther King day, or the newer Patriot Day, commemorating the 9/11 events), at times they also do the work of proclaiming public observances. Consider, for example, the main front page headline in *Ha'aretz* on 25 June 2010: 'Israel is today marking four years since the kidnapping of the soldier Gilad Shalit.' This statement has a representational-referential dimension, in that the coverage includes references to planned activities and events designed to mark four years of captivity for Gilad Shalit. However, the nationalization of this day (through the use of 'Israel' as the subject), the official language, and the fact that Shalit's anniversary in captivity is not an official national observance day make this headline more of a declaration than an assertive.

Sociologists of time have shown how time is socially divided, measured, marked and organized, and how this social construction of time serves as a basis for establishing national and group identities, with calendars arguably the best illustration of these processes (see, in particular, Zerubavel, 1985). In prominently marking special dates, which are defined less by current news developments and more by a certain temporal relation to events that happened in the past, the media play an important role in shaping the collective calendar and organizing collective time. In the above example, the framing and prominence of the coverage not only position the case of the captive at the top of the day's public agenda, but also make it part of the collective calendar. At the same time, it establishes the newspaper's social authority in relation to this national ritual.

Front page coverage of days that marked anniversaries or other meaningful time units (for example, a month, 100 days, a year, 1000 days) was found in the cases of Shalit, Betancourt and the French journalists (that is, in all cases except the three involving US citizens).

The journalistic practice of marking the time that had passed since the occurrence of past events, in particular anniversaries of significant historical events, was explored by scholars of journalism and collective memory in relation to events as diverse as the September 11 attacks, the JFK assassination, the Rabin assassination, Watergate, the liberation of Nazi concentration camps and Hurricane Katrina (Peri, 1999; Robinson, 2009; Schudson, 1992; Zelizer, 1992, 1998). However, it is important to differentiate between marking the time that has passed since the occurrence of important historical events and marking the duration of ongoing, unresolved news stories. It is the latter that relates to time passed in captivity. Here, the ritual is mission-oriented and the memory is directed toward future political action. Unlike 9/11 and the JFK assassination, when these stories are resolved (that is, when the captives return), those dates will no longer have meaning on the social calendar. This corresponds to the distinction between commemorative and mission-oriented rituals, the latter referring to rituals that attempt to repair, restore, or save the group rather than only re-present or reenact the past in the present (Marvin and Ingle, 1999). It is also a difference that relates to the distinction between retrospective and prospective memory, to be discussed below.

The ritual-performative dimensions of counting apply not only to the marking of anniversaries and other special dates, but also to consecutive counting, such as the daily countings in the French journalists' home newspapers. These daily consecutive countings – 'Abducted 92 days ago,' 'Abducted 93 days ago,' and so forth – have a performative dimension that the counting in larger intervals lacks. Like the collective ritual of counting out loud on New Year's Eve or the usually solitary ritual of counting the time while waiting for something to happen or to end, the daily counting of the number of days that have passed since an abduction is not only a means of marking a special date on the social calendar but a ritual practice in its own right. The readers seemingly join the newspaper in this daily counting ritual, and the fact that there is a parallel between the counting units and the newspaper's own time cycle creates a link between the counting ritual and the diminishing ritual of reading the newspaper.

The performance of collective counting can also be seen in the countdown featured on the front page of *Yedioth Ahronoth* four days before the return of Shalit (see Figure 6.2), following the signing of a prisoner-exchange deal between Israel and Hamas. '4 More Days,' reads the bright front-page headline which is laid over an illustration of a calendar page. The countdown signals the approaching end of a long

107

Figure 6.2 Countdown to Gilad Shalit's release (*Yedioth Ahronoth*, 14 October 2011, front page; main headline: '4 More Days'; caption of the logo at the upper-left corner: 'Waiting for Gilad'; in the picture: President Shimon Peres and Shalit's mother, Aviva. Photograph: Alex Kolomoisky)

collective wait, while also filling the narrative vacuum between the announcement on the deal between Israel and Hamas and the actual return of Shalit a week later. Time is thus used as a ritual and narrative resource in a mnemonic space that is a nexus of past and future within the present moment.

In addition to the counting of the time spent in captivity and the countdowns to important dates and events, another ritual of counting time was that of marking the captive's birthday. For example, on Shalit's fourth birthday in captivity, a front-page story in *Yedioth Ahronoth*, under the headline '23 years old, in captivity,' featured a picture of Shalit and his father from a childhood birthday party, as well as a birthday message from his mother (directed at 'Giladi,' Shalit's nickname). This front page reenactment of a family birthday party was associated with the symbolic construction of Shalit in Israel as 'everyone's child.' Like other examples in this section, it is a story whose performative-ritual function is more significant than its informative-factual value.

Time-counting as directive discourse

Beyond representing and organizing temporal reality, front page headlines such as 'Disappeared 19 Days Ago' (*Libération*, 24 January 2005), 'Abducted 69 Days Ago' (*Libération*, 15 March 2005), 'Malbrunot and Chesnot, Held Hostage in Iraq for One Hundred Days' (*Le Figaro*, 27 November 2004), or 'Tomorrow Marks Five Years of Captivity of Ingrid Betancourt' (*El Tiempo*, 22 February 2007) are reminders. So many days, so many years have passed, and the problem is still not solved. The hostages are still in captivity.

In Searle's classification of speech acts, reminders fall under the category of 'directives.' That is, they are attempts by the speaker 'to get the hearer to do something' (Searle, 1979: 13), in this case, to solve the problem of the hostages. Directives include a wide range of acts, from giving orders to asking questions. The uniqueness of reminders as directives is that they are memory-based. In other words, what one needs to act on is associated with past events, intentions and commitments. One needs to remember both what happened and what still needs to be done. Thus, when the news media repeatedly count the number of days that have passed since an abduction, they not only place the story on the public agenda and remind us over and over again what happened in the past (the fact of the abduction), but the combination of these two components urges us not to forget what is yet to be done – return the hostages home. Indeed, it is the news media's strategic location in relation to the social nexus of time and the fusion between their agenda-setting role and their functioning as agents of collective memory that uniquely positions them to issue such reminders.

The journalistic act of reminding what needs to be done, which connects past and future, collective memory and agenda setting, is captured by the notion of 'mediated prospective memory' (Tenenboim-Weinblatt, 2013a). In the psychological literature, retrospective memory refers to the recollection of past events and experiences, whereas prospective memory is defined as 'remembering to carry out intended actions at an appropriate time in the future' (McDaniel and Einstein, 2007: 1). The notion of mediated prospective memory encompasses the various media practices by which collective prospective memory tasks (such as gaining the release of the hostages) are shaped and negotiated. Counting time can be seen as a paradigmatic example of these practices. It connects in particular to the idea of time-based prospective memory tasks in which one should remember to execute the task after a certain amount of time has passed (to be differentiated from event-based prospective memory). In kidnapping and captivity cases there is clearly no non-arbitrary answer to the question of how much time in captivity is enough or too much (other than 'any amount of time'). In this context, anniversaries and other 'round' time units (such as 1000 days) are useful in anchoring the prospective memory. However, it is in combination with event-based reminders (for example, the release of videos of the hostages) that symbolic time markers become particularly potent.

Conclusion: journalism and spaces of collective waiting

This chapter has demonstrated how the mnemonic practice of counting time can serve as a rich discursive and narrative resource for journalists, allowing them to manage news stories over time, while connecting information, ritual and agenda setting, as well as retrospective and prospective remembrance. In the studied cases, multi-layered uses of time were both necessitated and enabled by the space of collective waiting created in anticipation of the return of the captives and the closure of the story. Waiting, as Harold Schweizer observes, is one of the most denigrated experiences in modern times, to be avoided at all costs. 'Those who wander in it,' writes Schweizer, 'find themselves in an exemplary existential predicament, having time without wanting it' (2008: 2). And yet Schweizer urges us to think of waiting not only as an aberration, inconvenience, or something to merely pass through, but as a creative space. As suggested by this chapter, mnemonic spaces of mediated collective waiting can also be used in this manner. These are spaces where time can be creatively shaped; where news conventions, for better and worse, are being subverted; and where journalists can enact, negotiate and fuse a wide array of social roles.

This is not to argue that practices of the type analyzed in this chapter are normatively desirable or offer a solution to the challenges facing mainstream journalism. However, this analysis does aim to provide a counterpoint to the conventional wisdom and academic strands that emphasize the ways in which time constrains and impedes journalism. Journalists are viewed as either chasing an ever-shrinking present, or, as suggested by Barnhurst (2011), as trapped in an older time regime. Either way, they are losing the battle to media players who are better adapted to the new temporal environment. Within this framework, the crisis facing mainstream journalism, and particularly print newspapers, is at least in part a crisis of time. Looking at the relationships between news and time from an alternative, complementary perspective, this chapter suggests that perhaps the challenge facing journalism is not necessarily how to overcome its 'temporal inferiority' in relation to other media actors, but how to claim time as a resource for creation and reimagination.

Notes

1. The newspapers include *El Tiempo* in Colombia; *Le Monde, Le Figaro* and *Libération* in France; *Yedioth Ahronoth* and *Ha'aretz* in Israel; and the *New York Times*, the *Washington Post*, the *LA Times*, *USA Today* and the *Christian Science Monitor* in the US.
2. In 'mediated speech acts' Kampf (2013) refers primarily to journalists' representation and framing of others' utterances (for example, reporting on politicians' statements). The analysis in this chapter suggests that journalistic direct or indirect speech acts are also constructed independently of 'external' utterances.
3. Assertives and directives belong to Searle's (1979) taxonomy of speech acts, which also includes commissives, expressives and declarations. The category of performatives, as used in this analysis, can be viewed as located between Austin's original and too-broad category of performatives and Searle's more restrictive category of declarations.

References

Andrews, W.L. (ed.) (2003) *Classic American Autobiographies*. New York: Penguin Books.

Austin, J.L. (1962) *How to do Things with Words*. Cambridge, MA: Harvard University Press.

Barnhurst, K.G. (2011) 'The Problem of Modern Time in American Journalism,' *KronoScope*, 11(1–2), 98–123.

Barthes, R. (1977) *Image, Music, Text*, trans. S. Heath. New York: Hill and Wang.

Bell, A. (1991) *The Language of News Media*. Oxford: Blackwell.

Bell, A. (1995) 'News Time,' *Time & Society*, 4(3), 305–28.

Berkowitz, D. (2011) 'Telling the Unknown Through the Familiar: Collective Memory as Journalistic Device in a Changing Media Environment,' in M. Neiger, O. Meyers and E. Zandberg (eds) *On Media Memory*. London: Palgrave Macmillan, pp. 201–12.

Betancourt, I. (2010) *Even Silence has an End: My Six Years of Captivity in the Colombian Jungle*. New York: Penguin Press.

Bird, S.E. and Dardenne, R.W. (1988) 'Myth, Chronicle, and Story: Exploring the Narrative Qualities of News,' in J.W. Carey (ed.) *Media, Myths, and Narratives: Television and the Press*. Beverly Hills, CA: Sage, pp. 67–86.

Boczkowski, P. (2010) *News at Work: Imitation in an Age of Information Abundance*. Chicago: University of Chicago Press.

Boyer, D. (2010) 'Making (Sense of) News in the Era of Digital Information,' in S.E. Bird (ed.) *The Anthropology of News & Journalism: Global Perspectives*. Bloomington: Indiana University Press, pp. 241–56.

Carey, J. (1989) *Communication as Culture: Essays on Media and Society*. Boston: Unwin Hyman.

Edy, J.A. (1999) 'Journalistic Uses of Collective Memory,' *Journal of Communication*, 49(2), 71–85.

Gonsalves, M., Howes, T. and Stansell, K., with Brozek, G. (2009) *Out of Captivity: Surviving 1967 Days in the Colombian Jungle*. New York: Harper Collins.

Grusin, R. (2010) *Premediation: Affect and Mediality after 9/11*. New York: Palgrave Macmillan.

Harvey, D. (1989) *The Condition of Postmodernity: An Enquiry into the Origins of Cultural Change*. Oxford and Cambridge, MA: Blackwell.

Kampf, Z. (2013) 'Mediated Performatives,' in J.O. Östman and J. Verschueren (eds) *Handbook of Pragmatics*. Amsterdam: John Benjamins.

Kitch, C. (2002) 'Anniversary Journalism, Collective Memory, and the Cultural Authority to Tell the Story of the American Past,' *Journal of Popular Culture*, 36(1), 44–67.

Klinenberg, E. (2005) 'Convergence: News Production in a Digital Age,' *Annals of the American Academy of Political and Social Science*, 597, 48–64.

Marvin, C. and Ingle, D.W. (1999) *Blood Sacrifice and the Nation: Totem Rituals and the American Flag*. New York: Cambridge University Press.

McDaniel, M.A. and Einstein, G.O. (2007) *Prospective Memory: An Overview and Synthesis of an Emerging Field*. Thousand Oaks, CA: Sage.

Meyers, O. (2007) 'Memory in Journalism and the Memory of Journalism: Israeli Journalists and the Constructed Legacy of Haolam Hazeh,' *Journal of Communication*, 57(4), 719–39.

Neiger, M. (2007) 'Media Oracles: The Political Import and Cultural Significance of News Referring to the Future,' *Journalism: Theory, Practice & Criticism*, 8(3), 326–38.

Oddo, J. (2013) 'Precontextualization and the Rhetoric of Futurity: Foretelling Colin Powell's UN address on NBC News,' *Discourse & Communication*, 7(1), 25–53.

Patterson, T.E. (1998) 'Time and News: The Media's Limitations as an Instrument of Democracy,' *International Political Science Review*, 19(1), 55–68.

Peri, Y. (1999) 'The Media and Collective Memory of Yitzhak Rabin's Remembrance,' *Journal of Communication*, 49(3), 106–24

Plasser, F. (2005) 'From Hard to Soft News Standards? How Political Journalists in Different Media Systems Evaluate the Shifting Quality of News,' *International Journal of Press/Politics*, 10(2), 47–68.

Richardson, B. (2006) 'Making Time: Narrative Temporality in Twentieth-Century Literature and Theory,' *Literature Compass*, 3(3), 603–12.

Rimmon-Kenan, S. (2002) *Narrative Fiction*. New York: Routledge.

Robinson, S. (2009) '"We Were All There": Remembering America in the Anniversary Coverage of Hurricane Katrina,' *Memory Studies*, 2(2), 235–53.

Roeh, I. and Feldman, S. (1984) 'The Rhetoric of Numbers in Front-Page Journalism: How Numbers Contribute to the Melodramatic in the Popular Press,' *Text*, 4(4), 347–68.

Rohde, D. and Mulvihill, K. (2010) *A Rope and a Prayer: A Kidnapping from Two Sides*. New York: Viking.

Rosenberg, H. and Feldman, C.S. (2008) *No Time to Think: The Menace of Media Speed and the 24-Hour News Cycle*. New York: Continuum.

Rushkoff, D. (2013) *Present Shock: When Everything Happens Now*. New York: Penguin Group.

Sayre, G.M. (2000) 'Introduction,' in G.M. Sayre (ed.) *American Captivity Narratives*. New York: Houghton Mifflin, pp. 1–17.

Schudson, M. (1992) *Watergate in American Memory: How We Remember, Forget, and Reconstruct the Past*. New York: Basic Books.

Schudson, M. (2005) 'Four Approaches to the Sociology of News,' in J. Curran and M. Gurevitch (eds) *Mass Media and Society* (4th edn). London: Hodder Arnold, pp. 172–97.

Schweizer, H. (2008) *On Waiting*. London and New York: Routledge.

Searle, J.R. (1979) *Expression and Meaning: Studies in the Theory of Speech Acts*. Cambridge: Cambridge University Press.

Tenenboim-Weinblatt, K. (2008) 'Fighting for the Story's Life: Non-Closure in Journalistic Narrative,' *Journalism*, 9(1), 31–51.

Tenenboim-Weinblatt, K. (2013a) 'Bridging Collective Memories and Public Agendas: Toward a Theory of Mediated Prospective Memory,' *Communication Theory*, 23(2), 91–111.

Tenenboim-Weinblatt, K. (2013b) 'The Management of Visibility: Media Coverage of Kidnapping and Captivity Cases around the World,' *Media, Culture & Society*, 35(7), 791–808.

Virilio, P. (2000) *Polar Inertia*, trans. P. Camiller. London: Sage.

Zelizer, B. (1992) *Covering the Body: The Kennedy Assassination, the Media, and the Shaping of Collective Memory*. Chicago, IL: University of Chicago Press.

Zelizer, B. (1998) *Remembering to Forget: Holocaust Memory Through the Camera's Eye*. Chicago, IL: University of Chicago Press.

Zerubavel, E. (1985) *Hidden Rhythms: Schedules and Calendars in Social Life*. Berkeley: University of California Press.

7
Reversed Memory: Commemorating the Past through Coverage of the Present

Motti Neiger, Eyal Zandberg and Oren Meyers

On the eve of Israel's Remembrance Day for the Holocaust and the Heroism (also known in Israel as 'Holocaust Remembrance Day' or 'Holocaust Day') 2012, the Israeli elite newspaper *Haaretz* published a provocative op-ed, written by Yoram Kaniuk, one of the country's prominent novelists, bearing the title 'Celebrate Holocaust Day.' Referenced both on the newspaper's front page and on its internet homepage the piece claimed that 'Holocaust Day should be a day of joy. Tens of thousands of people survived, returned to life, raised children and grandchildren... In Auschwitz, people became the greatest heroes in history... Holocaust Day should be a national holiday of joy, celebrating the rescue [and] the heroism of the survivors' (Kaniuk, 2012). A few days earlier, the popular daily *Yedioth Ahronoth* had published a feature story bearing the title 'We Took-Off Like the Phoenix' (Duek, 2012) that narrated the story of Holocaust survivors who became combat pilots in the Israeli air force (see Figure 7.1).

The visual image reflects the transformation of those who rose from the ashes and were re(air)born as Israeli fighter pilots: the yellow Star of David, the 'badge of shame' which Jews were forced to sew on their clothes in order to mark them as Jews in public during the Nazi era (as a metonym of the Holocaust), is balanced by the blue Star of David of the Israeli air force insignia (as a metonym of the State of Israel).

Both Kaniuk's op-ed and the story of the 'survivor pilots' draw the attention of readers from the pain of the traumatic past to the victorious present. It is a present that calls, as the media note, for a celebration of the overcoming of trauma, or even, implicitly or not, revenge for the ideas and perpetrators that caused the trauma. These two prime examples illuminate a well-known observation: collective memory concerns the present no less (or even more) than it refers to the past. Moreover,

Figure 7.1 'We Took-Off Like the Phoenix', an article from the Israeli newspaper *Yedioth Ahronoth* (12 April 2012) © *Yedioth Ahronot* and the photographer Tal Shahar

these examples emphasize the fact that in some cases 'the present of past events' – that is, new details or new developments regarding significant past occurrences – become the heart of the story and the main interest of the narrative, while the details of those past occurrences themselves are pushed aside, or, rather, into the background.

In the following chapter we wish to explore this phenomenon and suggest the concept of reversed memory: the cultural mechanism and journalistic practice of focusing on the present while commemorating a shared past. That is, reversed memory is a narratological device in which temporality works in a contrary direction: from the present to the past. Unlike the well-established argument that narratives of the past adapt 'the image of ancient facts to the beliefs and spiritual needs of the present' (Halbwachs, 1980 [1950]: 7), in the case of reversed memory the past is not merely narrated in the service of current objectives; rather, the *past is commemorated by means of the narration of the present.*

Fundamentally, collective memory deals with shared pasts 'there and then' while the news focuses on information concerning the present 'here and now'. Still, and despite its apparent oxymoronic nature, reversed memory enables the creation of narratives that qualify as news items as well as commemorative tools. Thus, shared manifestations of the past become part of the 'see it now' discourse of current events news coverage (Zelizer, 1992, 2008). News items that are constructed as emblems of reversed memory are more evident when they are part of several simultaneous and complementary rituals, such as national commemorative rituals, the media rituals that revolve around such 'national occasions' and, at the same time, the everyday, secular ritual of news production and dissemination.

This assertion becomes evident while exploring our main case study – the news media coverage of Israel's Holocaust Remembrance Day, which was established in 1951 and has become, over the years, one of the dominant rituals of Israel's civil religion (Liebman and Don-Yehiya, 1983). On such a symbolically charged day, the manifestations of reversed memory are positioned at the crossroads where several rituals meet: on Holocaust Remembrance Day, the news media need to prepare items that will pass both as news items and as commemorative tools. Such news items need to take into account two different, or even contradictory sets of values: on the one hand, professional journalistic norms (such as objectivity/ neutrality, newsworthiness and timeliness) and, on the other hand, the values that are intrinsic in collective memory construction processes, such as ethnocentrism and national solidarity. Finally, it is important to stress the organizational element central to the appearance of so many manifestations of reversed memory during times when mass social rituals are performed and observed: the dual social demands from the news media on such occasions leads to a heavy reliance on 'pre-scheduled news [items]' (Tuchman, 1973: 117), which can offer a conjunction between ritualistic significance and newsworthiness.

Narratives of collective memory always revolve simultaneously around the past and present (Zelizer, 1992; Meyers, 2007). And so, in such case, the present offers individuals and cultures a frame and a perspective for evaluating and understanding the past. When we address the concept of collective memory we usually focus on the narrative depiction of the past; nevertheless, when discussing this concept we must take into account that collective memory is not merely a narrative of the past, but rather a '(1) multi-directional process (between the past and present) of (2) concretizing a (3) narrative of the past into a (4) functional, (5) social-political construct' (Neiger, Meyers and Zandberg, 2011: 9). Moreover, in most cases, these processes and mechanisms are harnessed towards the advancement of dominant ideologies and the needs of the remembering collective. Within this context, reversed memory corresponds with Hirsch's conceptualization of postmemory

(2001), facilitating the understanding that the effect of past events continues into the present. In the specific case addressed in this chapter we refer to the shift in commemorative news reporting from a focus on the traumatic events of the Holocaust to a heightened emphasis on events that followed the Holocaust, and especially the establishment of the State of Israel and the lives of the survivors in their new homeland.

The past as a resource in news narratives: a typology

The process of emplotment of events into social narratives defines both news stories and collective memories. Although the common division assumes that newsmaking is about the present and collective memory focuses on the past, both of these social narratives involve complex interrelations between past and present (Tenenboim-Weinblatt, 2011). In line with previous research, we suggest the following typology of news items, according to their uses of *the past as resource*, that is, the visibility of the past in their narratives, and the way in which they construct the interrelations between past and present:

1. *The past as a curriculum.* Though routine news items focus on the 'here and now', they are always anchored within the assumed prior knowledge of news consumers, which bears critical significance to the ability of audiences to decipher news contents. Within this framework, the continual presence of the past in the news is 'the scene against which the events are played out' (Carey, 1989: 151–2). According to Carey, news organizations, as well as individual journalists, presuppose that news consumers are 'constant students' who have attended previous courses, and thus are able to turn the news they have consumed in the past into current usable knowledge. And so, even when such a connection is not directly manifested all news items are, in fact, related to a past that provides the deeper background against which current affairs unfold and future events and trends are explained (Neiger, 2007, 2012).
2. *The past as a yardstick.* News items that utilize the past as a point of reference to the present, that is, analogies that treat the past as a yardstick. Lang and Lang (1989) explored the use of collective memory as means of interpreting current events and Edy (1999) expanded this initial conceptualization by suggesting that journalists use collective memory in the news in order to commemorate, to produce historical analogies and to place current events within longitudinal contexts. In this kind of news coverage the past is more noticeable

than in the type of coverage discussed in the previous category; here, past events are consciously imported into the present in order to provide a meaningful context.

3. *The past as the focus of coverage.* The most evident presence of the past in the news occurs when coverage focuses purposefully on its commemoration. Such news reporting, demonstrated clearly in 'anniversary journalism' (Kitch, 2002) positions the past at the heart of the newsmaking process; it narrates socially significant past events while reading this past through the lenses of changing current convictions and perceptions (Meyers, 2002). Thus, in this type of coverage, the past occupies the foreground while the present and the future are constantly looming as interpretive background contexts.

These three categories illuminate the distinctions between various uses of the past as a resource and its changing degrees of visibility in news reporting: from the clear presence of the past in commemorative journalism, to the less salient appearance of the past in items that use it as an analogy, and finally to the clandestine yet ubiquitous presence of the past in everyday items focusing on current events. This categorization helps clarify the unique features of reversed memory as storytelling technique: news coverage that employs reversed memory logic deals, on the surface with the 'here and now', and thus resembles the covert use of the past as a curriculum. At the same time, the omnipresent commemorative context that surrounds and shapes such reporting infuses reversed memory with commemorative significance and meaning, just as in the case of any commemorative journalism items. Thus, reversed memory is most abundant when the news media take part in larger (mostly national) rituals that shape the meaning of the news of the day. Under such circumstances, news items do not necessarily have to reference the commemorated past in a direct manner and the items do not even have to imply their relations to the past; on such occasions the all-encompassing meaning of the ritual extends across the public sphere.

Such ritualistic instances position journalists in a professional dilemma: on the one hand, they cannot ignore commemorated past events, which stand at the heart of the national ritual; on the other hand, addressing this past time and again in the news is repetitive and cumbersome and it contradicts the notion of timeliness which news coverage is supposed to project. Moreover, on such occasions the continuous evocation of the past is to a large extent unnecessary: paradoxically, the ubiquitous presence of the past in the present and the utmost significance of such days minimizes the need for the news media to convey the historical detail; instead, such days stress the news media's role in bestowing current meaning upon familiar past events.

Finally, this characterization highlights the somewhat unexpected similarity between routine, present-centered coverage and reversed memory journalism: in both cases, the past is not necessarily directly addressed in the coverage of current events. At the same time, the prominence of the past-as-context distinguishes between the two phenomena: in the past as a curriculum case, news items anchor the past within the deep background, in a way that requires a reflexive-critical reading of the item in order to identify, or rather to extract the common knowledge that is assumed by news professionals; in contrast, in reversed memory items the past is the all-encompassing context – there is little need to address the past head-on, because on such extreme occasions it is simply all around; the density of the past in the communal atmosphere is at its peak.

Reversed memory as storytelling: time, space and protagonists

> We will talk about the Holocaust, we will talk about current events, and we will talk about the current Holocaust.
> (Anchor Dan Margalit, opening the 5 p.m. Channel 1 Holocaust Remembrance Day television newscast)

All narratives of collective remembrance are positioned somewhere on the spectrum extending between the 'there and then' and the 'here and now.' Specifically, all collective memory related reporting requires 'memory carriers' that enable the transformation of past events into current news items. We identify four prominent 'memory carriers' relevant for all collective memory accounts:

1. *People*: individuals or collectives who were directly related to events and can attest to their occurrence.
2. *Places*: locations that have become identified with the commemorated events – sites where events took place and/or sites where those events are commemorated.
3. *Objects*: emblematic artifacts that confirm the occurrence of events and symbolize them.
4. *Phenomena*: manifestation of social behavior or social attitudes that stood at the heart of past events, and thus became identified with those events.

Like all other narratives of collective memory, accounts of reversed memory require the presence of one or more of those four 'memory carriers.' In this section we wish to detail and explore the ways in which various conjunctions between these four types of 'memory carriers' shape different journalistic manifestations of reversed memory. We argue that the need to demonstrate both commemorative values and news values is the essential factor defining this type of coverage, positioned as it is on the matrix of narrative time and space.

Looking at Holocaust Remembrance Day news items in all media one notices the prominent role of Holocaust survivors as the dominant carriers of the memory of the Holocaust. Survivors possess a unique and exclusive authority to narrate the Holocaust as a result of several, different constraints. The first is the generational constraint: the number of Holocaust survivors is declining, and in a few decades there will be no one left who will be able to personally attest to the horrors of the Holocaust. Second is the cultural constraint: the fact that in Israeli culture (and elsewhere) survivors symbolize the memory of the Holocaust and have been socially granted the unique authority to tell the story of the Holocaust, as those who bear witness to the atrocities (Frosh and Pinchevski, 2009; Zandberg, 2010). Finally there is the specific genre constraint: professional news coverage conventions demand that news reports feature real-life people who speak in person; people whom the audience can trust, or mistrust, like or dislike. Moreover, the inability of news reports to present the past as though it were happening in the present – in contrast, for instance to scripted dramas – contributes to the frequent use of Holocaust survivors as the main narrative tool through which news stories are told. The mere presence in such news reports of survivors – unlike Holocaust victims who have perished, or individuals who did not experience the Holocaust – embodies a connecting link between the 'there and then' and the 'here and now.'

An analysis of the strategies employed in news items featuring Holocaust survivors as protagonists reveals that such items often construct victorious narratives of various kinds: one of the most common variations of the victory narratives featured on Holocaust Remembrance Day newscasts is the presentation of short interviews with Holocaust survivors and their families in which the survivors present the establishment of a family in Israel as their personal victory over the Nazis. Surviving the Holocaust and raising a family in Israel are thus presented as two inherently complementary successes; such a presentation links the past and the present while charging the life stories of the survivors with ideological meaning.

In the same vein, news items present survivors who epitomize what is considered to be the opposite of victimhood. For instance, Channel 2's newscast on the eve of 1996 Holocaust Remembrance Day reported on the story of Dr Felix Zandman, a Polish Jew who survived the Holocaust by hiding in a pit. In the years following the war, Zandman became a highly successful entrepreneur and established an electronics manufacturing empire. The news report followed Zandman as he visited some of his factories, including those operating in Poland. By doing so, the news item constructed a narrative link between the past survival story of the child who hid in a pit in Poland for 17 months and the present success story of a wealthy businessman, operating factories in that same country.

Another example of such a victorious narrative could be found in news items following Holocaust survivors and their families on journeys back to concentration camps, ghettos and hiding places. Such items present the family voyage as a victorious return, or even as an act of vengeance. Hence, for instance, a 2005 television news report, detailing such a journey, explained that the protagonist of the report is a survivor who 'took with her all the "tribe" she had founded in Israel, even her little great-granddaughter, and returned to Poland for a journey of retribution.' In such cases the combination of the televised presence of Holocaust survivors, a commemorative space (concentration camps, commemorative monuments in Poland, *Yad Vashem*) and commemorative time/ritual leads to the construction of reversed memory: when such conjunctions are created the need to speak directly and in detail about the past is redundant; on such days, the past is omnipresent in the public sphere in a way that enables stories focusing on the (victorious) present to occupy the journalistic forefront. Moreover, as demonstrated above, a complementary characteristic of reversed memory as a narratological device is the tendency to focus on the commemoration of events, rather than on the events themselves.

Holocaust Remembrance Day news coverage often uses commemorative sites in Poland as significant memory carriers. A visit to those sites is utilized in Holocaust Remembrance Day news items as a means of bestowing narrative commemorative authority, even upon those who are not directly related to the Holocaust. A prime example of this aspect of reversed memory could be found in the ongoing coverage of Israeli youth delegations participating in commemorative voyages to death camps in Poland. Since their emergence and continuous growth as a cultural phenomenon in the 1990s, these voyages have bestowed upon these teenagers the status of 'witnesses of the witnesses' (Feldman, 2008) and, thus, enabled them to take a central part in the process of shaping the current Israeli memory of the Holocaust. For example, the 1987 cover of the commemorative supplement issued by the popular daily *Yedioth Ahronoth* on Holocaust Remembrance Day featured a photograph of a concentration camp with the headline: 'I don't want to go back there ever again.' The headline did not quote, as one would expect a Holocaust survivor, but rather a teenage girl who had visited Auschwitz as a member of her school delegation. The main feature story in that particular supplement was based on the diary written by that student during her journey. Here again, the narrative focus was not on the suffering of Holocaust victims, but rather on the hardships experienced by those young Israelis during their trip to Poland. Hence, this feature story illuminated once again the tendency of current Holocaust discourse to shift from a discussion of the actual, historical events to their commemoration: the diary of Anna Frank has been replaced by the diary of a present-day Israeli schoolgirl.

Another reversed memory combination of memory carriers could be found in the annual visits of top Israeli officials, especially high ranking military personnel to commemorative sites. Hence, for instance, every year, on Holocaust Remembrance Day the Israeli General Staff conducts its weekly meeting in *Yad Vashem*. This potent measure associates the Israel Defense Forces, one of the most sacred symbols of modern Zionist revival and heroism, and the official Israeli commemorative authority in charge of preserving the memory of the Holocaust. Thus, for example, the 2011 Holocaust Remembrance Day homepage of the leading Israeli news site, *Ynet* featured an item covering this annual pilgrimage, focusing on the IDF's chief of staff, Beny Ganz, who during his *Yad Vashem* visit discovered new details about the fate of his family during the Holocaust. The news item quoted Ganz's assertion that 'genocidal enemies are still trying to destroy us.' The conjunction between the commemorative site, the ritualistic day and the specific speaker echoed and projected a mythical-circular perception of national time (Gross, 1985), in which ancient enemies reemerge, time and again, in modern form.

In 2004, during a similar *Yad Vashem* visit, the Israeli chief of staff was asked to comment about the killing of one of the leaders of the Hamas movement by the Israeli army. The general replied by asserting that 'this will be the fate of anyone who tries to attack Israel.' He then added: 'It is important to remember that the arch-terrorist Rantisi was a known denier of the Holocaust... we are in the midst of complicated warfare during which the army is required to act in a moral and ethical manner. We will not become murderers but we will also not become victims and what happened to us in the past will not happen again.' The combination of commemorative timing, the commemorative space and the broad nature of his comment forged a link between current events and collective recollection. On this specific occasion, the chief of staff's answer carried a message extending beyond the specific time and space in a manner that reflected and constructed reversed memory discourse. The specific context enabled journalists to take part in the national past-oriented commemoration by focusing on current events and on the coverage of the present.

Beyond the use of individuals and places as carriers of memory that enable the creation of reversed memory, objects can also be used as a connecting link between past events and current news items. Unlike people, objects cannot speak for themselves, so the journalists have to do so. Moreover, news professionals have to explain or even to justify to their audiences the newsworthiness of diaries, pictures, paintings and films, all anchored in the distant past. A 1999 Holocaust Remembrance Day newscast featured an item depicting five Holocaust survivors, who were shown watching film footage from the Łódź ghetto. The anchorman's accompanying text demonstrated the effort to position the item as newsworthy, as well as its complex construction of time – he stated that while everyday life in the ghetto is fixed in our memory in black and white, *new* color footage of the Łódź ghetto had recently been discovered. The anchorman went on to describe the Nazi photographer who had taken this footage and then presented the current reactions of ghetto survivors to the film. The item thus included several different time frames: the actual footage was filmed during World War II. The footage's newsworthiness was a result of the fact that it revealed the *first* existing color images of the Łódź ghetto, and it was only *recently* discovered. Interestingly, it was later made clear that a Polish director had in fact already made a film using the same footage (it had not, in fact, been so new). Additional newsworthiness appeal was manufactured by screening the footage to an audience of Israeli Holocaust survivors who were watching the film *at the present time* and for the *first* time. The combination of the 'recently discovered' footage from the past and the present screening for this specific audience constructed a narrative of reversed memory, focusing on a here and now occurrence in order to commemorate the there and then.

Finally, a fourth type of memory carrier, bridging the space between the past and the present, can be represented by phenomena such as social behaviors and attitudes which stood at the heart of past events. In our case study, anti-Semitism serves as the prime example of a social attitude that assists the construction of reversed memory. Every year, the Stephen Roth Institute for the Study of Contemporary Anti-Semitism and Racism at Tel Aviv University publishes 'The Annual Report on Anti-Semitism Worldwide.' The annual report is released on the eve of Holocaust Remembrance Day eve and it is widely cited in Holocaust Remembrance Day news media. The news stories covering the report rarely mention the Holocaust itself, but rather focus on the current state of anti-Semitism across the world. Nevertheless, the charged timing of the publication of the report connects it to the Holocaust and its memory. The report and its journalistic coverage thus serve the implicit notion that the Holocaust is an ongoing phenomenon. Typical news items quoting the reports focus entirely on the present and may mention current conflicts; such a presentation hints that the attitudes and behaviors that constituted the Nazi regime are still an active social phenomenon, and thus, that the Holocaust is not over yet.

Reversed memory and its political significance

This chapter introduced the concept of reversed memory, a storytelling strategy that enables news items to commemorate past events by narrating the present, thus maintaining these events as ongoing occurrences. An analysis of news items that were all part of a national commemorative ritual revealed how news professionals construct the newsworthiness of these items as well as their commemorative value. This dual demand yields a delicate professional balancing act: when the newsworthiness component seems to be more evident, journalists emphasize its commemorative value (for example, by juxtaposing the news text with images from the past); conversely, when the commemorative value is more apparent, journalists underline or rather construct the newsworthiness of the items by using phrases such as 'for the first time,' 'recently discovered,' 'never been seen before' and so on.

The dual-yet-complementary nature of reversed memory thus reflects and helps clarify a core communication research debate. Carey (1989) famously addressed the differences between the perception of the communicative process as a form of information transmission and its perception as a mass social ritual. Reversed memory features news items that clearly aspire to 'transmit' newsworthy and fresh information to audiences. At the same time, such items are salient emblems of a ritualistic view of the communicative process that 'conceives communication as a process through which a shared culture is created, modified and transformed' (Carey, 1989: 43).

Finally, the tendency of Holocaust Remembrance Day news items to commemorate past events while covering current ones delineates the political implications of the implementation of reversed memory rhetoric. Such an overt focus on present events eases the confrontation with a difficult past, especially when these narratives carry triumphal messages in their focus on the stories of survivors who built new lives in Israel, youth delegations to concentration camps marching as proud Israelis in commemoration of the memory of the Holocaust, generals and politicians in *Yad Vashem* pledging 'never again' and so on. These victorious accounts rise above the traumatic past; such items provide a narrative sweetener that eases the collective taking of the bitter, traumatic pill of the past.

Beyond the narrative relief, the praxis of creating news items bearing both newsworthiness and commemorative values leads to a propensity to commemorate the Holocaust via celebration of the mere existence of the State of Israel. By doing so, the news media reproduce and amplify the hegemonic national-Zionist narrative; a master commemorative narrative depicting the voyage of the Jewish people from exile to revival (Zerubavel, 1995). Although survivors are usually the main protagonists of reversed memory associated with Holocaust Remembrance Day, the real 'hero' standing at the heart of the items is the State of Israel. The state is thus portrayed not only as the proper moral 'response' to the Holocaust, but also as a guarantee that a second Holocaust will never take place. This overreaching narrative charges the private stories of Israeli Holocaust survivors with collective significance.

The centrality of the State of Israel is best illustrated in reversed memory rhetoric associated with Holocaust Remembrance Day during times of crisis, when the connection between the Holocaust and modern day Israel is intensified. On such occasions, news coverage constructs a continuity between the commemoration of Jewish victims 'there and then' and current Israeli hardships 'here and now,' especially armed conflicts and terror attacks (Zandberg, Meyers and Neiger, 2012: 73–4). By doing so, reversed memory 'stretches' temporal perceptions (Barnhurst, 2011) and constructs a 'past continuous' temporality, in which the Holocaust is a never-ending occurrence. Holocaust Remembrance Day therefore provides the 'perfect storm' for the confluence of a consensual theme, the context of a ritualistic mourning day (when other pressing issues are silenced) and the social consent that the Holocaust is important for the lives of current day Israelis – all of which lead to the framing of the Holocaust as an ongoing event.

In spite of the fact that in this chapter we have addressed the concept of reversed memory through the use of a highly charged example of

commemorative public memory, further research might track the operation of parallel mechanisms, constructing the past as an ongoing event,
outside the realm of state rituals. Thus we suggest looking for reversed
memory, even if on different scales, at the two ends of the spectrum: at
official commemorative (mostly national) rituals, in which the relations
between present events and the past are well-recognized by audiences,
and at non-commemorative collective memory, which is abundant in
routine news coverage (Schudson, 1997). At the non-commemorative
end of the spectrum stand news items such as a news report published
in *Yediot Aharonot* in August 2012 reporting that the German special
prosecutor's office had announced its recommendation that charges be
filed against a 87-year-old man alleged to have served as an SS guard
at Auschwitz during World War II. The story focused on current juridi-
cal procedures, yet the image that accompanied the story depicted the
infamous 'ARBEIT MACHT FREI' ['labor liberates'] sign placed across the
entrance to Auschwitz-Birkenau. Our argument is that in this example,
much as in Holocaust Remembrance Day cases, the news professionals
who created the story were driven to add commemorative value (the
sign) to coverage of the current event in order to balance newsworthiness and commemoration, thus framing the story as an ongoing event.

On a different level, one of the main questions that the presence of
reversed memory brings to the forefront of collective memory research
is when exactly is a past event socially understood to be over? When
does the past become a settled account? A done deal? Can society
address its past events as bygones, encapsulated in history, while live
news regarding its implications keeps streaming in?

The larger political context and significance of reversed memory is
thus strongly tied to these questions and to the struggle over framing
past events as continuous ones. Controversies over the interpretation of
salient past events are always anchored in the struggle between competing memory agents; and so, interpretive agents can gain political capital
by keeping past occurrences alive in the present public realm.

In the Israeli context, a prime example of the political struggle over
the finiteness of the past and the ongoing existence of seemingly-
bygone events could be found in the heated debate over the shaping
of the memory of the 1948 war (Israel's War of Independence; the
Palestinian *Nakba* [catastrophe]). Over the past three decades Israeli historians have been engulfed in a debate over the war and its outcomes,
with 'new historians' arguing that the veteran historical explorations
of the war were bluntly one-sided and that they avoided discussing
'uncomfortable' issues, such as the active Israeli role in the expulsion of

Palestinians during the war. As the debate over the 'new historiography' developed, the centrality of Israeli journalism to the argument became evident: most discussants seemed to agree that the debate was not only, or not even mainly, about the proper way to conduct historical research. Rather, the debate could only be adequately grasped through a consideration of its larger current political context: the dispute over Israel's past was an embodiment of the ongoing negotiation over Israel's present; and so, the seemingly academic debate constantly nourished the journalistic coverage of the ongoing Israeli-Palestinian peace process and especially the Palestinians' current demands for an implementation of the 'right of return' (Meyers, 2011).

Following the same vein, in the American context one can explore the commemoration of the 9/11 attacks and their presence in the news media. Such an investigation can look at commemorative coverage as well as the constant coverage of the American 'War on Terror,' as a mechanism through which the memory of the attacks is kept alive. Hence, an ongoing exploration of reversed memory manifestations could provide a better understanding of the processes through which communities manage their pasts, either through collective closure or through continuous discussion.

In Hanukah, Jews around the world recite blessings that thank God *'Who has done such miracles for our fathers and to us on those days at this time.'* Every year, in the Passover Haggadah Jews read that *'In each and every generation, a person is obligated to regard himself as though he actually left Egypt.'* Hence, just like the instructions found in ancient religious writings, reversed memory preserves the notion that major events are never really done; they are echoed time and again in history as well as in our everyday lives.

References

Barnhurst, K.G. (2011) 'The Problem of Modern Time in American Journalism,' *KronoScope*, 11(1–2), 98–123.

Carey, J.W. (1989) *Communication as Culture*. Boston: Unwin Hyman.

Duek, N. (2012) 'We Took-Off Like the Phoenix,' *Yediot Aharonot* (holiday supplement), 12 April, 14–17.

Edy, J.A. (1999) 'Journalistic Uses of Collective Memory,' *Journal of Communication*, 49(2), 71–85.

Feldman J. (2008) *Above the Death Pits, Beneath the Flag: Youth Voyages to Poland and the Construction of Israeli National Identity*. Oxford: Berghahn Press.

Frosh, P. and Pinchevski, A. (2009) *Media Witnessing: Testimony in the Age of Mass Communication*. Basingstoke: Palgrave.

Gross, D. (1985) 'Temporality and the Modern State,' *Theory and Society*, 14(1), 53–82.

Halbwachs, M. (1980 [1950]) *The Collective Memory*. New York: Harper Colophon Books. Translated into English by F.J. Ditter and V.Y. Ditter.

Hirsch, M. (2001) 'Surviving Images: Holocaust Photographs and the Work of Postmemory,' *Yale Journal of Criticism*, 14(1), 5–37.

Kaniuk, Y. (2012) 'Celebrate Holocaust Day,' *Haaretz*, 18 April, B1.

Kitch, C. (2002) 'Anniversary Journalism, Collective Memory, and the Cultural Authority to Tell the Story of the American Past,' *Journal of Popular Culture*, 36(1), 44–67.

Lang, K. and Lang, G.E. (1989) 'Collective Memory and the News,' *Communication*, 11, 123–39.

Liebman, C.S. and Don-Yehiya, E. (1983) *Civil Religion in Israel: Traditional Judaism and Political Culture in the Jewish State*. Berkeley: University of California Press.

Meyers, O. (2002) 'Still Photographs, Dynamic Memories: An Analysis of the Visual Presentation of Israel's History in Commemorative Newspaper Supplements,' *Communication Review*, 5(3), 179–205.

Meyers, O. (2007) 'Memory in Journalism and the Memory of Journalism: Israeli Journalists and the Constructed Legacy of *Haolam Hazeh*,' *Journal of Communication*, 57(4), 719–39.

Meyers, O. (2011) 'Memory in Journalism and the Memory of Journalism: Israeli Journalists and the Critical Reading of the National Past,' Annenberg Research Seminar, Annenberg School for Communication and Journalism, USC.

Neiger, M. (2007) 'Media Oracles: The Political Import and Cultural Significance of News Referring to the Future,' *Journalism: Theory, Practice & Criticism*, 8(3), 326–38.

Neiger, M. (2012) 'The Future is Present: The Media as an Agent of Collective Vision,' paper presented at the International Communication Association (ICA) conference, Phoenix, AZ, May.

Neiger, M., Meyers, O. and Zandberg, E. (2011). 'On Media Memory: Editors' Introduction,' in M. Neiger, O. Meyers and E. Zandberg (eds) *On Media Memory: Collective Memory in a New Media Age*. Basingstoke: Palgrave Macmillan, pp. 1–24.

Schudson, M. (1997) 'Lives, Laws, and Language: Commemorative Versus Non-Commemorative Forms of Effective Public Memory,' *Communication Review*, 2(1), 3–17.

Tenenboim-Weinblatt, K. (2011) 'Journalism as an Agent of Prospective Memory,' in M. Neiger, O. Meyers and E. Zandberg (eds) *On Media Memory: Collective Memory in a New Media Age*. Basingstoke: Palgrave Macmillan, pp. 213–25.

Tuchman, G. (1973) 'Making News By Doing the Work: Routinizing the Unexpected,' *American Journal of Sociology*, 79(1), 110–31.

Zandberg, E. (2010) 'The Right to Tell the (Right) Story: Journalism, Authority and Memory,' *Media, Culture & Society*, 32(1), 5–24.

Zandberg, E., Meyers, O. and Neiger, M. (2012) 'Past Continuous: Newsworthiness and the Shaping of Collective Memory,' *Critical Studies in Media Communication*, 29(1), 65–79.

Zelizer, B. (1992) *Covering the Body: The Kennedy Assassination, the Media, and the Shaping of Collective Memory*. Chicago: University of Chicago Press.

Zelizer, B. (2008) 'Why Memory's Work on Journalism does not Reflect Journalism's Work on Memory,' *Memory Studies*, 1(1), 79–87.

Zerubavel, Y. (1995) *Recovered Roots: Collective Memory and the Making of Israeli National Tradition*. Chicago: University of Chicago Press.

Journalism and Visual Memory

8
Hands and Feet: Photojournalism, the Fragmented Body Politic and Collective Memory

Robert Hariman and John Louis Lucaites

You cannot take a photograph of the past. This simple fact alters the relationship between journalism and collective memory. Journalism may be the 'first draft of history,' but others will be written as well, and the loss of immediacy may be of little consequence in distinguishing between earlier and later written accounts. As additional reports are collated, 'smoke everywhere' may become 'smoke filled the street for half a block.' Accuracy can improve and additional actors and perspectives can become part of the story.

Unlike the written reports, the photographs taken at the time will be the only visual documentation thereafter. There will be no second or third draft; instead, later documentaries will have to rely on the same images. Indeed, use of the photographic archive – at least since Ken Burns's 1990 documentary series on the American Civil War – has become a major means for establishing the authenticity of documentary film and other retrospective media productions such as commemorative issues of magazines. Of course, images are partial records that can mislead or be misinterpreted, and the written (and oral) reports remain vitally important for memory, history and political accountability. But photography provides the only draft for one type of documentary witness, and thus photojournalism might provide a relatively unique basis for understanding the role of the press in mediating a society's relationship with the past (Zelizer, 1998, 2004).

Images are used as aides-memoire in both private and public life, and specific practices have evolved in each realm. Private remembrance includes everything from baby pictures to putting images on cemetery headstones. Public remembrance includes press retrospectives, museum exhibitions, coffee-table books, posters, murals, roadside memorials and so forth. As we have argued previously, in the US a specific genre of photojournalism, the iconic photograph, has developed to play a prominent role in shaping and relaying collective memory (Hariman and Lucaites, 2007). Iconic photographs are understood to be essential representations of important historical events, they evoke strong emotional and symbolic connections, and they are reproduced across a wide range of media, genres and topics while people use them to manage political relationships such as citizenship. Along the way, images such as the flag raising on Iwo Jima or a napalmed girl running down a road in Vietnam have become key signposts in the collective memory of World War II, the Vietnam era and more.

Iconic images have their own problems, however, and can loom too large in a society's view of the past. Icons are necessarily oriented toward mainstream norms of social and aesthetic decorum which easily relay ideology; their suggestion of transcendental significance can lead toward mystification rather than critical reasoning; their continual reproduction can become too formulaic, leading to stock emotions while displacing a much wider range of experiences. A newspaper that used only iconic images would not really be a newspaper at all, any more than if it provided only editorials or weather reports. But the trend is toward more rather than less imagery, and journalism provides other visual images that, although relatively under the radar in terms of critical study, offer intriguing examples of how collective memory works visually.

This chapter will focus on one, small, somewhat peculiar technique that can be found throughout contemporary photojournalism in the US and the UK and particularly in coverage of national and international politics. That technique is to frame or crop images to feature otherwise disembodied feet or hands (see Figure 8.1).

Examples include prisoners' hands holding the bars of a prison cell, a child's hand protruding from the rubble of a bombing, black shoes in a row at a congressional hearing and combat boots at a memorial service; and bare hands, calloused hands and hands that are gloved, painted, or otherwise adorned or stained; and bare feet, crippled feet, and socks, shoes, work boots and cowboy boots; and also prostheses for hands and feet, and – sure sign that a convention is active – images whose rhetorical power comes from the display of missing limbs.[1] In all of these photographs the feet or hands, whether present or absent, are salient, and they are often the more so because the individuals' heads or bodies are *not* shown.

This compositional technique functions as a rhetorical figure because it is a deviation from standard usage for added effect. Just as the Shakespearean 'to the well, go,' is distinctive because of how it varies

Figure 8.1 A woman holds on to a truck containing food for distribution in Iraq. Petr David Josek, Associated Press

the standard usage of 'go to the well,' so does an isolated foot or hand vary from the usual practice of showing the whole or upper half of the body while featuring the face (Hariman and Lucaites, 2008). All photojournalism will provide a sense of politics as an embodied practice – indeed, that may be one of its more important functions – but against that background, figures of bodily fragmentation may acquire additional rhetorical power.

Even so, a small gain in effect from occasional use of a minor technique would seem to be of little significance. News images are no more going to be dominated by close shots of hands or feet than they are going to be limited to iconic photos. What is forgotten, however, is how most photographs do not show the full body outline, much less what would be seen from the reverse angle, and how any photograph is but a thin slice of a larger event. Most news images are of body parts that are seen as whole bodies, and all images are of single events that are taken to be episodes in a larger story. Thus, the obvious bodily fragment exemplifies tacit features shared by all photography: fragmentation of some larger whole and separation from context (Sontag, 1977: 105–6). These characteristics of the medium have been targeted by its critics and used to assert the professional necessity of anchoring news images with verbal captions. It seems obvious, then, that increased fragmentation would further threaten the narrative continuity supposedly essential for a community of memory. We won't challenge that idea outright, but we will suggest that something else could happen as well: these fragmentary images become a form of gestural communication articulating a body politic that is the more accurate and inclusive for not being whole.

Bodily fragmentation and the elocutionary function

Political speech is littered with references to body parts, many of them gendered. Those with political muscle will strong-arm others, unless someone has the backbone or guts or balls supposed to provide political will. When leaders do get their hands on the levers of power, they may hit the deck running or issue a call to arms, while dissenters will argue that big government should get its hands out of taxpayers' pockets or reduce an environmental footprint. If leaders are not responsive, voters may give them the boot. All of this will be reported by talking heads.

These and other metonyms for representing power are all exceedingly conventional. They may also be examples of *enargia*, or the use of speech to create visual images. Obviously such images need not be the equivalent of a great work of art. They must be doing something, however, and their persistence as a common code within public discourse suggests that they are being used to mediate and negotiate political relationships. George Lakoff and Mark Johnson, as well as a few others, have demonstrated that bodily coding within political speech can have considerable structural and social significance – say, in constituting civic status within patriarchal relationships (Lakoff and Johnson, 1980; Holland, 2001). The question remains, however, as to how such figural images work when they really are *images* – that is, when the bodily coding of public opinion occurs via photojournalism, television news and other visually intensive media.[2]

Our contention is that the display of fragmentary images of feet and hands in photojournalism exemplifies the way in which modern image production reprises the classical rhetorical canon of delivery (*hypocrisis* in the Greek, *actio* in the Latin). That is, we are witnessing the transfer of an *elocutionary function* from one public art to another. More simply, bodily gestures are used to communicate both in support of and in lieu of speech, and photographs can not only relay an intentional movement but can become an equivalent form of voiceless speech.

In classical rhetoric, gestures were considered essential to persuasion because they were the means to engage the emotions directly.

Just as one learned to use one's native language, a speaker could draw on the 'language' of gestures to communicate to a public audience. As Quintilian emphasized:

As for the hands, without which all action would be crippled and enfeebled, it is scarcely possible to describe the variety of their motions, since they are almost as expressive as words. For other portions of the body merely help the speaker, whereas the hands may almost be said to speak. Do we not use them to demean, promise, summon, dismiss, threaten, supplicate, express aversion or fear, question or deny? Do we not employ them to indicate joy, sorrow, hesitation, confession, penitence, measure, quantity, number and time? Have they not power to excite and prohibit, to express approval, wonder or shame? Do they not take the place of adverbs and pronouns when we point at places and things? In fact, though the peoples and nations of the earth speak a multitude of tongues, they share in common the universal language of the hands.

(Quintilian, 1979: 11.3.85–7)[3]

The point was not lost on later writers on delivery, who typically channeled the classical rationale while claiming to offer a distinctive program of instruction. For example, the late nineteenth-century pedagogue Albert Bacon detailed 56 gestures for the right hand that, commensurate with related bodily movements, would 'furnish a vocabulary of gesture commensurate with the realm of thought and feeling' (Bacon, 1892: 11).

It is easy to ridicule the elocutionary tradition, but also mistaken. Certainly it provides evidence of how claims to universality are culture-bound: Quintilian and later writers discuss in exhaustive detail the semiotic and emotional valances of specific configurations of the fingers, yet the signs are no longer intelligible. Likewise, the systems of articulation quickly explode as the many thousands of technical options are multiplied by endless variations in speaker, subject, occasion and audience. But there is more to the elocutionist's theory, which begins to emerge with this statement by Quintilian: 'Nor is it wonderful [amazing] that gesture which depends on various forms of movement should have such power, when pictures, which are silent and motionless, penetrate into our innermost feelings with such power that at times they seem more eloquent than language itself' (Quintilian, 1979: 11.3.67). What may seem a stretch (so to speak) in the art of oratory is in fact the natural attitude of the visual arts. The expressive power of painting, for example, depends on our emotional response to bodies and correlatives of bodily experience. Those responses depend on both culturally specific iconographies (whether of Renaissance portraiture or Cubist painting), and on reception that seems direct, unmediated and universal precisely because it involves bodies, shapes, lines, colors and other sensory elements without language. The iconographies will blend together both universal features of bodily experience (arms but not antennae) and encultured conventions of depiction (two arms in Europe, multiple arms in India).

Photography is particularly representative in this regard. It is focused predominately on bodies while capturing in close detail costume and gesture as they comprise the encultured surface of everyday experiences. Thus, images of hands and feet, as with images generally, are understood to be emotionally evocative precisely because they are corporeal rather than verbal. And just as gesture is used in oratory to provide emotional inflection and emphasis to the verbal message, gestural images will do the same. This is one reason why neither oratory nor journalism relies on verbal meaning alone. The emotionally evocative gesture provides a simple, effective vehicle for communicating with a large public audience, and the gestural photograph does the same.

What is distinctive about the photographic image is that it can both relay another's gesture – as when a political leader waves to the crowd – and create a gesture not necessarily intended by the subject of the photograph – as when a dead child's hand protrudes from the wreckage of a bombing. Such images might merely activate stock emotions, but they can also be highly evocative. One might consider a parallel structure with the production of collective memory, in which media can both activate known memories – prior experiences held in common – and lay down new memories – other experiences that now are condensed into simple, vivid, memorable images (Hirsch, 1997). (The process is more complex, of course, as stock images can acquire renewed significance in a particular setting, and innovative imaging often fails to have wide appeal.) Whether amplifying another's gesture or creating a new gestural statement, the image of the body part, like photography generally, provides a moment of embodied cognition powerfully suited to both public communication and collective memory.

Like all gestural communication, the photographic gesture is nothing if not conventional. And like the use of gesture in public speech, images of hands, feet, or other body parts become legible and effective as they address conventional relationships and concerns of collective association. We believe that images of disembodied feet and hands work in this way by providing a political iconography – that is, even if selected for sheer visual salience, the images of hands and feet serve as a small sign system for political communication. This repertoire stems from an initial limitation: anonymous hands and feet are better able to reveal social types than they are to describe individuals. This is also part of a larger distribution of meaning: typically the face is the register of individuality and personality, the head signifies cognition and authority, the body is indirectly a means for social classification because of the clothes that cover it, and feet and hands provide stance and gesture and therefore experience, agency, relationality and commonality. Images of hands and feet are not studies in individuality; instead, they operate as signs of communication and action among groups.

This iconography is used to articulate political relationships, as when the elected official reaches out to the electorate or when parliamentary opponents clasp hands in ritual affirmation of the democratic process. These images of leadership are reinforced by images of citizenship, which involve hands that vote, pledge allegiance, salute, share and otherwise work together. The gestural economy is particularly evident in representations of dissent. The hands (and arms) and feet (and boots and shoes) that are highlighted in photographs of demonstrations ensure that those events are seen as populist movements striving to communicate what otherwise is unvoiced or unheard. Typical images include hands reaching upward from the crowd, fists or V-signs held high, hands touching memorials, hands painted with blood or holding peace symbols aloft, clasped hands, jostling hands, marching feet and so forth. The state, which otherwise is represented by portraits and ceremonial groupings of officials, is often now signified by police boots or gloved hands holding clubs.

The iconography of protest presents a troubled mixture of force and speech: the voice of the people is expressed not in words but by massed bodies and defiant gestures, while the state's legitimacy is reduced from reasoned discourse to its monopoly on force. When speech is given over to gesture, and when mass movements are represented by fragmented bodies, the desire to communicate becomes pathetic in several senses: obviously emotional, lacking proper authority, venue, or skill, and unlikely to be met in full if at all. These images are also powerful, however, because the gestural iconography of photojournalism does intensively what the medium does generally: it communicates bodily experience, and particularly a democratic form of experience – that is, experience that is collective rather than idiosyncratic or personal. Images of stance and gesture carry with them palpable limits that in turn can become the shape of experiences likely to be shared by others in that predicament. A wave of the hand can be brief but poignant, and feet always answer to the hard common denominator of the ground. The photograph communicates that hard-won experience as a basis for judgment of political leaders, policies and institutions. Images of victims and mourning obviously are the most telling in this regard: a mangled foot belies the supposed daintiness of foot binding; hands prostrate on a coffin suggest the utter incapacity to bring back the war dead. Other images seem to exist to feature the primacy of experience itself: an image of field workers' toughened, dirty feet splayed out on the grass to rest articulates the bare life of third world labor (Figure 8.2).

Figure 8.2 also demonstrates how the focus on body parts carries with it a specific danger: not unintelligibility or romanticism, although these are potential problems, but rather objectification. The virtual dismembering of the alien body can make it into a specimen, which carries with it the most dangerous asymmetry of power between observer and observed.[4] To guard against this bias, one must ask how the photographic fragment works in conjunction with other tropes, not least the metaphor of the body politic.

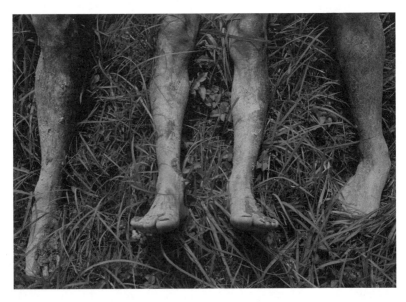

Figure 8.2 Nepalese farmers resting. Narendra Shrestha, European Pressphoto Agency

Fragmenting the body politic in a liberal democratic society

The gestural image is figural rather than literally descriptive. The body part articulates social types, political relationships, evocative emotions and collective experience, but indirectly. The primary figural operation is metonymy, but it operates in tandem with a metaphoric register. Some of the time the metaphor is superficial, as when we see a helping hand. Some of the time the iconography activates both dimensions powerfully: we see both the metonymic reduction of a complex reality to visible markers of experience, commonality and responsibility, and a corresponding analogy with the body politic. Although no longer a significant concept within political theory or public speech, the figure of the body politic lives on visually. Interestingly, pre-modern political discourse features not so much the whole body as its parts, and principally hands and feet (Hale, 1973). The hands and feet together could signify the common people in Rome, while in the medieval period the hands represented the nobility or soldiers and the feet the peasantry. In the Renaissance, one could be reproved that the foot must not be the judge of the head, for rulers are not to be judged by subjects. In all periods, the various members should work in concert, as Paul averred: 'The eye cannot say to the hand, "I have no need of you," nor again the head to the feet, "I have no need of you." . . . Now you are the body of Christ and individually members of it' (Paul: 1 Cor. 12.21, 12.27; *New Oxford Annotated Bible*: 1994).

Thus, we see that the body – which, of course, largely remains under wraps – is quickly known metonymically through its members, which in turn provide a convenient schema for figural depiction of the segmentation of the political order. The specific associations (head with leadership and feet with the common people) are in fact reproduced continually in modern representational practice, albeit with the nuanced inflections that come from the modern democratic association of political legitimacy with egalitarian norms. The result can be used in either direction, of course: to confront leaders with the experience (if not the voice) of the common people, or to maintain a traditional hierarchy separating political elites and masses while allowing the former to display the common touch. But we should not conclude that mediation is so easily manipulated. The intersection of metonymy and metaphor provides not only the rhetorical engine for continual production of these images, but also the capacity in any one image, however fragmented, partial, or banal, to activate an entire set of political relationships, emotions and actions.[5] The connection between visible body part and invisible body politic makes the gestural iconography a vehicle for the political imagination.

There could be several reasons for the persistence of the pre-modern trope in public representation. One answer would note the conservative bias in the metaphor: either conservative ideas are underrepresented in liberal societies and so likely to emerge in subordinate venues (images rather than official discourse, for example), or the elite determination of political representation continues through all available means and is all the better hidden for becoming visual. These answers can suffice some of the time, but other factors bear consideration as well. Rather than seeing the body politic as a pre-modern vestige in the modern medium, we think it mediates tensions inherent within modern political representation, particularly as representation has to work visually.

The tensions all follow from the constitutive terms of modern democracy: the leaders are not sovereign (only the people are sovereign); the people are not an individual (and thus cannot be placed); the public is not a social group (no social ascription can signify the public); no one person or thing can be comprehensively plural (social totality can never be represented fully because political representation is always incomplete).[6] In addition, speech cannot be shown and so has to be pantomimed for those who are seeing rather than hearing or reading public performances. In light of these conditions, the stock images of talking heads, audiences, buildings, ceremonies and the like could seem less fitting than the image of a fragmentary body part. Let us consider, then, how the trope of disembodied hands and feet might have developed to finesse two related problems of contemporary public life: how to suture the local and the global, and how to represent a heterogeneous public sphere.

There need not be a contradiction between any particular thing and broader, even universal reference, as one can see the laws of nature in a grain of sand. The local, parochial, encultured reality of human life, however, turns more on difference and contingency than universality. Communication in particular is thought to be fully legible, effective and ethical only when it is thoroughly situated in respect to a particular audience. At the same time, the transportation and communication technologies of modern societies drive all cultures toward standardized forms of exchange. The expansion in scale to a global communications environment – whether in fact or as a social fact – only adds fuel to the fire. So it is that media arts are going to include a number of strategies for capturing both local meaning and globally intelligible articulation. Iconic images are one strategy; the iconography of stance and gesture is another.

It can seem that in this case photojournalism offers a 'natural' alignment between image, medium and function. The image of a gesture, the transparency of the photographic medium and the projection of the body politic would seem to be correspondingly universal attributes. Human beings do use a rudimentary, unschooled 'sign language' for pointing, begging and similarly elemental tasks across cultures. Photographs are continuous with ordinary sight, and more familiar than other media of representation across cultures. The metaphor of the body politic persists across all historical periods, and a lexicon of bodily terms is used continually across cultures to describe political behavior. Thus, one might conclude that the gestural images are an obvious development as communication goes global. By showing only the foot or featuring the hand, the image depicts something that is obviously particular, local and situated, and it communicates modally that this thing should be universally recognizable. One sees a small part of a specific locality, and obviously is not being asked to understand the whole, and yet is 'gestured to' as someone who can immediately see, relate, empathize or otherwise connect with that part of the whole that can be directly experienced without the mediation of language or the hermeneutical skill required to negotiate the scene as a whole. By contrast, familiar head shots, photos of buildings and other stock images, while actually more recognizable formally, are already codified as situated and addressed to those within the institutions, scenes, roles and gambits constituting the social space of the particular newspaper or newscast. Ironically, they are often the more generic images, whereas the gestural fragments are more finely situated and in greater need of captioning, but the difference in composition signals very different terms of address.

If seeing only the hand or foot, there may be little there; by seeing and thinking *with* the hand or foot (Burnett, 2004), one activates a traditional way of thinking about politics – the body politic – as that has been adapted to the conditions of public representation: it appears to be fragmented rather than totalizing, realistic rather than idealized, and provisional rather than essentialist. Body parts communicate relationships of contiguity that may be contingent, which is why hands and eyes can get out of synch or head and feet be at cross purposes. Most important, the dismemberment of the body implies a body politic that is no longer whole yet still active. This plural, shape-shifting, motive mass known only through dismemberment and pantomime could be monstrous but never becomes so because it is never seen. In fact, it never exists whole, but only in parts.

An assemblage of parts can appear to be kitsch or otherwise offensive to modernist aesthetic norms. Public art is by nature compromised, however, and these mixed and muddled media are so in part because of the work they have to do. The image of a bodily fragment signifies the distributed body of modern social organization, the pluralistic body of modern civil society, the multicultural body of a transnational public sphere. This is the body that resists the abstraction and political symbolism dominating official discourse, but always indirectly, through figures of embodiment that are already dismembered. This is a rhetoric of bodily experience, but not the personalized experience of identity politics or the *faux* intimacy of infantilized citizenship (Berlant, 1997). These images have proliferated when official authority is already discredited, and they are used both to contest that authority and finesse the problem of maintaining public legitimacy.

To see how the body part can be used to represent a community that was trying to become a polity unencumbered by conventions of political coherence, consider a photograph that appeared in a slide show on the Occupy Wall Street Movement (Figure 8.3). According to the caption, the photograph was taken in Zuccotti Park and shows the protestors charging high-capacity boat batteries that have been retrofitted

Figure 8.3   Occupy Wall Street protest, Zuccotti Park, New York City. John Minchillo, Associated Press

with small manual generators after their gas-powered generators were confiscated by the police.

No faces are shown, and the *bricolage* of equipment isn't entirely clear either (where are the batteries?). Around the cluttered center of the image are arrayed some of the Occupy crowd, with one person working and the others apparently spectators (like those viewing the photograph). In place of identifiable individuals, we are shown their shoes – and several different shoes, including a work boot, an ankle boot and a black oxford. (There may be a sneaker in the background, though it is hard to be certain.) The reduction of protestors to their shoe styles calls attention to a pluralist world that precedes political organization. Thus, the photograph is in some measure an allegory for the body politic. But instead of an organic, idealized, or essentialist political body marked by an 'official spokesperson,' we see a body politic that is fragmented, realistic, provisional and known by its gestures. Some will bemoan what is seemingly being abandoned, but one can also see how this image is an example of adaptation to the social conditions and representational habits of the contemporary period. In short, the photograph shows a conception of public life that is no longer whole – in the most traditional sense – but is nevertheless active and engaged and in its own way successful. It is, in short, an image of a *pluribus* without an *unum*, a plurality that need not be reduced to a stultifying One: what William Corlett has called 'community without unity' (Corlett, 1989; Zerilli, 2000). This is a public that is animated by common needs and goals without either ignoring or being reduced to stylized differences.

Remembering in part

The words are usually heard at Christian weddings, but that formulaic recitation doesn't diminish their deep appeal:

> For now we see in a mirror, dimly; but then we will see face to face. Now I know only in part; then I will know fully, even as I have been fully known.
>
> (Paul: 1 Cor. 12.13)

A great deal of photography might be thought of as an attempt to bring people 'face to face' across the barriers of distance, time and culture (Peters, 1999). Ordinary people use it daily to communicate with family and friends, and when the subjects of these photos wince at the camera's accuracy, transparency seems natural. As critics of the medium point out, however, the experience is always condemned to fragmentation and separation: a tiny slice of space and time, a virtual encounter, a material object, a substitution of image for reality, a message without a code, lacking context and lost to dissemination – the photograph offers and then betrays the deep desire to communicate without mediation, directly, purely, in perfect relation with the other.

As photography is an art, it possesses the capacity both to enhance this offer and convert its limitations into a means for even more significant expression. The enhancement is evident in the standard conventions of focusing on people and then on faces, and on people looking at and so communicating with one another or, via the image, with the viewer. These conventions are of course taken for granted, but they are also on occasion disrupted. So it is with images of feet and hands. These images exemplify photography's inherent fragmentation of perception, and the mute separation of any image from the event recorded, and the difficulty in making a connection between those seeing and those being seen. For precisely this reason, they provide an opportunity to reflect on the construction of collective memory, which is also plagued by fragmentation, separation and the pathos of communication.

Just as cropped bodies are often seen as whole, so are memories actually cropped, partial, broken fragments of what was. The incompleteness of memory is not news within memory studies, but the extent to which wholeness is valued needs additional reconsideration (Huyssen, 1995; Sturken, 1997: 17). Like the complete image of the body politic, collective memory is a useful fiction summarizing a more troubled and generative process of representation. Nor is this difference captured by arguments about exclusion and inclusion, as the concept of potentially comprehensive representation persists. By contrast, if one considers that full representation is impossible, then a different accounting of how memory works becomes available. In this conception, verbal narrative and a process of continuing revision remain important, but not privileged. Likewise, photographs remain fragmentary images in need of literal and imaginative contextualization, but not subordinate for all that.

Memory work becomes no easier, however, and a tendency toward fragmentation does carry its own difficulties. The gains to be had from relying on an iconography of gesture in a globalized digital media environment may be offset by other losses. Critically important contextual information could be lost. Coherence might be harder to sense, much less to articulate. Images could become illegible more quickly as small signs are lost to changes in fashion. A small disruption in pictorial conventions might have larger consequences over time, not least because the past can never be photographed again.

Even so, the primary task of photojournalism and an important function of collective memory is to equip people to live together in the present. As an iconography of boots, shoes, feet, hands, gloves, prostheses and absent limbs builds up a world of political relationships represented only in part, a particular type of public culture becomes more readily available. That culture is both inherently heterogeneous and answerable to common denominators of human bodily experience. In place of the bourgeois subject of the modern public sphere, embodied in individual portraiture, the contemporary citizen is known only in part. In place of a culture of consensus, the public culture becomes a far more uneven thing of radically democratic membership. In place of a community of memory always haunted by what has been lost, remembrance can be dedicated to understanding what remains. Public arts today, at their best, provide collective representation without totality and community without unity. If we are comfortable within that culture, it may be in some measure because of how photojournalism has been shaping the public consciousness though unwitting representation of a body politic that is best known, and remembered, only in part.

Notes

1. The authors have collected hundreds of examples – so many that after a while we quit collecting most of them – from several major papers, where they occur in print or in digital slide shows continuously. See also the posts under the category of 'Boots and Hands' at our blog, http://www.nocaptionneeded.com.
2. Work on the relationship between the human body, social representation and power is voluminous, with attention to the raced body, the gendered body and so on. For a survey of such work see Shilling (1993); Gatens (1997); Cavarero (2002), especially 99–120; and Fraser (2005). On the relationship between the body and visual culture see Sobchack (2004) and Casper and Moore (2009). The broad array of such work notwithstanding, we have encountered little on the visual depiction of body parts as representations of public culture.
3. Quintilian begins the discussion of delivery by noting, first, the relative interchangeability of voice and gesture, and, second, the connection to emotional response (11.3.1). For a gloss of Quintilian's discussion of gesture, see Graf (1991).
4. These images may provide particularly apt examples of how many photographs can contain contradictory articulations of both virtual citizenship and biopolitical subjugation. On how photography extends citizenship to the photographic subject, see Azoulay (2008).
5. On the intersection of metaphor and metonymy in textual composition, see de Man (1979: 3–19).

6. On the distinction between the public and social identity, see Warner (2002). On full political representation being impossible, see Ankersmit (1996).

References

Ankersmit, F.R. (1996) *Aesthetic Politics: Political Philosophy Beyond Fact and Value*. Stanford: Stanford University Press.

Azoulay, A. (2008) *The Civil Contract of Photography*. New York: Zone Books.

Bacon, A.M. (1892) *A Manual of Gesture; Embracing a Complete System of Notation, Together with the Principles of Interpretation and Selections for Practice*, 7th edn. New York: Silver, Burdett & Co.

Berlant, L. (1997) *The Queen of America Goes to Washington City: Essays on Sex and Citizenship*. Durham, NC: Duke University Press.

Burnett, R. (2004) *How Images Think*. Cambridge, MA: MIT Press.

Casper, M.J. and Moore, L.F. (2009) *Missing Bodies: The Politics of Visibility*. New York: New York University Press.

Cavarero, A. (2002) *Stately Bodies: Literature, Philosophy, and the Question of Gender*. Ann Arbor: University of Michigan Press.

Corlett, W. (1989) *Community without Unity: a Politics of Derridian Extravagance*. Durham, NC: Duke University Press.

de Man, P. (1979) *Allegories of Reading: Figural Language in Rousseau, Nietzsche, Rilke, and Proust*. New Haven: Yale University Press.

Fraser, M. (ed.) (2005) *The Body: A Reader*. New York: Routledge.

Gatens, M. (1997) 'Corporeal Representation in/and the Body Politic,' in K. Conboy, N. Medina and S. Stanbury (eds) *Writing on the Body: Female Embodiment and Feminist Theory*. New York: Columbia University Press, pp. 80–9.

Graf, F. (1991) 'Gestures and Conventions: The Gestures of Roman Actors and Orators,' in J. Bremmer and H. Roodenburg (eds) *A Cultural History of Gesture*. Ithaca, NY: Cornell University Press, pp. 36–58.

Hale, D.G. (1973) 'Analogy of the Body Politic,' in P.P. Wiener (ed.) *Dictionary of the History of Ideas*. New York: Scribner's, pp. 67–70.

Hariman, R. and Lucaites, J.L. (2007) *No Caption Needed: Iconic Photographs, Public Culture, and Liberal Democracy*. Chicago: University of Chicago Press.

Hariman, R. and Lucaites, J.L. (2008) 'Visual Tropes and Late-Modern Emotion in U.S. Public Culture,' *POROI*, 5(2), 47–93.

Hirsch, M. (1997) *Family Frames: Photography, Narrative, and Postmemory*. Cambridge, MA: Harvard University Press.

Holland, C. (2001) *The Body Politic: Foundings, Citizenship, and Difference in the American Political Imagination*. New York: Routledge.

Huyssen, A. (1995) *Twilight Memories*. New York: Routledge.

Lakoff, G. and Johnson, M. (1980) *Metaphors We Live By*. Chicago: University of Chicago Press.

The New Oxford Annotated Bible, ed. B.G. Metzer and R.E. Murphy, New Revised Standard Version. New York: Oxford University Press.

Peters, J.D. (1999) *Speaking into the Air: A History of the Idea of Communication*. Chicago: University of Chicago Press.

Quintilian (1979) *Institutio oratoria* vol. 4, trans. H.E. Butler, Loeb Library. Cambridge, MA: Harvard University Press.

Shilling, C. (1993) *The Body and Social Theory*. London: Sage.

Sobchack, V. (2004) *Carnal Thoughts: Embodiment and Moving Image Culture*. Berkeley: University of California Press.

Sontag, S. (1977) *On Photography*. New York: Picador.

Sturken, M. (1997) *Tangled Memories: The Vietnam War, the AIDS Epidemic, and the Politics of Remembering*. Berkeley: University of California Press.

Warner, M. (2002) *Publics and Counterpublics*. New York: Zone Books.

Zelizer, B. (1998) *Remembering to Forget: Holocaust Memory through the Camera's Eye*. Chicago: University of Chicago.

Zelizer, B. (2004) 'The Voice of the Visual in Memory,' in K.R. Phillips (ed.) *Framing Public Memory*. Tuscaloosa: University of Alabama Press.

Zerilli, L. (2000) 'Democracy and National Fantasy: Reflections on the Statue of Liberty,' in J. Dean (ed.) *Cultural Studies and Political Theory*. Ithaca, NY: Cornell University Press, pp. 167–88.

9
Journalism, Memory and the 'Crowd-Sourced Video Revolution'

Kari Andén-Papadopoulos

This chapter considers how the nature of journalistic memory work is changing in our 'new memory ecology' (Brown and Hoskins, 2010; Hoskins, 2011), when smartphone-carrying citizens are replacing professional journalists as on-site eyewitnesses to breaking news stories and, consequently, filling in as key producers of images that linger as historical markers of disruptive events. Camera images, still and moving, are critical 'technologies of memory' (Sturken, 1997): key representations through which public memories are created, questioned and given meaning. This is also to say that the significance of journalism as a key institution of mnemonic record, and its centrality in broader cultural memory formation, hinges on the special potential of images for shaping public understanding and memory.

A defining aspect of the current shift towards what is variously called 'participatory,' 'convergent' or 'networked' journalism is the exceptional status assigned to eyewitness photographs and videos contributed by citizens in the production of crisis news (Andén-Papadopoulos and Pantti, 2011). Insofar as journalism now increasingly relies on such imagery to record and remember nodal news events, the memory implications of this shift call for closer examination than they have typically received in scholarship on journalism and memory to date.

Although the significance of journalism as a main site for public memory construction is by now widely recognized, it has remained largely unexplored within the larger field of collective memory studies (Edy, 1999; Zelizer, 2008). Also, as Zelizer notes, the key role played by images in shaping public memory 'has been asserted rather than explicated' (2003: 157) by scholars on collective memory. However, within the sub-field of collective memory research that has indeed explored the role of the news media in shared processes of remembering and forgetting, the role of the visual in the construction of journalistic memory has been the subject of important scholarly work (for example, Meyers, 2002; Tenenboim-Weinblatt, 2008; Zelizer, 1998, 2002, 2010). Still, much of the existing literature on journalism's memory work has yet to recognize and resolve the shifts that are under way in a mobile media environment that operates in real time and on a global scale, and in which public media and personal communication increasingly merge. I suggest that these shifts necessitate a critical re-evaulation of the role of journalism in shaping 'the first draft of history' which, in effect, tends also to become a final one (Berkowitz, 2011: 203). As Carolyn Kitch writes, the initial draft that journalism provides of current events is 'also the first draft of memory, a statement about what should be considered, in the future, as having mattered today' (2008: 312).

My chapter, then, takes as its point of departure the recognition that we cannot think about the symbolic – and thus mnemonic – power of news reporting without considering the distinct power of certain news images to 'lay down the tracks' with regard to how we receive and remember critical world events. A common critique of professional photojournalism concerns its complicity in the reproduction of oppressive global power relations, and its limited and inadequate exposure of distant suffering in ways that tend to 'trivialize the victim's experience or inflict an injustice on them' (Linfield, 2010: 87). It is, at least partly, against this skepticism of photojournalism's ability to construct a moral imaginary and memory of the pain of others that the incorporation of crowd-sourced footage into professional crisis reporting has been hailed as adding to the authenticity, and thereby moralizing force of journalistic witnessing. As opposed to the model of detachment, images taken by involved citizens summon an affective and embodied experience from 'inside' the event that is believed to impose a particular moral and political obligation on the consumers of news (Andén-Papadopoulos, 2013). If the appeal of such imagery, then, is that it differs in some critical ways from professional photojournalism or other 'official' genres, this is again something that has been asserted rather than carefully studied. My chapter thus addresses the following questions. Can we identify an alternative ethics and aesthetics of authenticity in these images, one that is altering traditional forms and standards for the visual coverage of news? Insofar as crowd-sourced video now helps forge and reforge how, why and what journalism remembers, to what extent can we read this as a democratizing intervention that expands journalism's power to relay the human drama that enhances our understanding of and engagement with the past? Using the amateur cellphone footage of the

killing of Neda Agha Soltan during the 2009 Iranian post-election protests as a critical point of reference, I set out in this chapter to analyze
the 'aesthetic registers and ethical discourses' (Chouliaraki, 2008: 339)
through which citizen footage constructs its truth claims. The chapter
draws on the idea that the moral and aesthetic values of this imagery are
interdependent – that is, that the moral value of crowd-sourced video is
contingent on the specific, embodied and affective gaze of the citizen
videographer which, in turn, is encoded in the distinct aesthetic features of this imagery. While the on-the-ground authenticity of crowd-
sourced footage now endows the news with a new moralizing potential,
I conclude that it is not enough in itself to provide a meaningful and
credible mnemonic record. Rather, it precisely demonstrates the value
that professional journalists can add to crowd-sourced content, not only
in giving it global visibility and significance but also in mitigating the
issues of reliability, accuracy, verifiability and also of security and dignity that are raised in the new circulatory memory-scape.

Journalism in a new media/memory ecology

What and how we remember in today's digital news environment is
changing as new mobile media are upending traditional hierarchies
of communicative power. Journalism's exclusive role in shaping what
is recognized as and becomes 'memory' is challenged in an increasingly converged media landscape, where new tools of digital recording
and dissemination enable individuals to turn their personal memories
into a public record that can be archived, annotated, appropriated and
recirculated in new and powerful ways. The example of the viral circulation of the cellphone footage of the killing of Neda Agha Soltan is suggestive of the ways in which mediated memories today are increasingly
on the move: they may be personally and hyper-locally produced, before
being mobilized both 'vertically' from the on-site witness to media
organizations and prosumers and 'horizontally' between citizens via
mobiles and social networking sites (Reading, 2011: 250), swiftly traveling across media, geographic, national and cultural boundaries. Agha
Soltan was killed by a single gunshot wound to the chest in Tehran on 20
June 2009 during the Iranian post-election protests. Her final moments
were captured by at least three bystanders with mobile phone cameras,
and the footage was instantly uploaded to social networking sites and
forwarded to CNN, the BBC, the *Guardian* and other news media around
the world. News organizations commonly hailed the camphone imagery
as 'the defining moment' of the battered uprising against the Iranian

regime, and they promptly canonized Agha Soltan as an 'instant symbol,' 'icon' or 'martyr' of the opposition movement (Mortensen, 2011). At the same time, the footage was pulled through multiple circuits of subcultural and political appropriations as Agha Soltan inspired the creation of various memorial websites, a Twitter icon, Facebook groups, poems, songs, documentary films, videos and placards used in anti-regime protests within Iran and beyond (Zelizer, 2010: 8–12). The example of Agha Soltan is thus indicative of what Hoskins (2011: 279) calls a 'connective turn' in the cultures of news and cultures of memory, as the affordability of mobile technologies and networks enable ordinary people to make significant input to the news production process and also to re-circulate and radically re-purpose existing news material.

The global news industry is in the midst of a 'crowd-sourced video revolution' (Sasseen, 2012: 4) that is altering both information flows and the nature of news work. Traditional journalists no longer have a monopoly on the footage that is shot and broadcast from zones of conflict and crises around the world. Instead, citizen journalists, political activists and human rights workers are now filling in as critical eyewitnesses to unjust and disastrous developments worldwide. News organizations are, in response, increasingly giving up attempts to lead on breaking news, focusing instead on verifying and re-mediating the stream of crowd-sourced images and information provided by on scene witnesses. In the case of the post-election protests in Iran 2009 and the Arab uprisings that began in 2010, professional newsrooms became heavily reliant on protesters and citizen journalists in their coverage, due to lack of on-the-ground access and the speed of unfolding events. Current research suggests that collaboration between newsrooms and citizen journalists changed notably between 2009 and 2011: while journalists have become more comfortable and confident in using what they prefer to call user-generated content (UGC), citizen videographers and lay journalists have become more aware of editorial processes and now strategically tailor their content to meet professional requirements, thereby becoming increasingly 'able to shape the news agenda' (Hänska-Ahy and Shapour, 2012: 13).

As major news organizations now extensively rely on such imagery, citizen videographers have taken on a new and vital role in shaping the news and the newsworthy and in mediating understanding of specific events, both at the time of their original publication and subsequently. In many cases, the crowd-sourced image or video itself *is* the news event – as the footage of the shooting of Neda Agha Soltan exemplifies. Yet journalism's extensive reliance on images created by unknown citizens, who do not abide by the ethical standards and responsibilities of the news trade, presents potentially devastating challenges to conventional journalistic notions of truth-telling (including fact-checking and source criticism). Importantly, this is a context in which journalism cannot distance itself from amateurs and other non-journalistic actors. For a news organization to reject available and newsworthy visuals would seriously undercut its credibility, while including them, in effect, often means risking violation of editorial control and standards. Journalists negotiate this dilemma by employing various discursive strategies for incorporation that seek to 'normalize' citizen imagery to suit existing norms and practices (for example, Singer, 2005).

Under such pressures, recent studies indicate that the 'professional logic of control' may be slowly shifting towards a revised logic of 'adaptability and openness,' which breaks away from the professional understandings of objectivity and truth (Lewis, 2012: 851; see also Andén-Papadopoulos and Pantti, 2013). Following Chouliaraki (2010), the subcontracting of the role of the eyewitness to private citizens can be seen to constitute a break not only with the monopoly of journalistic storytelling but also with professional discourses of objectivity. In replacing the journalist with the citizen as a guarantor of the authenticity of witnessing, she argues, it is no longer only the verification of facts and sources that makes for the trustworthiness of news but the authority of genuine emotion and first-person experience. It follows that journalism's claim to authority in shaping society's stories of the past, which traditionally has been built precisely on journalists' eyewitness relationships to events in the real world, is being altered by this move towards more participatory modes of witnessing.

The un/reality of photojournalism

A relevant starting point for discussing the distinct moral and aesthetic values of crowd-sourced footage is the skepticism expressed toward the capacity of professional photojournalism to adequately and appropriately bear witness to distant crisis. Hariman and Lucaites (2007) demonstrate that photojournalistic images provide a distinctly effective means for shaping public understanding, motivating action and framing public memory. Following Sturken, journalistic images, particularly those that are awarded iconic status, can be characterized as 'technologies of memory': key representations through which memories are shared, produced and contested (1997: 9). Photojournalistic images are commonly held, among professionals and the public alike, to have an extraordinary capacity to embody and create memories (for example,

Guerin and Hallas, 2007; Sturken, 2007; Zelizer, 1998, 2002, 2010). This potency derives from the visual image's privileged epistemic status: camera images in particular are considered as an authentic 'record of the real' that verifies and brings an event into iconic presence. Also, in their focus on bodily expression, journalistic images provide viewers with powerful evocations of emotional experience, thus placing the spectator in an affective relationship with the people depicted (Hariman and Lucaites, 2007: 35). If the news and other media need emotive visual embodiment and interaction in order to compel public attention and create a sense of shared reality and memory, it is crucial to note that news images simultaneously function as important 'sites of struggle' for the interpretation of historical events (Perlmutter and Wagner, 2004: 93). As Campbell stresses, the power of the image 'depends in the first instance on its public circulation' (2004: 67), and this circulation need not reflect a broad consensus or fixed meanings but can also include diverse and often inconsistent forms of viewer response.

However, the overall structure of today's global news ecology is still dominated by Western news media who reflect national and geopolitical distributions of power, privileging 'some disasters as worthy of Western emotion and action while leaving others outside the space of appearance' (Chouliaraki, 2010: 306). Those crises which do get reported are characterized by restricted visual repertoires that primarily serve to support versions of events that have already been established in public discourse by powerful political interests. Moreover, news images in the context of conflict and crisis tend to bolster a Euro-American-centered viewpoint that often provides an overt visual objectification of 'others' as enemy or inconceivable subjects, frequently identified with a passive and pathetic victimhood. Photojournalism's portrayal of suffering has, accordingly, been dismissed as 'tableaux of profound abjection' (Squiers, 1999; quoted in Linfield, 2010: 10) that undermine the possibilities for an audience engagement beyond either voyeurism or narcissistic identification. Industry standards have also effectively sanctified a system of self-censorship that regulates the representation of atrocity, which means that disturbing sights of bodily injury and death have been prevented from entering mainstream media platforms. Much visual current affairs coverage, then, has been complicit in producing what Campbell calls a 'horrific blindness' which, he concludes, 'constitutes a considerable injustice with regard to our collective understanding of the fate of the other' (2004: 71).

It is, at least partly, against this skepticism of traditional photojournalism's ability to be either politically or ethically potent that the rise of mass mediated visual self-publication has been hailed as a potentially democratizing force. Citizen video documenting human and civic rights abuses promises to bring previously silenced histories to light, to record otherwise undocumented atrocities and to grant a more diverse, grassroots range of actors access to the news. Images captured by on-the-scene citizens are perceived to be authentic, 'more real and less packaged' than the formulaic, distancing reports from professional journalists (Williams, Wardle and Wahl-Jorgensen, 2011). Yet, it is critical to remember that these representations are not transparent, but constitutive elements in the construction of testimony. It is to an analysis of crowd-sourced imagery as a distinct mode of witnessing that constitutes its own claim to truth that I now turn.

The aesthetics of authenticity in citizen imagery

Citizen video is characterized by a low-tech and verité aesthetic that distinctly breaks with the traditional representational conventions of photojournalism. The perceived immediacy of citizen footage is thus partly an aesthetic effect of its framing and production, as its often poor visual and audio quality codes it as 'authentic' rather than professionally produced. It is this very amateurism, then, that heightens the effect of 'realness' and 'closeness' already so powerfully signified by the sense of viewing events from the involved perspective of those who lived or experienced a crisis as it was actually happening.

The most widely reproduced footage of the shooting of Neda Agha Soltan, a 40-second clip, shows her collapsing in front of a parked car at the side of the street. A large pool of blood is collecting on the pavement beneath her. Two men are seen frantically trying to revive the dying woman. As the videographer moves closer and zooms in on her face, Neda's eyes roll over to the side and meet the camera in a distant stare as she apparently loses consciousness. Blood begins to pour from her mouth and nose and literally covers her vision. She radiates an uncanny calmness in the midst of the desperation and panic surrounding her. People are screaming out loud and a third man kneels down beside her in a futile attempt to save her life. He can apparently be heard saying: 'Neda, don't be afraid .... Neda, stay with me!'

Using this clip as a critical example, I distinguish four main characteristics of the aesthetics of crowd-sourced footage: *hypermobility, opacity, non-narrativity* and *'raw' audio.*

Hypermobility. The hallmark of citizen footage is the shaky and 'hypermobilized' camerawork (Tait, 2009: 343), with frantic and disorienting pans and zooms (compare Niekamp, 2011). In contrast to the steady camera shots that indicate professionalism, citizen video is distinguished by highly mobile, sudden and seemingly aimless camera movements. Hence, citizen-shot imagery is chaotic and indiscriminate; it does not draw viewer attention to a particular point of interest. The notion of hypermobility extends not only to the motion of the camera, but also to the motion of the citizen photographer, who physically pursues and takes the place of people caught up in affecting life-and-death situations. The camphone footage of the shooting of Agha Soltan is marked by the manic efforts of the videographer to frame and hold the image as he hastily moves in on the scene with the young woman lying in a pool of blood. The camera then circles around the body on the ground, apparently attempting to zoom in on the victim's face. The video is shaky, mostly out of focus and with constant back-and-forth pans and zooms. While the haphazard camerawork clearly codes the scene with authenticity – as a signifier of proximity and participation in a moment of crisis or danger – it also partly blocks our access to the scene recorded, at times poising the image on the edge of legibility.

Opacity. The aesthetics of crowd-sourced footage is identified by an orientation toward visual opacity: the 'medium' explicitly comes forth as the 'message' in the typically blurry, dim and grainy quality of citizen-shot video. This imagery compromises the representational process by means of accidental forms of inscription, such as fuzziness, low resolution, poor lighting, ellipses and interferences within the field of vision – in the case of the Agha Soltan clip, people running to the rescue of the fatally wounded woman also move frantically in and out of the frame, occasionally blocking sight of the main subject. We are thus positioned at a threshold of knowledge, confronted with an uncertain form of representation that flickers between figure and abstraction, transparency and opacity.

Non-narrativity. Citizen video is distinctly set apart from professional photojournalism in that it breaks away from the prevailing journalistic norm of storytelling. The chaotic, fragmentary and incoherent clip of Agha Soltan's death radically disrupts the fundamental structure of narrative (a story with proper beginning, middle and end, a coherence working to enact closure). The professional photographer typically seeks to identify 'the decisive moment' and carefully composes the shot according to preexisting conventions so as artfully to construct a sense of emotional closeness and identification. In contrast, crowd-sourced footage has been described as a form of 'spraypainting': the camera is just rolling, pointing in all directions as the photographer frantically and indiscriminately tries to capture everything that is happening around him or her. As a result, central events are often taking place off-screen and a particular focus of attention is conspicuously lacking. It is precisely this seemingly spontaneous, unstaged quality of citizen video, that is, its open refusal of 'the morally suppressive force of narrative' (Orgad, 2012: 197), that codes it with authenticity – as well as with ambivalence.

'Raw' audio. The reality effect of crowd-sourced video is a also a result of the unedited sound, which is key to creating a sense of 'being-there' and, as the Agha Soltan clip illustrates, of getting access to the rawness of the event. The desperate yelling and screaming at the scene of Agha Soltan's death intensifies the sense of drama and also of attendance – of being there in the midst of the affected crowd.

The ethics of authenticity in citizen imagery

Insofar as crowd-sourced video has a particular moral and political purchase on audiences, this is the result not only of *how* it represents an event, but also of *who* records *what*, and *why*. As opposed to the professional convention of objectivity, citizen videography represents a localized, subjective and embodied rendering of experience. This situatedness is vital not just in that it can emotionally engage viewers but also in vouching for the ethical and epistemological credibility of those represented. I here distinguish three main principles that variously serve to construct – but potentially also compromise – citizen footage's claim to reality and morality: *subjectivity*, *affectivity* and *partisanship*.

Subjectivity. One key source of the power of the now-notorious cell-phone footage of the death of Neda Agha Soltan is that it affords a deeply emotive insight into the tragedy as it impacted upon her fellow citizens who, just like her, were an integral part of the protest. The individual who shot this footage evidently took a great personal risk in being physically present at the protest, and also in recording this act of indiscriminate state violence. These clips draw us into an empathic relationship with people in pain – the victim and her distressed rescuers – partly because they provide a strongly subjectivized point of view, one that conjures an embodied presence and response *within* the traumatic event.

Citizen images thus locate their truth value precisely in their marked subjectivity and situatedness, that is, in their apparent location in a particular moment and place, which serves to align the viewer with the position of a direct eyewitness. Such visuals provide testimony not to fact but to an intensely personal experience: 'I was there, this is what I saw.' This actuality, then, is as unassailable as it is ambiguous, suggesting that issues concerning truth, morality and authenticity take on a complexity otherwise unaddressed by assertions about the potential of citizen imagery to foster a global imagination and ethics of care.

Affectivity. The Neda Agha Soltan footage exemplifies the fact that the rhetorical power of memorable citizen imagery comes in large measure from the way it concentrates and directs raw feelings. Such imagery departs from a conventional journalism of facts in that it reflects and feeds a broader shift towards emotions and personal expression as authentication of news.

The most powerful affective appeal in the 40-second recording of Agha Soltan's death is without doubt her gaze, the fact that she casts her eyes toward the camera as she takes her final breaths. Her eyes meet ours while blood covers her vision; life is literally pouring out of her as we watch. Whoever comes to see this is directly addressed by the agonizing look of the dying woman, urging us to identify with the terrible pathos of her unjust loss. Her look is a direct demand for accountability and compensatory action, the force of which is only heightened by her muted stillness in the midst of the loud-voiced panic swirling around her. Again, the resounding cries of pain from the male bystanders are amplified by the quietude of the traumatized woman before them. They become her ventriloquists, giving voice to the violated body that can no longer speak. The outcries of the men struggling to bring Agah Soltan back to life are more than a sign of personal affect, for their screams bespeak the deep social rupture that occurs when a government murders its own citizens for exercising their civil rights. The emotions attain additional significance because they become political emotions, drawing us into an explicitly political scenario (compare Hariman and Lucaites, 2007). Hence, because it fuses political dissent with a moment of intense individual agony and public grief, the cellphone footage can be seen to have afforded global news publics a space to connect viscerally with the escalating political crisis in Iran, which is also to say that it builds its claim to reality precisely on the authority of embodied affect.

Part of the truth value of the Neda Agha Soltan footage is also that it disrupts one of photojournalism's strongest conventions, which is to withhold documentary scenes of death and horror from public view. The amateur clips of this young woman's death document the raw violence of the killing, showing the fatally wounded woman in a way that accentuates the damage to her body. They feature the thick stream of blood gushing from Neda's chest wound across the pavement, and zero in on her face with blood pouring from her mouth and nose – drawing viewer attention to the terrible passion of the dying woman.

Partisanship. In contrast to a professional journalism of detachment, citizen videographers are characterized by the fact that they typically report as both observers and parties to a contested situation. Hence, it is rarely the case that people who publicize their testimony to a particular crisis or conflict are simply seeking to be heard. More often they are attempting to get a particular message across. It follows that the line between citizen journalism and political action at times is altogether blurred, as citizens and activists increasingly participate in both the media and the critical event through their strategic self-representation.

Despite the reluctance on the part of mainstream media and bloggers to attribute the word 'propaganda' to information spread by apparent supporters of the Iranian opposition, the instant mobilization of Agha Soltan as a martyr for the opposition's cause indeed suggests a coordinated effort by anti-regime groups in Iran and beyond to create a figure that could revitalize the opposition to president Ahmadinejad. In mass demonstrations in Tehran and around the world, portraits of her were carried aloft like religious icons to the rallying cry of 'We are Neda.' The demonstrators thus gave notice to the world that the ideals of justice for which Neda Agha Soltan had laid down her life had not died with her, but were resurrected in the renewed resolve of the people who had witnessed her wrongful killing. Agha Soltan became a public symbol of defiance; and the recordings of her unjust death were strategically fed back into the political dynamic of the conflict itself, functioning to unite and revive the battered opposition to the Iranian government. Yet, the main point to consider here is that the honesty of citizen video which makes explicit its political stance becomes a category of value, one that is associated with claims to authenticity. Citizen imagery that acknowledges its invested perspective is thus often perceived as more truthful and sincere than the 'professional' appeal to a principle of detachment which underpins the news image's claim to offer a neutral reflection of 'things as they are.'

Conclusions

This chapter has traced a shift in the representation of authenticity in crowd-sourced images of newsworthy events, one that is recasting professional crisis reporting as a political, affective space that exceeds normative renderings of impartiality and detachment. Using the mobile-phone footage of the killing of Neda Agha Soltan as a critical case, I have identified four main characteristics of the aesthetics of citizen imagery – hypermobility, opacity, non-narrativity and 'raw' audio – and three defining aspects of the values by which it constructs its claim to reality and morality, namely subjectivity, affectivity and partisanship. Drawing on the idea that the moral and aesthetic values of citizen images are interdependent – in that the distinct aesthetics of this imagery testifies to the very specific materialized gaze of an involved participant-videographer – I have identified and analyzed the ways in which crowd-sourced footage breaks with the journalistic gaze and its professed capacity to be impersonal, detached and dispassionate in its renderings. As professional news organizations become more reliant on citizen eyewitness images that claim partiality and subjectivity as the route to 'truthfulness' so too might a different kind of journalism emerge that is more audience-centred and recognizes the limitations of the enduring occupational norms of objectivity and impartiality (Fenton and Witschge, 2011).

Granted, (photo)journalism has long been ethically underwritten by the idea of 'bearing witness,' which draws attention to a crucial function of the news not only as reporting 'the facts' but as engaging people's potential to care. Chouliaraki, among others, has highlighted the paradoxical coexistence of 'the objective' and 'the testimonial' requirements within news journalism, that is, that its narratives 'should appear both as objective information that respects the values of the news organization and as testimonial accounts that touch their publics into action' (2010: 308; see also Tait, 2011). Crowd-sourced footage nevertheless departs from testimonial conceptions of journalism insofar as its authority of moral commitment draws on a 'situated', emotive and contingent rather than an objectivist truth claim. It is precisely because they are perceived to be closer to an actual experience, less mediated than professional storytelling formats and therefore more raw and real, that citizen eyewitness images have come to endow the news with a new moralizing potential.

Set against the unique news value afforded to audience eyewitness footage in the context of crisis reporting, the fact that Agha Soltan's bloodied face was made a symbol of the Iranian uprising suggests that citizen-created footage can bring about profound changes in the power of political representation. Such high-profile cases, including the killing of Saddam Hussein and the capture of Muammar Gaddafi, speak to the potential of the current crowd-sourced video revolution to give new and diverse voices a chance to enter the news and thereby reshape its memory-scapes. Yet it has also raised new concerns about issues such as veracity, representativeness and accuracy, as it has often proven difficult – or indeed impossible – for news organizations to verify by whom, why and where a particular video was shot. This points to a paradox that lies at the heart of the crowd-sourced video revolution: the figure of the citizen videographer is positioned as intensely important to the claims this imagery has to embodied authenticity, while simultaneously being effectively erased as a named witness. In a move to defuse the potentially devasting challenges that images from non-institutional settings pose to the epistemic authority of journalism, news organizations tend to 'de-authorize' such images by attributing them to news agencies and content-sharing sites. As Saugman Andersen observes, this is a means of 'emphasising institutional legitimacy while totally hiding the author' (2012: 330). This begs the question, then, of whether the shift to convergent news indeed bears out the promise of allowing unknown citizens a voice in representing and remembering political crisis.

In addition, the democratic appraisal of the crowd-sourced video revolution often occludes issues of security, dignity and consent (Gregory and Zimmermann, 2011). As the example of Agha Soltan suggests, the public remediation of citizen video featuring people in pain raises pressing issues about the right to privacy in death, re-victimization through circulation and the ethics of re-purposing. In a new digital mediascape of interactivity and participation, the mnemonic audio-visual record produced by journalism has shifted from a fixed object to a fluid participatory discourse that travels through viral online networks of circulation, aggregation and remix. Yet in this world of mutating viral economies there remains, more than ever, a sense that effective democracy requires precisely those experienced professionals whose value lies in their knowing how to critically report on new information, not merely recirculate it. At the same time, commercial pressures place increasing constraints on journalists' ability to conduct the ideal of journalism as embodied in the ethical framework of objectivity, impartiality and public interest (Fenton and Witschge, 2011). In effect, news organizations are often caught up in the practice of remediating user-generated visuals with minimal verification, thus undermining the very professional values that could best serve to sustain their business in a world of communicative abundance.

In an environment of a mass plurality of information and harsh market pressures, news journalism that purports to provide accurate and factual information and to serve the public interest is too important to be allowed to disappear. Still, this implies that journalistic ethics have to be reimagined to catch up with this new thing called the crowd-sourced video revolution. Professional journalists might have to accept more willingly a 'critical objectivity and reflexive impartiality' (Fenton and

Witschge, 2011: 160) that plays down objective reporting in favour of an increased awareness of subjectivity as a category of value in journalistic reporting and remembering.

References

Andén-Papadopoulos, K. (2013) 'Citizen Camera-Witnessing: Embodied Political Dissent in the Era of "Mediated Mass-Self Communication,"' *New Media & Society*, online 31 May 2013, doi: 10.1177/1461444813489863.

Andén-Papadopoulos, K. and Pantti, M. (2011) 'Introduction,' in K. Andén-Papadopoulos and M. Pantti (eds) *Amateur Images and Global News*. Bristol and Chicago: Intellect Books, pp. 9–20.

Andén-Papadopoulos, K. and Pantti M. (2013) 'Re-Imagining Crisis Reporting: Professional Ideology of Journalists and Citizen Eyewitness Images,' *Journalism*, 14 (October), 960–77, doi:10.1177/146488491347905.

Andersen, R.S. (2012) 'Remediating #IranElection. Journalistic Strategies for Positioning Citizen-made Snapshots and Text Bites from the 2009 Iranian Post-election Conflict,' *Journalism Practice*, 6, 317–36.

Berkowitz, D. (2011) 'Telling the Unknown through the Familiar: Collective Memory as Journalistic Device in a Changing Media Environment,' in M. Neiger, O. Meyers and E. Zandberg (eds) *On Media Memory: Collective Memory in a New Media Age*. Basingstoke and New York : Palgrave Macmillan, pp. 201–12.

Brown, S.D. and Hoskins, A. (2010) 'Terrorism in the New Memory Ecology: Mediating and Remembering the 2005 London Bombings,' *Behavioral Sciences of Terrorism and Political Aggression*, 2(2): 87–107.

Campbell, D. (2004) 'Horrific Blindness: Images of Death in Contemporary Media,' *Journal for Cultural Research*, 8(1), 55–74.

Chouliaraki, L. (2008) 'The Symbolic Power of Transnational Media: Managing the Visibility of Suffering,' *Global Media and Communication*, 4(3), 329–51.

Chouliaraki, L. (2010) 'Ordinary Witnessing in Post-Television News: Towards a New Moral Imagination,' in L. Chouliaraki (ed.) *Self-Mediation: Citizenship and New Media*, special issue *Critical Discourse Studies*, 7(3), 305–19.

Edy, J. (1999) 'Journalistic Uses of Collective Memory,' *Journal of Communication*, 49(2), 71–85.

Fenton, N. and Witschge, T. (2011) '"Comment is Free, Facts are Sacred": Journalistic Ethics in a Changing Media Scape,' in G. Meikle and G. Redden (eds) *News Online: Transformation and Continuity*. Basingstoke: Palgrave Macmillan, pp. 148–63.

Gregory, S. and Zimmermann, P. (2011) 'Speculations on the Virtual and the Viral Witness to Human Rights Crises,' *Mediascape*, Winter, available at http://www.tft.ucla.edu/mediascape/Winter2011_HumanRights.html (accessed 14 October 2013).

Guerin, F. and Hallas, R. (eds) (2007) *The Image and the Witness: Trauma, Memory and Visual Culture*. London: Wallflower Press.

Hariman, R. and Lucaites, J.L. (2007) *No Caption Needed. Iconic Photographs, Public Culture, and Liberal Democracy*. Chicago and London: Chicago University Press.

Hoskins, A. (2011) 'Anachronisms of Media, Anachronisms of Memory: From Collective Memory to a New Memory Ecology,' in M. Neiger, O. Meyers and

E. Zandberg (eds) *On Media Memory. Collective Memory in a New Media Age.* Basingstoke and New York: Palgrave Macmillan, pp. 278–88.

Hänska-Ahy, M. and Shapour, R. (2012) 'Who's Reporting the Protest? Converging Practices of Citizen Journalists and Two BBC World Service Newsrooms, from Iran's Election Protests to the Arab Uprisings,' *Journalism Studies*, 14(1), 29–45.

Kitch, C. (2008) 'Placing Journalism Inside Memory – and Memory Studies,' *Memory Studies*, 1, 311–20.

Lewis, S. (2012) 'The Tension Between Professional Control and Open Participation: Journalism and its Boundaries,' *Information, Communication & Society*, 15(6), 836–66.

Linfield, S. (2010) *The Cruel Radiance. Photography and Political Violence.* Chicago and London: Chicago University Press.

Meyers, O. (2002) 'Still Photographs, Dynamic Memories,' *Communication Review*, 5(3), 179–205.

Mortensen, M. (2011) 'When Citizen Photojournalism Sets the News Agenda: Neda Agha Soltan as a Web 2.0 Icon of Post-Election Unrest in Iran,' *Global Media and Communication*, 7(1), 4–16.

Niekamp, R. (2011) 'Pans and Zooms: The Quality of Amateur Video Covering a Breaking News Story,' in K. Andén-Papadopoulos and M. Pantti (eds) *Amateur Images and Global News.* Bristol: Intellect Books, pp. 113–28.

Orgad, S. (2012) *Media Representation and the Global Imagination.* Cambridge: Polity.

Perlmutter, D.D. and Wagner, G.L. (2004) 'The Anatomy of a Photojournalistic Icon: Marginalization of Dissent in the Selection and Framing of "A Death in Genoa,"' *Visual Communication*, 3(1), 91–108.

Reading, A. (2011) 'Memory and Digital Media: Six Dynamics of the Globital Memory Field,' in M. Neiger, O. Meyers and E. Zandberg (eds) *On Media Memory: Collective Memory in a New Media Age.* Basingstoke and New York: Palgrave Macmillan, pp. 241–52.

Sasseen, J. (2012) *The Video Revolution. A Report to the Center for International Media Assistance.* Washington, DC: Center for International Media Assistance.

Singer, J.B. (2005) 'The Political J-Blogger: Normalizing a New Media Form to Fit Old Norms and Practices,' *Journalism: Theory, Practice and Criticism*, 6(2), 173–98.

Sturken, M. (1997) *Tangled Memories. The Vietnam War, the AIDS Epidemic and the Politics of Remembering.* Berkeley and Los Angeles: University of California Press.

Tait, S. (2009) 'Visualizing Technologies and the Ethics and Aesthetics of Screening Death,' *Science as Culture*, 18(3), 333–53.

Tait, S. (2011) 'Bearing Witness, Journalism and Moral Responsibility,' *Media, Culture & Society*, 33(8), 1220–35.

Tenenboim-Weinblatt, K. (2008) '"We will Get Through This Together": Journalism, Trauma and the Israeli Disengagement From the Gaza Strip,' *Media, Culture & Society*, 30(4), 495–513.

Williams, A., Wardle, C. and Wahl Jorgensen, K. (2010) '"More Real and Less Packaged": Audience Discourses on Amateur News Content and Their Effects on Journalism,' in K. Andén-Papadopoulos and M. Pantti (eds) *Amateur Images and Global News.* Bristol: Intellect Books, pp. 195–209.

Zelizer, B. (1998) *Remembering to Forget: Holocaust Memory Through the Camera's Eye*. Chicago: Chicago University Press.

Zelizer, B. (2002) 'Finding Aids to the Past: Bearing Personal Witness to Traumatic Public Events,' *Media, Culture & Society*, 24(5), 697–714.

Zelizer, B. (2003) 'The Voice of the Visual in Memory,' in K.R. Phillips (ed.) *Framing Public Memory*. Tuscaloosa: University of Alabama Press, pp. 48–68.

Zelizer, B. (2008) 'Why Memory's Work on Journalism Does Not Reflect Journalism's Work on Memory,' *Memory Studies*, 1, 75–83.

Zelizer, B. (2010) *About to Die. How News Images Move the Public*. New York: Oxford University Press.

10
The Journalist as Memory Assembler: Non-Memory, the War on Terror and the Shooting of Osama Bin Laden

Anna Reading

News of the shooting by US security forces of the leader of Al Qaeda, Osama Bin Laden, was broken via the micro-blogging site, Twitter. The event was significant in terms of marking a watershed in the intersecting practices of mobile and social media with journalism, with the Bin Laden story 'marking a new reference point' in media coverage (Filloux, 2011).

I take this example to show how journalism in relation to memory and to media witnessing in particular now takes place within 'a globital memory field.' In addition, I suggest that the use of a range of modalities and points of contact by journalists and non-journalists to report events requires us to recognize the importance of journalism's 'incomplete, ambiguous, suggestive and unstable relays to the world' (Zelizer, 2010: 323).

The media witnessing of the killing of the leader of Al Qaeda, Osama Bin Laden, on 1 May 2011 is particularly revealing in this regard. After initial news broke via Twitter various versions of the story rapidly emerged, despite the attempt by the US to deny any direct witness to the events by preventing public access to images of the shooting itself and to images of the dead body, reportedly buried at sea within 12 hours. However, the connective cultures of globalization with digitization means that journalists and non-journalists sought to assemble an alternative 'witnessing' of the shooting to compensate for the absence of images of the shooting and the dead body.

Below I examine international news reportage through the practices associated with reporting the events of that day, addressing the way in which the professional work of the journalist now intersects with those of non-journalists as they 'assemble' and 'reassemble' witnesses to the story, even in the absence or withholding of digital witness images, in this case, images of the shooting itself. This is particularly evident in the practices of journalists and non-journalists in relation to the image of 'The Situation Room' which the Pentagon uploaded onto the photo-sharing site Flickr.

The chapter begins with a brief critical overview of media witnessing and journalism and then outlines a framework for digital analysis that takes into account the new media ecologies of connective cultures and digitization that are changing journalistic practices.

Witnessing, media and memory

The mass media have long been established in their role as broadcasting history in the making (Dayan and Katz, 1992). Journalists, and photo journalism in particular, have played a critical role in shaping both pub-lic memory and public forgetting (Zelizer, 2002). With digitization, jour-nalism has become an even more important component of collective memory, with the digitization of newspaper archives, the availability online of an archive of digitized news broadcasts and photojournalism, and the remediation by journalists themselves of earlier now digitized versions of related events (Bolter and Grusin, 2000). What is particularly important as a subset of this is the particular role of journalism and journalists in the immediate witnessing of events (Ellis, 2000) or what is more accurately termed 'media witnessing' (Frosh and Pinchevksi, 2009a, 2009b).

Written in 2001, and thus prior to the impact of social and mobile technologies on journalism, John Durham Peters defined witnessing itself as involving a three-way process involving the person who bears witness, the testimony and the audience to the testimony. Research on images and photographs as witnessing practices in relation to atroc-ity, especially the Holocaust, often emphasize the repetitive nature of images which can result in saturation (Sontag, 1989; Kaplan, 1993), which is then explained in terms of 'postmemory' (Hirsch, 2001), as well as representing a way of publically remembering in order to for-get (Zelizer, 1998). However, new media ecologies are reshaping the relationships between journalists, texts and consumers (Frosh and Pinchevski, 2009b: 2). Digital witnessing involves processes of assem-blage made up of material practices and discursive formations which are subject to change through (de)territorialization (Reading, 2011a, 2011b). Developing this thesis further, I argue here that digital witness-ing in journalism involves a dynamic and polylectic process in which the journalist, or non-journalist, who witnesses the event, assembles a text, which may then be reassembled by prosumers in different places and reassembled by different journalists.

The globital memory field

A number of scholars have observed that globalization and digitization may be changing the ways in which the intersection of memory and media is articulated (Assman and Conrad, 2010; Morris-Suzuki, 2005; Van Dijck, 2007; Garde-Hansen, Hoskins and Reading, 2009). Journalistic practice in relation to memory needs to be understood as being reshaped within a media ecology that is unevenly digitized and globalized and that we may term the 'globital memory field' (Reading, 2011a, 2011b).

The term 'globital memory field' draws on the established concept in relation to cultural production and consumption of the 'field,' developed by Pierre Bourdieu (1993). Bourdieu argued that cultural production and consumption take place within a field of activity in which cultural agents are engaged in an uneven struggle for resources. With the emergence of the new globital memory field, journalists and non-journalists, as agents of memory, struggle to secure and mobilize a record of events within a field that is unevenly globalized and digitized – hence 'globital'.

Building on Barbie Zelizer's (2010) argument that we need to pay more attention to the importance of 'contingency' within journalism and journalistic practices, the conceptualization of the globital memory field suggests an approach to thinking about journalistic practices and memory that recognizes the importance of processes of assemblage and trajectory. These dynamics in terms of journalistic practice then work across and between the private and the public, the individual and collective, the digital and the analogue, the energetic and material, the professional and the non-professional in new ways. The term punctuates the word global with the computing term 'bit', suggesting how within journalistic practice, text and prosumption, the analogue is in dialogue with the digital through the mobilities of the hidden language of algorithm and energetic transfers and interchanges of bits and bytes. This enables an intermeshing and intersecting of the collective and the individual, the cultural with the social, the mediated and non-mediated in new ways that implicate the understanding of memory and journalistic practice.

Furthermore, the globital memory field requires methods for understanding the relationship between journalism and memory that are dynamic rather than only static and that add to approaches that emphasize the meaning and content of discrete texts or particular organizations of journalistic production. Media witnessing in the globital memory field, I would suggest, may be examined through and across six key dynamics. The first is the extent to which the journalist works across different media, transferring stories from one medium to another: this is the dynamic of transmediality. Second is the speed or time in which journalists assemble stories across the electric, algorithmic, geographic and psychic dimensions of the field: this is the dynamic of velocity. Third is journalistic practice in relation to the limit and reach of assemblage from the historical point of origin: this is the dynamic of extensity. Fourth is journalists' professionalized sets of patterns, forms and protocols, which may then assert or deny the possibility, impossibility, or as Zelizer (2010) puts it 'contingency,' or necessity of the assemblage's content: these are the modalities of the story. Fifth is journalistic practice in terms of the number of bonds or sticky points that journalists create between their assemblage and other assemblages: this is its valency. Sixth, as suggested by Bauman's (2000) idea of liquid modernity, is journalistic practice in relation to the assemblage's internal resistance to flow or change: this is the practice of viscosity. Table 10.1 offers an overview of these six key dynamics.

In the next section I examine journalistic practices within the globital memory field tracing the dynamics of transmediality, velocity, extensity, modality, valency and viscosity across multiple axes in relation to media witnessing of the shooting of Osama Bin Laden in May 2011.

The new dynamics of journalistic assemblage

Historically, the processes of dying and death within news journalism have been captured through the practices of war artists, professional war photographers and journalists and military photographers. More recent work, such as that by Susan Sontag (2003), Barbie Zelizer (1998, 2002), John Ellis (2000) and John Durham Peters (2001), emphasize how the particular act of witnessing has become a mass mediated experience. Increasingly, however, death and dying are also captured through the mobile and social witnessing of ordinary citizens who make a visual or data record on their mobile phones and then transmit the images or tweets to blogs, social networking sites and mainstream news organizations. The attacks by Muammar Gaddafi's military on the civilian population in Libya (2011), attacks by the state on civilian protestors in Syria (2011), bombs by terrorist groups in London (2005), Mumbai (2008) and Moscow (2010), as well as catastrophes such as the Japanese

Table 10.1   Journalism and memory within the globital memory field: six dynamics of analysis

Dynamic of analysis	Definition	Journalistic practice
(Trans)mediality	The extent to which assemblage travels and is transformed into and between different media	How do the non-journalist and journalist assemble the story across different media?
Velocity	Speed with which the assemblage travels across the electric, algorithmic, geographic and psychic dimensions of the field	What is the speed with which the non-journalist and journalist develop the assemblage?
Extensity	Limit and reach from the historical point of origin	From where to where do the non-journalist and journalist assemble and disseminate the assemblage?
Modality	Journalistic forms, protocols or conditions that may assert or deny the possibility, impossibility, contingency or necessity of content	How are professional journalistic forms, protocols or conditions challenged with the processes of assemblage?
Valency	The number of bonds between the assemblage and other assemblages	What bonds do the journalist and non-journalist create between the assemblage and other assemblages?
Viscosity	The assemblage's internal resistance to flow or change	How do the journalist and non-journalist respond to changes in the assemblage?
Axes	*X = composition of material and discursive formations* *Y = mobilization and securitization*	

earthquake and tsunami in 2011, have all been witnessed using mobile phones and social networking sites. In situations of conflict or natural disaster the mobile and social witnessing of killing, dying and death is thus now the norm within the globital memory field. As we shall see this was also to some extent the case with the witnessing of the shooting of Osama Bin Laden. Yet the US also attempted to create a deliberate media void or 'non-memory' that to some extent backfired through the ability of journalists and non-journalists publically to modify the void through the dynamics of assemblage journalism.

First let us trace multiple dynamics by focusing on the speed with which journalists and non-journalists sought to disseminate transmedial assemblages of the events. At 7.24 p.m. Eastern Standard Time on 1 May 2011 a tweet from former naval intelligence officer Keith Urbahn stated, 'So I am told by a reputable person that they have killed Osama Bin Laden: Hot Damn' (Filloux, 2011). At 10.40 p.m., the *New York Times'* national security team and its Washington bureau ran one line on Bin Laden's death. Ten minutes later, journalists had updated the website with the headline, 'Bin Laden Dead, US Official Says.' At 10.45 three US TV networks interrupted their programming to break the news. At 11.30 Barack Obama addressed the nation. Journalists around the world picked up the story to broadcast the news that the leader of Al Qaeda had been killed by US Special Forces (Filloux, 2011).

The US Special Forces operation took place not in a cave in the mountains of Afghanistan but in a house in a compound near a military base in Abbottabad, Pakistan. Journalists reported that the body had been buried at sea within 24 hours according to Muslim tradition. On 2 May a photograph was uploaded onto Flickr by the Pentagon titled 'The Situation Room.' Journalists reported initially that the photo depicted 'the witnesses' of the security operation, Barack Obama and Hillary Clinton along with top military personnel, watching live as the 79 Navy Seals carried out the operation in Osama Bin Laden's compound. Two days later, five videos were released by the Pentagon which journalists reported had been found in the compound during the mission. One was described as a recording of Osama Bin Laden watching himself on television. Audiovisual news and newspaper journalists gave huge amounts of coverage to the events, with UK broadcasters continuing to treat it as 'news' a week later.

Analyzing journalistic practice in relation to the dynamics of velocity, extensity and transmediality reveal that journalists are able rapidly to exploit the possibilities of the globital memory field to create multiple bonds between immediate witnessing and other digitized connective resources including archived news stories. Further, this journalistic assemblage practice involves putting together digital forms that have non-journalistic protocols and conditions of production such as Google Earth, 3D graphics, propaganda videos and images from family photograph albums. Thus journalists working within broadcast and online television news organizations produced stories within minutes and hours, which themselves drew on digital archives and were subsequently archived and made available on YouTube. Journalists at Aljazeera English, for example, had drawn on the online resources of

Google Earth to assemble a digital map of the town of Abbottabad with a witness talking about a helicopter and gun fire (Aljazeera English, 2011). At ABC News' *Good Morning America*, under the programming title 'Osama Bin Laden Dead: Inside the Top Secret Operation,' journalists rapidly created a graphic digital reconstruction of the mission, assembling it with images of cheering crowds at Ground Zero (ABC, 2011a) and a statement by a journalist outside the White House (ABC, 2011b). BBC journalists on 'Osama Bin Laden is Dead' assembled images of the compound where Osama Bin Laden was killed, followed by shots of cheering crowds at Ground Zero, and the speech to the US nation by Barack Obama (BBC News, 2011a). Within a couple of hours, journalists had accessed digital news archives to create a news feature showing a 'retrospective' of Osama Bin Laden's life beginning with the now well-known photo of him as a rich Saudi teenager, which was put together with archive video of 9/11 and archive camera phone images from the 7/7 London bombings. The feature ended with an image of Osama Bin Laden not in military gear or with a gun, but in white robes, lit in a way that connoted a religious icon, as a voice-over stated, 'Osama bin Laden may be dead, but his ideas are not' (BBC News, 2011b). Journalists at *Russia Today* drew on satellite images of the compound, which were then assembled with documentary footage of the town of Abbottabad and buildings, calling it a 'custom made hide-out.' It was then connected to a 3D digital graphic diagram depicting compound walls, a purposefully made rubbish burning area, opaque glass and so on. This was in stark contrast to BBC journalists who emphasized the banality or ordinariness of the compound. *Russia Today*'s journalists followed their news assemblage with Ahmed Quarashi's 'Project for Pakistan in the 21st Century' about how the action provided a positive face-saving way for the US to get out of Afghanistan, shot over cheering crowds at Ground Zero. The *Russia Today* journalists then used archive video of Osama Bin Laden in military gear, followed by a discussion by 'experts' of the decision to bury Osama Bin Laden's body at sea to prevent people paying homage to him. Journalists questioned the 'lack of transparency of evidence' regarding his body, in comparison with the trial and hanging of Saddam Hussein (*Russia Today*, 2011).

Assemblage modalities and non-memory

Within these poly-medial assemblages reporting the shooting of Osama Bin Laden, it is thus highly significant that journalists had no actual images of his dying moments or his dead body. It is also significant that within this context of absence one of the most viewed online images was the 'The Situation Room,' the 'witness' photograph of the White House operations room with Barack Obama and Hillary Clinton present as security services monitored the operation through live action video (Figure 10.1).

Looking at the media coverage of the death of Osama Bin Laden what is evident in journalistic practice in relation to witnessing within the new dynamics of the globital memory field was firstly the extent to which journalists routinely practiced transmediality: news was broken through one medium, Twitter, a micro-blogging site, which was then connected to mainstream news organizations which rapidly assembled and mobilized archival photographic and video images related to Bin Laden's life and death, including a rapid retrospective BBC biography. This is similar to witnessing practices that I have analyzed elsewhere, such as the reporting of the shooting of Neda Agha Soltan (Reading, 2011a, 2011b). It shared with this earlier example of media witnessing a characteristic extensity of reportage, with the modality of embodiment in which journalistic practice was then rapidly mobilized as public performance on the streets, with demonstrations as well as celebrations in different towns and cities around the world.

The media witnessing of the shooting of Osama Bin Laden, however, was also subject to a dominant discursive strategy deliberately mobilized by the US in order to secure a 'non-memory,' or deliberate media

Figure 10.1   'The Situation Room' (Flickr, 3 May 2011)

void within a declared state of exception, the 'enemy,' in this case the Al Qaeda leader. This was sought by ensuring that journalists and pro-sumers would not have any access to video or photographs of the actual killing or the enemy's dead body. This, I suggest, ties in with a thesis put forward by Holger Potzsch (2010, 2011) which draws on Judith Butler's idea of 'grievable and ungrievable lives' (Butler, 2009: 38). In Potzsch's analysis of feature films about war he argues that audiovisual war culture uses particular discursive logics to create epistemological barriers to produce a 'ubiquitous absent – hidden, inaccessible, incom-prehensible yet potentially omniscient as a deadly threat' (Potzsch, 2011: 5). The narrative usually starts with an 'evil deed': in the news narrative of the global War on Terror this is the 9/11 terrorist attack on the World Trade Center by Al Qaeda. But to Potzsch's account, I would add that there is a critical legal protocol that states invoke in relation to memory and non-memory. This derives from Giorgio Agamben's (2005) observation that during a 'State of Exception,' such as was invoked by the US in relation to the War on Terror, the value of a human life can be reduced to 'Homo Sacer' or bare life, no longer warranting legal protec-tion by the state. The 'State of Exception' in news media terms not only allows the possibility of the creation of a legal void but also implies the supposed 'right' by a state to assert that the enemy does not have the moral right to representation by journalists and should not be remem-bered. Within the 'State of Exception,' journalists must then work to assemble a story around the ubiquitous absence, in which 'the other is de-humanised and de-subjectified, and the killing of it is implicitly justified' (Potzsch, 2011: 5).

Within the dynamic of modality of the protocols of the US there was thus an attempt to secure 'non-memory' or an absence within media memory in relation to the killing of the enemy, Osama Bin Laden. The modality of the assemblage was such that the state sought not so much to censor content, but rather to deny the legal right to any content being necessary. No images of the man's dying, death or body were released to the public, ostensibly in order to prevent commemorative rituals or shrines being built where his body was buried. Only a chosen few were allowed to view images that depicted the shooting and the body, result-ing in the Associated Press rapidly filing a demand to see the photos under the Freedom of Information Act (Borger, 2011). However, around the edges of the deliberately created absence or void of representation, journalists worked within the available resources of the globital memory field, using archives, news footage, other witnesses, imagined graphic scenarios and the image of the Situation Room to assemble their story.

The result was that there were ongoing journalistic ambiguities and instabilities that disrupted the attempt to secure non-memory through absence of the visual record of the body: this occurred both within official discourse and outside of it via interpretations by journalists, responses by non-journalists and then further responses by journalists. 'The Situation Room' image, for example, produced a range of interpretive comments by journalists and was subject to re-assemblage and modification by non-journalists. There were claims that the image transformed the way in which the US President was represented, because a now official image showed a black man and two white women in positions of power, signifying the greater gender and racial equality of US democracy, as well as the 'feminine' side of the President. Thus, one journalist in 'What the Situation Room Reveals About Us' wrote, 'It is a snapshot of how much this nation's attitudes about race, women and presidential swagger are changing' (Blake, 2011). Blake argued that the flak-jacketed swaggering 'Protector-in-Chief' had been replaced by a complex image in which presidential machismo was softened since he was not in the centre of the picture and was shown looking worried and anxious rather than confident and cool (Blake, 2011)

One blogger pointed out the exceptional position of Brigadier General Marshall B. Webb in the image:

> Webb holds, in the true sense of the word, an *exceptional* position in the photograph: he is the only person whose full military uniform is visible, he is sitting at the top end of the table further underlining his elevated position within the room, but most importantly, he is, unlike everyone else, not looking at the screen but at a laptop in front of him.
>
> ('Deconstructing the Situation Room,' 2011)

Journalists also commented on the position of Hillary Clinton which was said to highlight the gender horizons of the image: the men were interpreted as largely emotionless and distant; Hillary, in contrast, was interpreted as in a state of shock or awe with her hand over her mouth, an interpretation which she quickly rebuffed, claiming she was using her hand to stifle a cough.

Further, the image itself was subject to a number of discursive battles arising from journalists and non-journalists modifying the assemblage. Firstly within the press itself, there was the example of journalists at the New York Hasidic newspaper *Der Zeitung* digitally deleting the women from the picture and displaying the edited photo on its front page.

This modality was then reported as the result of adhering to the policy of the newspaper, whose editor claimed, 'because of laws of modesty, we are not allowed to publish pictures of women, and we regret if this gives an impression of disparaging to women, which is certainly never our intention' (Bell, 2011). The editor also apologized, stating that the journalist responsible for the deletion of the women had not noticed in the rapid reporting of the events that the White House had explicitly stated that the 'photograph may not be manipulated in any way' (The White House, 2011; Bell, 2011). The modified image received much journalistic and blogger comment (Price, 2011) with journalist Angela Watercutter at Wired.Com developing an online competition to develop the best modified image. The collection included a shocked cat, Obama playing a video game, a version with all Obama, and one with a dinosaur. Journalist Alexis Madrigal of the *Atlantic* responded, 'The Situation Room has been colonized. It's part of our world' (Madrigal, 2011). The website Free Williamsburg, as a response to the women's images being deleted by *Der Zeitung*, then deleted all the men from the Situation Room image and showed only the two women, resulting in further comment by a journalist for the National Public Radio Blog 'Two Way' (Memott, 2011). Other modifications produced by non-journalists through Tumblr, but then picked up by news journalists in ABC and CNN and Channel Four in the UK, included one showing all the participants wearing Princess Beatrice's hat from the other major event of the week, the British Royal Wedding (Tit for Tat, 2011). Another version showed the Situation Room recreated by film student Alex Eylar, using Lego. The modified photo was picked up by Pacificoast.com news and then became picture of the week in the UK's *Telegraph* (Eylar, 2011).

Journalists also engaged in a process of reinterpretation of what exactly was being witnessed by those in the image. To begin with, journalists reported the official line that the state witnesses were watching the actual shooting dead of Osama Bin Laden, but later this was changed to a story that they were watching the lead-up to the operation. Because the subject of the witnessing remained unknown and therefore ambiguous, it allowed for speculation as to what the President was actually watching.

Non-journalists engaged with the non-memory of the shooting in other ways. In Egypt it was reported that in the absence of an image of Osama Bin Laden, both men and women were changing their Facebook personal profile images to that of Osama Bin Laden (Khalil, 2011). In the US, journalists at the newspaper *Indian Country Today* asked Facebook users to change their profile images to that of the Native

American Chiricua Apache Geronimo to honour him and to protest against the US Navy Seals appropriating his name by calling their Operation 'Geronimo.'

Other journalists sought to create contingencies around the ubiquitous absence of the killing of Osama Bin Laden through the use of satire. One response in the UK by a *Guardian* columnist was to create a fictional Osama Bin Laden diary, with the claim that it had been discovered amidst the reported finds of data memory sticks in the compound. The *Guardian* published the spoof diary with selected entries from the past couple of years with a fictional entry for 14 August 2009 that read, 'Watched TV for a few hours to see if there were any stories about me. Nothing today. I did see that temptress Sarah Palin on CNN though, practically naked as usual' (Dowling, 2011)

Conclusion

This chapter has reviewed journalistic practices in relation to memory in terms of the media witnessing of the shooting of Osama Bin Laden in May 2011. The case is significant because it marked a watershed in journalistic practice in that initial and subsequent news coverage drew significantly on social networking and micro-blogging sites. It also illustrates how journalism in relation to memory and to media witnessing in particular now takes place within what has become 'a globital memory field.' In order to capture some of the changing practices within the field I suggested an analytical framework that focuses on six dynamics. It highlights that the witnessing work of journalists in the globital memory field is transmedial, rapid in time and globalized in extensity; it involves assembling stories from 'live' micro-blogging texts as well as digital archives, and it comes from multiple sources that are reassembled by other journalists and non-journalists working vertically and horizontally. The journalist and non-journalist make use of the multiple valencies or sticky qualities of digital media to enable multiple bonds with other elements. The journalist and non-journalist in this case work polylectically to rapidly respond to modifications and mobilizations of the original assemblage.

The US refused to allow journalists access to images of Osama Bin Laden's dead body, whilst also planting its own 'witness image,' 'The Situation Room,' on Flickr. Its publically declared intention was to prevent public martyrdom and memory of Osama Bin Laden. Yet the globital memory field means that the activities of journalists and non-journalists now have many more points of contact and many more digital resources at hand. Consequently, rather than a non-memory of the event, audiences and readers are left with many questions and a strong sense of the contingencies of the story. This at least partially disrupted the attempt to secure a non-memory or deliberately created absence by the US in the media witnessing of the shooting of Osama Bin Laden.

Acknowledgement

With thanks to Associate Professor Dr Colin Harvey for our ongoing discussions of these and other ideas.

References

ABC (2011a) Good Morning America; ABC News: Osama Bin Laden Dead: Ground Zero Crowds Cheer All Night. YouTube, 2 May, available at: http://www.youtube.com/watch?v=ge0nUfUzR6k&feature=relmfu (accessed 8 May 2012).

ABC (2011b) Good Morning America; ABC News: Osama Bin Laden Dead: Inside the Top Secret Operation. YouTube, 2 May, available at: http://www.youtube.com/watch?v=8yhX1NNSnh4&feature=related (accessed 9 May 2012).

Agamben, Giorgio (2005) *The State of Exception*. Chicago: University of Chicago Books.

Aljazeera English (2011) A Witness Account of Bin Laden's Death. Aljazeera English. YouTube, 2 May, available at: http://www.youtube.com/watch?v=lW7OywJlT8o&NR=1 (accessed 9 May 2012).

Assman, Aleida and Conrad, Sebastian (eds) (2010) *Memory in a Global Age: Discourses, Practices and Trajectories*. Basingstoke: Palgrave.

Bauman, Zygmunt (2000) *Liquid Modernity*. Oxford: Polity.

BBC News (2011a) 'Osama Bin Laden Is Dead1.' Shows compound where Osama Bin Laden killed; cheering crowds at ground Zero, and speech by Barack Obama. YouTube, available at: http://www.youtube.com/watch?v=2u_fWAqu0_4 (accessed 2 June 2011).

BBC News (2011b) 'Osama Bin Laden Is Dead2.' The retrospective of Osama Bin Laden's life begins at 3 minutes 4 seconds. YouTube, available at: http://www.youtube.com/watch?v=IqnVIdqCQ_A&NR=1 (accessed 2 June 2011).

Bell, Melissa (2011) 'Hillary Clinton, Audrey Tomason go missing in Situation Room photo in *Di Tzeitung* newspaper.' *Washington Post* blogpost, 5 September, available at http://www.washingtonpost.com/blogs/blogpost/post/hillary-clinton-audrey-tomason-go-missing-in-situation-room-photo-in-der-tzitung-newspaper/2011/05/09/AFfJbVYG_blog.html (accessed 8 May 2012).

Blake, John (2011) 'What the Situation Room Says About Us.' CNN, 5 May, available at http://edition.cnn.com/2011/US/05/05/iconic.photo/index.html (accessed 10 May 2011).

Bolter, Jay and Grusin, Richard (2000) *Remediation: Understanding New Media*. Cambridge, MA: MIT Press.

Borger, Julian (2011) 'Who Gets to See the Photos of Osama Bin Laden Dead.' *Guardian*, 11 May, available at http://www.guardian.co.uk/world/2011/may/11/pictures-osama-bin-laden-dead?intcmp=239 (accessed 11 May 2011).

Bourdieu, Pierre (1993) *The Field of Cultural Production*. Cambridge: Polity.

Butler, Judith (2009) *Frames of War: When is Life Grievable?* New York: Verso.

Dayan, D. and Katz, E. (1992) *Media Events: The Live Broadcasting of History.* Cambridge, MA: Harvard University Press.

Dowling, Tim (2011) 'Osama Bin Laden's Diary: Are Dishwasher's Blasphemous? 14 August 2009'. *Guardian*, 12 May, available at http://www.guardian.co.uk/world/2011/may/12/osama-bin-laden-diary-blasphemous?INTCMP=SRCH (accessed 13 May 2011).

'Deconstructing the Situation Room' (2011), available at http://visualculture blog.com/category/politics/ (accessed 8 May 2012).

Ellis, J. (2000) *Seeing Things: Television in the Age of Uncertainty.* London: I.B. Tauris.

Eylar, Alex (2011) 'Lego Situation Room.' Pacific Coast News Com. On The Week in Pictures. *Telegraph*, 20 May, available at http://www.telegraph.co.uk/news/picturegalleries/theweekinpictures/8526890/The-week-in-pictures-20-May-2011.html?image=3 (accessed 8 May 2012).

Filloux, Frederic (2011) 'Lessons from the Coverage of the Bin Laden Story.' *Guardian*, 9 May, available at http://www.guardian.co.uk/technology/2011/may/09/lessons-from-bin-laden-coverage?intcmp=239 (accessed 13 May 2011).

Frosh, Paul and Pinchevski, Amit (2009a) 'Crisis Readiness and Media Witnessing,' *Communication Review*, 12(3), 295–304.

Frosh, Paul and Pinchevski, Amit (2009b) 'Introduction: Why Media Witnessing? Why Now?,' in P. Frosh and A. Pinchevski (eds) *Media Witnessing, Testimony in the Age of Mass Communication.* Basingstoke: Palgrave Macmillan, pp. 1–22.

Garde-Hansen, Joanne, Hoskins, Andrew, and Reading, Anna (eds) (2009) *Save As… Digital Memories.* Basingstoke: Palgrave.

Hirsch, Marianne (2001) 'Surviving Images: Holocaust Photographs and the Work of Postmemory,' *Yale Journal of Criticism*, 14(1), 5–37.

Kaplan, Alice (1993) *French Lessons.* Chicago: University of Chicago Press.

Khalil, Yasser (2011) 'In his death Osama Finds Sympathy.' *Dawn*, 10 May, available at http://dawn.com/2011/05/10/in-his-death-osama-finds-sympathy/ (accessed 10 May 2011).

Madrigal, Alexis (2011) 'The Situation Room Meme: The Shortest Route from Bin Laden to Lulz.' *Atlantic*, 3 May, available at http://www.theatlantic.com/technology/archive/2011/05/the-situation-room-meme-the-shortest-route-from-bin-laden-to-lulz/238251/#slide10 (accessed 8 May 2012).

Memott, Mark (2011) 'The Situation Room Meme Continues; This Time All the Men are Removed.' *National Public Radio NPR Two Way Blog*, 13 May, available at http://www.npr.org/blogs/thetwo-way/2011/05/13/136271340/situation-room-meme-continues-this-time-all-the-men-are-removed (accessed 8 May 2012).

Morris-Suzuki, Tessa (2005) *The Past Within Us: Media, Memory and History.* London: Verso.

Peters, J.D. (2001) 'Witnessing,' *Media, Culture & Society*, 23(6), 707–23

Potzch, Holger (2010) 'Challenging the Border as Barrier: Liminality in Terrence Malick's The Thin Red Line,' *Journal of Borderlands Studies*, 25(1), 67–79.

Potzch, Holger (2011) 'Borders, Barriers, and Grievable Lives: The Discursive Production of Self and Other in Film and Other Audio-Visual Media,' *Nordicom Review*, 32(2), 75–94.

Price, Rebecca (2011) 'Where did Hillary and Audrey Go? Writing Women Out of History.' *Huffington Post*, 5 October, available at http://www.huffingtonpost.

com/rebecca-price/hillary-clinton-photoshop_b_860083.html (accessed 8 May 2012).

Reading, A. (2011a) 'Memory and Digital Media: Six Dynamics of the Globital Memory Field,' in M. Neiger, O. Meyers and E. Zandberg (eds) *On Media Memory: Collective Memory in a New Media Age*. Basingstoke and New York: Palgrave Macmillan, pp. 241–52.

Reading, Anna (2011b) 'Globital Witnessing: Mobile Memories of Atrocity and Terror from London and Iran,' in Katharina Hall and Kathryn Jones (eds) *Constructions of Conflict: Transmitting Memories of the Past in European Historiography, Literature and Culture*. Oxford: Peter Lang, pp. 83–69.

Russia Today (2011) 'Satellite Images, Video of Osama Compound in Abottabad, Pakistan.' YouTube, 3 May, available at http://www.youtube.com/watch?v=BlZVT5gGrSc (accessed 25 September 2013).

Sontag, Susan (1989) *On Photography*. New York: Anchor Doubleday.

Sontag, Susan (2003) *Regarding the Pain of Others*. New York: Farrar, Straus and Giroux.

Tait, Robert and Weaver, Mathew (2009) 'The Accidental Martyr: How Neda became the Face of Iran's Struggle,' *Guardian*, 22 June, p. 1 and p. 15.

The White House/Pete Souza (2001) P050111PS-0210 (the Situation Room), *Flickr*. 3 May, available at http://www.flickr.com/photos/35591378@N03/5680724572 (accessed 8 May 2012).

Tit for Tat (2011) When Two Worlds Collide, 6 May, available at http://www.txt4t.com/2011/05/when-two-worlds-collide.html (accessed 12 May 2012).

Van Dijck, Jose (2007) *Mediated Memories in the Digital Age*. Stanford: Stanford University Press.

Zelizer, Barbie (1998) *Remembering to Forget: Holocaust Memory Through the Camera's Eye*. Chicago: Chicago University Press.

Zelizer, Barbie (2002) 'Photography, Journalism, Trauma,' in B. Zelizer and S. Allan (eds) *Journalism after September 11*. London: Routledge, pp. 48–68.

Zelizer, Barbie (2010) *About to Die: How News Images Move the Public*. New York: Oxford University Press.

11

A New Memory of War

Andrew Hoskins

On the mediality of memory

Just as personal memory functions through matching the here-and-now with an intelligible there-and-then, by shifting context, re-framing meaning and massive selectivity, journalism has long held – and imagined – a larger aperture of social memory. This relationship – between journalism and social memory – is riven with the news values of rupture and catastrophe, paradoxically tinting the journalistic lens by framing incoming uncertainties with the historical certainties of the survival of societies and the continuities of the past. In this way the journalistic churning of late twentieth and early twenty-first-century history is particularly entangled with the contemporary memory boom(s) or 'turn to memory,' with an increasing premium being placed on historical discourses and memories of warfare in modern societies (Huyssen, 2003; Winter, 2006). At the same time, the salience of journalistic schemas – premised on the scarcity of journalists, their experience and their embodiment of the 'matching of context' – has suddenly been devalued. The 'connective turn' (Hoskins, 2011a and b) – the massively increased pervasiveness and accessibility of digital technologies, devices and media – has ushered in a 'post-scarcity culture' and charged a wholesale reappraisal of the nature and the value of journalism.

In this chapter I explore the dynamic relationship between journalism, memory and conflict, subject to the connective turn. My focus is on photojournalism, given both the significance of the visual in forging memory and the fluidity of digital and digitized visual content that transforms the 'infrastructures' of information and archives from which memory and history are made. If we take journalists as formerly comprising a relatively bounded and professionally exclusive 'living

179

archive' of information and interpretation, what difference does the unbounding of journalism today have on social memory as it is forged through visual schema?

Is it not the case that whereas once we could conceive of journalists as 'agents of memory' (Zelizer, 2008), this agency (in assembling, interpreting, publishing news-of-the-world) is now diffused to the many, rather than the few, of the digital network? Following from this, surely the information avalanche of post-scarcity culture should at least loosen, if it does not undermine, the tight coupling of iconic trajectories of twentieth-century warfare from the ways in which recent and emergent catastrophes and conflicts are seen and embedded in journalism and remembered today? In what follows I consider why these digital expectations do not as yet appear to have been quite fulfilled and why the contemporary memory boom, driven by photojournalistic trajectories of vision and re-vision, still appears to be in full swing.

A great deal is being claimed about the advent of the digital in shaping whatever journalism is and does today and what that means in handing over influence to non-professionals. In addition to the 'citizen,' we have news of the amateur and the emergent 'asymmetric' power of 'information doers' (Gowing, 2009). The metaphors of liberation fall thick and fast; journalism is today prefixed in terms of 'multimedia' (Deuze, 2004), 'digital' (Jones and Salter, 2011) (including a new journal entitled *Digital Journalism*), 'participatory' (Singer et al., 2011), 'citizen' (Allan and Thorsen, 2009; Wall, 2012) and 'citizenship' (Tunney and Monaghan, 2009).

This liberation of journalism is seen to be – in part at least – liberation from the institutional media monsters, the world of conglomerates, moguls, and that which Dan Gillmor (2006) calls 'Big Media' – the CNNs, News Corps, Reuters and the picture agencies.

'Small media,' then, consisting of highly mobile and networked recording and communication devices increasingly packaged as 'smart phones,' shape a new flux of amateur content that both challenges and stimulates contemporary journalism. Such accessible, affordable and pervasive technologies are seen to complicate the dominance of Big Media in determining what is seen and not seen as 'news.' As Merrin (2008) puts it, 'The top-down provision of information is replaced by peer-produced relationships with news of the world being replaced by news of the self.' Suddenly that which was once sourced, edited and distributed by the few for the many is complicated by a 'new mass' (Hoskins and O'Loughlin, forthcoming) of routine and everyday editing, posting, circulating, linking, liking, mixing and remediating digital content so even that which was once established and recognized as 'news' in the late twentieth century has become strange.

But what does all of this digital flux add up to? Are the established images of war made through and by an era when there was only Big Media journalism diminished by the emergent multitude, redefined by the digital and/or actually reinforced in their digital reincarnation? For example, Geoff Bowker argues that 'Each new medium imprints its own special flavor to the memories of that epoch' (2008: 26). And yet, post-scarcity culture produces a kind of equivalency – not in the aesthetic and other representational features of the photograph, video, or film, for example, through which each visual epoch has tradition-ally been defined (black-and-white, sepia, clarity, and all of the markers of deterioration) – but rather in terms of *mediality* (compare Richard Grusin, 2004, 2010). So, rather than representationality and the nature, objectivity or accuracy of an image being put foremost, in post-scarcity culture the medial force of images, video and the like is increased by their being consumed, posted, forwarded, circulated, edited, linked, liked, tagged, archived, and by all the new 'work' associated with the mediation and remediation of the digital.

The 'agency' of journalists as makers of memory is then reconfigured with the mediality of images and footage uploaded and downloaded by a whole gamut of 'users,' including journalists themselves, all of which is constitutive of a new 'extended present' (Nowotny, 1994) or an afterlife of media and memory. To mention one example of the new mediality of an iconic image of war: the 1968 Eddie Adams's photo-graph of the execution of a member of the Vietcong, which freezes the fractional moment just before the act of execution. Today, this image is plugged in as part of a continuous 'chain of memory' (Hervieu-Léger, 2000) hyperlinked in time and space through the mediality of the inter-net. As Fred Ritchin (2009: 140) suggests, 'If the reader clicked on the famous photograph... he or she could see the images that preceded and followed it. If the reader clicked on the man doing the shooting, he or she could find out that he later opened a pizzeria in Dale City, Virginia.'

The 'special flavor to the memories' of post-scarcity culture is mediality – a hyperconnectivity of past and present that challenges traditional modes of representation from which individual and social memory has long been forged and reforged. And yet, at the same time, the traditional modes of media that furnished the iconic twentieth-century images of warfare – photojournalism and television journalism – while of course changed by mediality, offer a 'chain of memory' that is in some ways resistant to techno-cultural change. This is particularly salient in the contemporary news reporting of warfare, given how suddenly and deeply mediality appears now to define a new visibility of and from the front line (compare Hoskins and O'Loughlin, 2010). I now turn to explore further this seeming dichotomy and the persistence of a mainstream vision of warfare after the connective turn.

Mainstream past and present

The contemporary representation of warfare is probably one of the most intense sites of the dichotomy between and interpenetration of the persistence of a 'mainstream' news media, on the one hand, and a sense of flux, of everything being connected, remediated and networked in an all-equivocating mesh of mediality, on the other. Over the past two decades, perceptions in and by modern societies have shifted from the occasional and distant occurrence of nodal conflicts to a stream of more connected and seemingly co-present wars demanding continuous attention (Shaw, 1996: 2). For example, a series of twenty-first-century terrorist attacks and the wars in Iraq and Afghanistan are embedded in a connective turn: the massively increased pervasiveness and accessibility of digital technologies, devices and media shape a new knowledge base – an 'information infrastructure'[1] (Bowker and Star, 2000) – through which wars are planned, fought, understood, (de)legitimized, remembered and forgotten. These in turn shape new symmetries in the discourses on and the capacities for the waging of war and are a significant driver of claims about a shift in the very character of contemporary warfare (for example, Münkler, 2005; Shaw, 2005; Hoskins and O'Loughlin, 2010). Thus warfare has become more medial.

Modern warfare is shaped by two different types of mediated memory. The first concerns the continuity of the past through its constant referencing and re-referencing in a journalistic déjà vu. The second offers memory as unfinished, unsettled and mobile. This is not to say that the latter (flux) doesn't carry the former (continuity) but that it shapes a 'new memory' that comprises both a clash and mesh of media. What I am questioning here is what this new memory is and what it does. What is its force compared with preceding kinds of media memory? To this end I now turn to consider 9/11 – one of the most iconic catastrophes of the twenty-first century, whose mediation occurred prior to the full force of the connective turn but was nonetheless subject to a new critical mass of circulating media images of the event, framed in relation to prior (twentieth-century) conflict.

From his analysis of the covers of 400 daily American newspapers from the 11th and 12th of September 2001, Clément Chéroux found that the front page photographs fall into six image types (see Truc, 2010). He makes the point that: 'September 11 is undoubtedly the most photographed event in the history of photojournalism. Yet coverage of the event seems to have been the least diversified' (Chéroux, 2012). Big Media are clearly part of the explanation for this convergence of vision, with the Associated Press responsible for 72 percent of the photographs from the front pages examined in Chéroux's study.

However, this phenomenon in itself is relatively unremarkable, known in journalism as picture or image 'clustering,' where photojournalists tend to use or take identical or very similar photographs of the same phenomenon. And, as Chéroux acknowledges, the scale of this conformity around 9/11 can be explained by the consolidation of Big Media image agencies since the 1990s. However, more interesting for Chéroux is a different temporality of the repetition of images, namely that extending across a historical timescale. He calls this 'intericonicity,' drawing upon Gérard Genette's definition of 'intertextuality' as 'a relation of copresence between two texts or among several texts – that is to say, eidetically and typically as the actual presence of one text within another' (Genette cited in Chéroux, 2012: 269).

Chéroux points to work that shows that media coverage of 9/11 was defined by an 'essential *topos*' of the World War II Japanese attack on Pearl Harbor both through image comparisons and iconographic rhetoric (2012: 263). Interestingly, there is a long history of work on the somewhat similar phenomenon of the role of 'media templates' (Kitzinger, 2000; Hoskins, 2004a and b; Hoskins and O'Loughlin, 2007, 2010). Media templates are the frames, images and, more broadly, discourses (presumed by journalists, news editors and producers to be familiar to their audiences) that are routinely employed as sometimes near-instantaneous prisms through which current and unfolding events are described, presented and contextualized. But templates are not always benign, as Kitzinger suggests: 'Media templates are a crucial site of media power, acting to provide context for new events, serving as a foci for demands for policy change and helping to shape the ways in which we make sense of the world' (2000: 81).

Furthermore, the importance of templates is often signified by their absence, or when they fail to live up to the task for which they are employed. Templates sometimes require a great deal of explicit and overt working through, where an image or video has to be churned over and reiterated until a lens with enough relevance or force can be found to make an unfolding event intelligible. This was certainly the case in the US on 11 September 2001, when television news anchors and commentators struggled to find a template of sufficient magnitude and meaning that would hold a point of comparison to the unfolding news coverage of 9/11 (Hoskins, 2005). Television journalists at least initially struggled in their use of the templates of Pearl Harbor and the Vietnam War, for despite their presence in American historical consciousness they both seemed to lack the force of catastrophic memory required to render 9/11 quickly intelligible.

And yet, intelligible it became. This was achieved in part through repetition (compare Silverstone, 2002), with 9/11 remaining headline news across most US media for the following 12 months.

However, 9/11 marks the last major catastrophic media event of an era occurring on the cusp of the connective turn. The wars and other terrorist attacks (related and unrelated) which have followed are subject to the immediacy and volume of a different scale. This is due to the profound mobility and connectivity of digital media content, which, rather than fixing a trajectory of memory, puts it out there, opens it up and renders it mutable. What then of the icons and templates of the mainstream in this environment?

The persistence of vision

I now turn to the idea that rather than post-scarcity culture leading to new ways of seeing the present and past, mainstream media trajectories appear actually to have consolidated amidst the uncertainties of the speed and flux of the digital. For example, in terms of popular culture, Jaron Lanier (2010: 131) draws upon the anthropologist Steve Barnett's term 'pattern exhaustion', to bemoan 'a phenomena in which a culture runs out of variations on traditional designs... and becomes less creative' (compare Lovink, 2012: 9).

Perhaps this is a critique that can be leveled at journalism itself.

So much has been written on the shifting visual content of war reporting and representation and its claimed effects and lack of effects that it is impossible to summarize in the scope of this chapter. However, I will say that there has occurred a small but discernable turn in conflict photojournalism or photography away from 'pattern exhaustion' towards a kind of 'media archaeology' of warfare and other catastrophes. Alex Danchev, in a review essay, traces this development in part to the shifting character of warfare:

> Now the old wars are over, more or less, and the old breed has gone. In an age of terrorism and tribalism, obliteration and occupation, war too has been brought home. No man's land migrates, from

Lower Manhattan to Babylonia itself. As if to ape Don McCullin, war photography has turned to still life and landscape. The finest practitioners in the world today conduct a kind of autopsy. Gilles Peress traces the bones, the most reliable witnesses to atrocity. Simon Norfolk fixes the afterburn, using a wood and brass field camera, with tripod, magnifying glass to focus, and blanket over the head. Stupendous images slowly form on negative plates. They contain few people but many remains.

(Danchev, 2005: 215)

Given this characterization, I want to develop the perspective of Simon Norfolk who considers that war journalism does suffer from a kind of pattern exhaustion (Norfolk, 2012). Norfolk is an award-winning landscape photographer whose work over the last decade or so has probed the notion of 'battlefield' in all its forms. His work, taken in some of the world's worst war zones and refugee crises, is as much archaeology as photography, revealing the fossilization of time. For example, Norfolk (following Bakhtin) calls a collection of his work on Afghanistan 'Chronotopia' – where space and time come together to forge a single frame or chronotope. Norfolk's study of Afghanistan reveals the layering of the sedimentations of over 30 years of warfare, with the scars and remains of the landscape as the only evidence of the carnage of such persistent modern war in one place.

Norfolk's argument is useful to consider as a practitioner's perspective on the dichotomy set up here, between the flux of the new and the persisting trajectories of the old, and how this tension and transition produces both new interpenetrations and contestations of social memory.

In terms of the journalistic representation of warfare, Norfolk considers the ways in which new technologies of warfare are challenging the representation of war. He conceives that the way war is photographed and fought – two realms that used to be intimately connected – have spent the last 40 years or so falling away from each other. Norfolk points us to the visual politics site 'BagNews' and the work of Michael Shaw to illustrate this argument.

Shaw (2011) observes that three separate Western mainstream news organizations – *Time*, the *Toronto Star* and the *New York Times* – sent three of the leading photojournalists in the business – James Nachtwey, Louie Palu and Tyler Hicks, respectively – to Afghanistan. And they all returned with virtually the same picture, all publishing their photo-stories within a two-week period in January 2011 (Shaw, 2011). These pictures all depict wounded US marines in the rear of a military 'medevac' helicopter being airlifted out of the Afghan warzone to safety.

Subsequently, Shaw found a number of similar photographs published in 2010, 2011 and 2012 across a range of mainstream media. In drawing attention to what he calls 'redundancy,' Shaw makes clear that his intention is not to disrespect the photographers, the soldiers, or the medevac missions and their saving of lives. Instead, he argues, 'this is a stunning display of American chauvinism given the intimate framing of the war in such a redundantly heroic narrative, all eyes on our warriors as saviors on high. And then, what does it mean that such high-profile redundancy can occur with hardly a notice?' (Shaw, 2011).

Norfolk characterizes the effect of this redundancy across photojournalism as 'running down tramlines.' Despite the array of photographs that could be taken and potentially published from the war in Afghanistan, there appears a particularly persistent expectation (on the part of picture editors, photojournalists and other newsworkers) of what a mainstream version of warfare looks like. Norfolk argues that 'these are the award winning pictures, the pictures the magazines expect to see, so the problem with memory starts with what is being generated on the battlefield.'

But significantly, the 'tramlines' Norfolk speaks of are not merely synchronic to Afghanistan in early 2011 but rather follow a much longer mainstream photojournalism trajectory of the medevac image, embedded in earlier US wars. He argues that this includes David C. Turnley's World Press Photo of the Year, which, in turn, is a 're-shoot' of the iconic Larry Burrows's Vietnam photograph on the cover of *Life* magazine in April 1965: 'The photographers are photographing the same thing: they're re-photographing a picture that was made 50 years ago. Those pictures from the Vietnam War are 50 years old. The photographers are looking for 50 year old photographs in the modern electronic cyberwarfare battlefield' (Norfolk 2012). The persistence of this mainstream photojournalistic visioning of warfare is partly explicable through the emergent challenges of picturing developing technologies of war. (This is part of a longer history in the development of distancing technologies of warfare and the emergence of a new 'logistics of military perception' (Virilio 1989: 7).) Norfolk offers the example of computer viruses as a significant emergent part of cyberwarfare which is not representable in the same way as traditional warfare: 'How do you photograph a drone flying over Yemen at 40,000 feet and firing a missile into a car in the middle of nowhere? You can't photograph it. How do you photograph satellite warfare or submarine systems, or cyberwarfare? That's how the war of the future is being fought, that is where the money is being spent... I don't know how to photograph any of that stuff' (Norfolk, 2012).

So, as new technologies facilitate a 'militarized regime of *hypervisibility*' (original italics; Gregory 2011: 193), enabling an increasingly remote (although not necessarily less intimate) means of locating and killing the enemy, the copresence of journalists and consequently their capacity to represent warfare is increasingly compromised. In this way, the trajectories of the icons of twentieth-century war fill the mainstream representational void. This is evident both in the 'tramlines' of photojournalism identified by Norfolk and in the disjunctures of the mediated and political templates of warfare. For example, the US Defense Secretary Leon Panetta, highlighting cyber attacks and the growing threat posed by them to US interests, recently declared 'the collective result of these kinds of attacks could be a cyber Pearl Harbor.' And this part of the speech was precisely the headline used in the reporting of the story by BBC News online (BBC News, 2012). A selective memory of twentieth-century warfare is thus re-articulated through the difficulties in both escaping its legacy – in US political and media consciousness – and in finding a means of visual representation and political rhetoric that gives a sufficient materialization and measure of the threat of emergent war without media/memory. In sum, the photojournalism of war has narrowed the aperture of social memory at least in its defining of certain image trajectories or 'tramlines.' This seems oddly counter to post-scarcity culture's unbounding of journalism's living archive of information and interpretation. But what exactly is the new living archive of warfare, and what kind of memory does it produce in contesting or reinforcing the persistence of a particular vision of the wars of today and twentieth-century conflict?

Memory of the long tail

The immediacy of digital technologies and social media drives an acceleration of the circulation of information and the production of news, stealing the clothes of broadcast media. And this immediacy renders memory, as I suggested above, as spontaneous, unfinished, unsettled and mobile, in contradistinction to the seemingly more orderly, contrived and continuous journalistic living archive. The reality is that these two kinds of distinct and separate memory are also blended together. The mediality of war memory is apparent, for example, with the ready availability of media content of the war in Afghanistan. A quick search of

YouTube reveals a panoply of samples of both the mainstream remediated and the unofficial and unauthorized – 'raw combat footage,' 'helmet cam footage,' 'sniper kill shot,' 'marine sniper, one shot one kill, Afghanistan' – not jostling for a punctual or simultaneous audience but instead awaiting their algorithmic return from the searches of users.

This is just a fragment of the effect that Geoffrey Bowker calls a *'databasing of the world'* (original italics; Bowker, 2007: 22). (Databases here are the 'set of traces...available and searchable on the Internet' (Bowker, 2007: 36, n1).) For Bowker, the databasing of the world marks a shift 'from the era of recorded memory to one of potential memory' (2007: 26), so that remembrance is possible should the need ever arise. This is memory of the long tail – where there are an almost infinite number of variations of aggregation from the endlessly remediated and recontextualized right down to the untouched, unfound and forgotten.

Memory of the long tail begs the question: what is the threshold for a collective or social memory of warfare after the connective turn? Certainly, the trajectories of warfare embedded in twentieth-century frames and icons are traceable over time. For example, Michael Griffin's (2004) study of US mainstream magazine photo coverage of the Iraq War found that the number of combat photographs (from the front line) comprised 10 percent of published pictures, which is perhaps surprising given the scale and (political and military) success of 'embedding' with this war. And David Campbell (2011: 153) suggests that this work 'demonstrates that news pictures are less concerned with the first-hand recording of events and more with the repetition of familiar subjects and themes.' In other words, mainstream media trajectories serve the 'official' war narrative (ibid.).

But magazine photojournalism and other visual media such as television (including their online variants) are embedded in medium-specific histories, through which they see (or don't see) the emergent world of war. To what extent, then, is the generational journalistic memory of warfare being broken up and fragmented, so that the familiar trajectories are disrupted and disconnected?

Databasing the world can be seen as a 'process of disembedding information that was once more tightly bound to professional communities, with their tightly controlled forms of accreditation and membership' (David, 2007: 177). Will the unbounding of journalism – in terms of the availability of digital recording and publication in post-scarcity culture – also ultimately lead to an unbounding of memory, and, in Zelizer's (2008) terms, diminish journalists as 'agents' of memory?

In sum, and currently at least, there appears to be both convergence and coexistence here, between a trajectory of a journalistic vision of what warfare looks like and that which is driven by the flux of the digital. So, just as the tightly-bound journalistic information is disembedded (by the so-called 'amateur' and via digital technologies and media), the mediality of memory is in turn appropriated by journalists and re-embedded into a mainstream accounting of war.

However, mediality, in the databasing of the world and the editing, posting, circulating, linking, liking, mixing and remediating of digital content, nonetheless offers more immediate modes of remembering that seem to occur 'on-the-fly' (Hoskins, 2009). This is in contrast to being rendered as settled, stable or derived from a fixed space and/or trajectory of remembrance (archive, museum, journalist).

The established and emergent modes of representation and mediation – from journalistic schemas to mediality – appear to consume the memory of conflict and catastrophe. Yet, these different and even oppositional features of the contemporary memory boom provoke counter-memorial imaginations and practices. The work of Simon Norfolk, for instance, is indicative of an emergent media archeology in an era characterized by excess (of media, memory and war) that challenges and reveals a memory of warfare with new resonance and force.

Note

1. See also Lievrouw and Livingstone (drawing upon Star and Bowker, 2002) who set out the parameters of a 'new media infrastructure' as: 'The artefacts or devices used to communicate or convey information; the activities and practices in which people engage to communicate or share information; and the social arrangements or organizational forms that develop around those devices and practices' (2002: 2).

References

Allan, Stuart and Thorsen, Elinar (eds) (2009) *Citizen Journalism: Global Perspectives*. New York: Peter Lang.

BBC News (2012) 'Leon Panetta warns of "cyber Pearl Harbour."' *BBC News*, 12 October, available at http://www.bbc.co.uk/news/technology-19923046 (accessed 1 October 2013).

Bowker, Geoffrey C. (2007) 'The Past and the Internet,' in Joe Karaganis (ed.) *Structures of Participation in Digital Culture*. New York: Social Science Research Council, pp. 20–36.

Bowker, Geoffrey. C. (2008) *Memory Practices in the Sciences*. Cambridge, MA: MIT Press.

Bowker, Geoffrey C. and Star, Susan Leigh (2000) *Sorting Things Out: Classification and its Consequences*. Cambridge, MA: MIT Press.

Campbell, David (2011) 'How has Photojournalism Framed the War in Afghanistan?,' in John Burke and Simon Norfolk (eds) *Burke and Norfolk: Photographs from the War in Afghanistan*. Stockport: Dewi Lewis Publishing, pp. 153–5.

Chéroux, Clément (2012) 'The déjà vu of September 11: An Essay on Intericonicity,' trans. Hillary Goidell, in Felix Hoffman (ed.) *The Uncanny Familiar: Images of Terror*. Köln: Walther König, bilingual edition, pp. 261–87.

Danchev, Alex (2005) 'War Stories,' *Journal of Military History*, 69(1), 211–15.

David, Shay (2007) 'Toward Participatory Expertise,' in Joe Karaganis (ed.) *Structures of Participation in Digital Culture*. New York: Social Science Research Council, pp. 176–96.

Deuze, Mark (2004) 'What is multimedia journalism,' *Journalism Studies*, 5(2), 139–52.

Gillmor, Dan (2006) *We the Media: Grassroots Journalism By the People, For the People*. Sebastopol, CA: O'Reily Media, Inc.

Gowing, Nik (2009) '"Skyful of Lies" and Black Swans: The New Tyranny of Shifting Information Power in Crises,' Reuters Institute for the Study of Journalism working paper, University of Oxford.

Gregory, Derek (2011) 'From a View to a Kill: Drones and Late Modern War,' *Theory, Culture and Society*, 28(7–8), 188–215.

Griffin, Michael (2004) 'Picturing America's "War on Terrorism" in Afghanistan and Iraq: Photographic Motifs as News Frames,' *Journalism: Theory, Practice and Criticism*, 5(4), 381–402.

Grusin, Richard (2004) 'Premediation,' *Criticism*, 46(1), 17–39.

Grusin, Richard (2010) *Premediation: Affect and Mediality After 9/11*. Basingstoke: Palgrave Macmillan.

Hervieu-Léger, Danièle (2000) *Religion as a Chain of Memory*, trans. by Simon Lee. London: Polity Press.

Hoskins, Andrew (2004a) *Televising War: From Vietnam to Iraq*. London: Continuum.

Hoskins, Andrew (2004b) 'Television and the Collapse of Memory,' *Time and Society*, 13(1), 109–27.

Hoskins, Andrew (2005) 'Flashframes of History: American Televisual Memories,' in John Beck and David Holloway (eds) *American Visual Cultures*. London: Continuum, pp. 299–305.

Hoskins, Andrew (2009) 'Digital Network Memory,' in Astrid Erll and Ann Rigney (eds) *Mediation, Remediation, and the Dynamics of Cultural Memory*. Berlin: Mouton de Gruyter, pp. 91–106.

Hoskins, Andrew (2011a) 'Media, Memory, Metaphor: Remembering and the Connective Turn,' *Parallax*, 17(4), 19–31.

Hoskins, Andrew (2011b) '7/7 and Connective Memory: Interactional Trajectories of Remembering in Post-Scarcity Culture,' *Memory Studies*, 4(3), 269–80.

Hoskins, Andrew and O'Loughlin, Ben (2007) *Television and Terror: Conflicting Times and the Crisis of News Discourse*. Basingstoke: Palgrave Macmillan.

Hoskins, Andrew and O'Loughlin, Ben (2010) *War and Media: The Emergence of Diffused War*. Cambridge: Polity Press.

Hoskins, Andrew and O'Loughlin, Ben (forthcoming) *The New Mass*.

Huyssen, Andreas (2003) *Present Pasts: Urban Palimpsests and the Politics of Memory*. Stanford: Stanford University Press.

Jones, Janet and Salter, Lee (2011) *Digital Journalism*, London: Sage.

Kitzinger, Jenny (2000) 'Media Templates: Key Events and the (Re)construction of Meaning,' *Media, Culture & Society*, 22(1), 61–84.

Lanier, Jaron (2010) *You Are Not a Gadget: A Manifesto*. London: Allen Lane.

Lievrouw, Leah A. and Livingstone, Sonia (2002) 'Introduction,' in Leah A. Lievrouw and Sonia Livingstone (eds) *Handbook of New Media*. London: Sage, pp. 1–14.

Lovink, Geert (2012) *Networks without a Cause: A Critique of Social Media*. Cambridge: Polity Press.

Merrin, William (2008) 'Media Studies 2.0,' at: http://mediastudies2point0. blogspot.com/.

Münkler, Herfried (2005) *The New Wars*. Cambridge: Polity Press.

Norfolk, Simon (2012) 'Simon Norfolk in conversation with Andrew Hoskins,' Open Eye Gallery, Liverpool, 3 May, available at http://www.mixcloud.com/ OpenEyeGallery/simon-norfolk-prof-andrew-hoskins-in-conversation-art-memory-landscape-genocide/ (accessed 12 October 2013).

Nowotny, Helga (1994) *Time – The Modern and Postmodern Experience*. Cambridge: Polity Press.

Ritchin, Fred (2009) *After Photography*. New York: W.W. Norton & Company.

Shaw, Martin (1996) *Civil Society and Media in Global Crises: Representing Distant Violence*. London: Continuum.

Shaw, Martin (2005) *The New Western Way of War: Risk-Transfer War and its Crisis in Iraq*. Cambridge: Polity.

Shaw, Michael (2011) 'Big Media Sent 3 Of My Favorite War Photographers to Afghanistan And What They Brought Back Were The Near-Same Medevac Shots,' *Bagnews*, 16 January, available at http://www.bagnewsnotes.com/2011/01/ big-media-sent-3-of-my-favorite-war-photographers-to-afghanistan-and-what-they-brought-me-back-were-the-near-same-medevac-shots/ (accessed 1 October 2013).

Silverstone, Roger (2002) 'Mediating Catastrophe: September 11 and the Crisis of the Other', available at http://www.infoamerica.org/documentos_pdf/silverstone07.pdf (accessed 12 October 2013).

Singer, Jane B. et al. (2011) *Participatory Journalism: Guarding Open Gates at Online Newspapers*. Oxford: Wiley-Blackwell.

Star, Susan Leigh and Bowker, Geoffrey (2002) 'How to Infrastructure,' in L. Lievrouw and S. Livingstone (eds) *Handbook of New Media: Social Shaping and Consequences of ICTs*. London: Sage, pp. 151–62.

Truc, Gérôme (2010) 'Seeing Double: 9/11 and its Mirror Image,' *Idess*.fr. available at http://www.booksandideas.net/IMG/pdf/20090911_truc_EN.pdf (accessed 1 October 2013).

Tunney, Sean and Monaghan, G. (eds) (2009) *Web Journalism: A New Form of Citizenship?* Brighton: Sussex Academic Press.

Virilio, Paul (1989) *War and Cinema: The Logistics of Perception*. London: Verso.

Wall, Melissa (ed.) (2012) *Citizen Journalism: Valuable, Useless or Dangerous?* International Debate Education Association.

Winter, Jay (2006) *Remembering War: The Great War Between Memory and History in the Twentieth Century*. New Haven: Yale University Press

Zelizer, Barbie (2008) 'Why Memory's Work on Journalism Does Not Reflect Journalism's Work on Memory,' *Memory Studies*, 1(1), 79–87.

Journalism and Institutional Memory

12

The Late News: Memory Work as Boundary Work in the Commemoration of Television Journalists

Matt Carlson and Daniel A. Berkowitz

In his masterpiece on medieval politics, *The King's Two Bodies*, Kantorowicz (1957) examines the vexing relationship between individual mortality and institutional continuity. The king embodied the state, but was also embodied himself and destined to the same fate as any commoner: death. To rectify this disjuncture, the king came to occupy a symbolic presence advancing beyond his bodily presence. Chants of 'The king is dead! Long live the king!' sum up this duality. Individuals – even important ones – die, but institutions endure.

We do not need to look to antiquity to observe how the deceased are put to work as symbols joining past, present and future. Instead, we only need to consider television news. While not quite imbued with perquisites of royalty, the ascension of television in modern culture has resulted in television journalists possessing popularity exceeding their print predecessors (Meltzer, 2009). Known nightly or weekly to millions of viewers, these journalists have attained a level of authority closely connected to their familiarity. The fusion of television journalists with the stories that they report further cements their place in collective memory – to remember the assassination of President John F. Kennedy or Neil Armstrong landing on the moon is to remember its announcement by CBS News anchor Walter Cronkite.

Of interest in this chapter is how television journalists commemorate their departed colleagues. The death of prominent television journalists occasions a professional rite in which past and present journalists revisit their careers through montages of past stories and personal recollections. But, more importantly for understanding journalism, the television news community uses memories of deceased journalists to construct symbolic boundaries delineating acceptable forms of practice. In this professional moment, mediated remembrances turn from the external world to gaze inward, securing current practice firmly in place or legitimating a boundary shift for future practice. In essence, this rite shores up cultural authority in the face of a tumultuous present and an uncertain future: by doing so, memory work becomes boundary work. As such, the deceased is made to serve the continuity of a whole set of practices.

The news anchor is dead. Long live the news anchor.

Memory as boundary work

Despite their deep-seated obsession with being as up-to-date as possible, journalists often serve as agents of memory. Whether it is drawing from the past to interpret the present or commemorating bygone events, memory is ever-present in news discourse. So too is memory present in how journalists talk about their profession.

For journalists, memory is more than recollection. It forms a core part of how journalists understand themselves as an interpretive community (Berkowitz and TerKeurst, 1999; Zelizer, 1993). Journalists situate themselves within a history paralleling the rise of democratic institutions, drawing on this longevity to legitimate their social role. For example, the lore surrounding Bob Woodward and Carl Bernstein's Watergate reporting became a 'sustaining' myth within journalism (Schudson, 1992: 124), including the corollary mythologizing of the unnamed source 'Deep Throat' (Carlson, 2010). For those uninvolved in the story – or even unborn – Watergate is held up as a watershed moment and a source of continual pride for journalism despite an embellishing of Woodward and Bernstein's role in the eventual resignation of President Richard Nixon. Nonetheless, the heralding of their work provides the interpretive community with a mnemonic reservoir to support watchdog journalism in the present – and therefore journalism's central role. Stanley Fish argues that for any interpretive community, 'its perspective is interested rather than neutral' (1980: 14). For journalism this includes a defense of norms and practices underlying the production of news.

Journalists' reliance on memories of their own profession to support their work demonstrates the close ties between memory and cultural authority (Connerton, 1989). Even as journalists act as an interpretive community, they do so within a wider context of competing interests. To possess the cultural authority to produce and relay truthful accounts requires convincing the sources and audiences for this news of its merit and importance (Carlson, 2012; Eason, 1988; Zelizer, 1992). Yet the means by which journalistic authority is established and defended needs more attention. One way forward is to connect journalists' use of collective memory with what Weber calls the 'traditional grounds' for authority (Weber, 1947: 328). In this diachronic iteration, the legitimacy of institutions is closely bound up in their continuity within society.

We argue that the memory work journalists undertake in regard to their own profession should be understood as a form of boundary maintenance. This claim stems from the work of Gieryn (1983, 1999) in the sociology of science. No one would reasonably dispute the existence of science or scientists, but Gieryn's problem centered on excavating how the borders between science and non-science came to be. If one looks across time, it is clear that the social role of science has been enlarged, but by what mechanism does this occur? Beyond the material work of doing science lies a rhetorical layer legitimating this work as science while, simultaneously, dismissing other work as non-science. The terrain of science as a social practice is a contested one, requiring attention to how territorial struggles are mounted. This question gives rise to a conception of boundary work as 'the discursive attribution of selected qualities to scientists, scientific methods, and scientific claims for the purpose of drawing a rhetorical boundary between science and some less authoritative residual non-science' (Gieryn, 1999: 4–5). The simple substitution of 'journalist' for 'scientist,' 'journalistic' for 'scientific' and 'non-journalism' for 'non-science' begins moving us to key questions regarding journalism as a particular social practice.

However, for Gieryn's model of boundary work to be rendered useful for journalism, another substitution is needed in the above definition. Our concern with journalistic boundary work lies not in its entanglement with what Gieryn termed 'residual' practices, but rather in what we might call 'emergent' practices, in reference to Raymond Williams (1973). This shift emphasizes boundary work as something always ongoing as the conditions for social practices change. Journalism, in particular, suffers from what Todd Gitlin (2011) labels a 'surfeit of crises' ranging from economic and material crises to crises of authority and deference.

The struggles for television news in the US are visible through a number of markers. During the 1960s and 1970s, the evening news broadcasts – the flagship programs for network television news – grew to become a shared cultural experience for millions of households. In an era of three networks with limited competition, television news became a dominant source of information (Prior, 2007). At the same time, the evening news became a ritual carefully timed to coincide with evening meals and the liminal shift from work to leisure (Selberg, 1993). The changing media landscape, first with the arrival of cable television and later with online news, has led to steep declines in evening news viewership, with the average nightly audience for ABC, CBS and NBC falling from 50.1 million in 1981 to 23.7 million viewers thirty years later in 2011 (Project for Excellence in Journalism, 2012). The remaining audience tends to skew towards older viewers – making it less attractive to the advertisers who ultimately fund news costs. Against these declines, the growth of cable news has ushered in pundit-centered programs presenting an alternative format stressing opinions over newsgathering, a trend exacerbated online.

Against this backdrop, working and retired journalists have responded to the deaths of their colleagues by restating core norms and asserting the cultural centrality of television journalism. The discourse that emerges among the journalistic interpretive community is by no means uniform or entirely coherent. Yet looking across a decade's worth of reactions reveals a number of recurrent themes that elucidate deep-seated anxieties among journalists.

This chapter contributes to research on collective memory, boundary work and cultural authority. A growing literature within journalism studies has examined how journalists use memory to enhance their authority (Carlson, 2006, 2007, 2010; Carlson and Berkowitz, 2012; Schudson, 1992; Zelizer, 1992). Another set of research has examined boundary work within journalism (Bishop, 1999; Lewis, 2012; Schudson and Anderson, 2009; Winch, 1997). However, the overlap between these two bodies of research has been scant to date. The evidence presented here suggests the need to better connect memory work and boundary work.

'How much the news mattered': memory work as boundary work

Shortly after the death of Walter Cronkite, columnist and regular television pundit Margaret Carlson remarked that watching old clips of the longtime news anchor 'reminded me how much the news mattered and how much he mattered to the news' (*Countdown*, MSNBC, 17 July 2009). The past tense here is telling; Carlson and other journalists remembered Cronkite nostalgically as they spoke admiringly not only of his career but of the news environment in which he worked. At the outset, it should be recognized that public discourse pertaining to the death of prominent journalists constructs images both of the individual journalists and of the medium in a larger sense. How this occurred and how it is used to talk about the present is the crux of why this discourse is important.

The following sections examine recurring trends arising within the commemoration of prominent television journalists (date of death in parentheses): NBC *Huntley-Brinkley Report* anchor David Brinkley (11 June 2003), *ABC World News Tonight* anchor Peter Jennings (7 August 2005), *CBS Evening News* anchor Walter Cronkite (17 July 2009) and *60 Minutes* anchor and correspondent Mike Wallace (7 April 2012). Reactions in both television and newspapers were analyzed for the ways in which they constructed the memories of these journalists and for how these efforts created boundaries of acceptable practices. We also take the opportunity to present a case of delayed commemoration of Edward R. Murrow. Decades after his death in 1965, Murrow was capitalized upon by not only broadcast journalism's elite, but by media outside the mainstream fold which presented much broader 'boundary skirmishes.'

Journalists as cultural actors

The death of any prominent figure touches off waves of public remembrance that go beyond merely rehashing the individual's accomplishments to instead reinforce their significance and worthiness for veneration. For television news anchors, this meant turning to the cultural role occupied by the deceased. Such remembrances conflated the journalist with a litany of major stories he covered, suggesting that the journalist was more of a guide or fellow witness than simply a medium through which news traveled. For example, according to MSNBC's David Shuster (*Countdown*, MSNBC, 17 July 2009), Cronkite's significance lay not just in relaying news, but also in assuming a deeper role as 'the voice and the prism through which so many people experienced the Kennedy assassination, or Vietnam, or the floods, or the landing on the moon, or Watergate, or political conventions.' Similarly, current NBC news anchor Brian Williams summed up Mike Wallace's career through listing a diverse sample of his interviews: 'He interviewed presidents and Salvador Dali, Jack Kevorkian, Frank Lloyd Wright, Malcolm X, Johnny Carson, Barbra Streisand, and a ton of shady characters' (*Nightly News*, NBC, 6 April 2012). Such recollections closely connect the deceased journalists and the stories with which they come to be conflated in memory (Carlson, 2012).

The response to the sudden death of Peter Jennings elicited this type of reaction. Jennings had competed for decades alongside Tom Brokaw at NBC and Dan Rather at CBS before the latter two retired in 2004 and 2005 respectively. Jennings's abrupt disappearance from the screen and subsequent death from cancer led journalists to expand remembrances to encompass the cultural role of all three anchors. The *New York Times* linked these anchors to the stories they covered:

> For more than two decades, the magnitude of a news event could be measured, at least in part, by whether Mr. Jennings and his counterparts on the other two networks showed up on the scene. Indeed, they logged so many miles over so many years in so many trench coats and flak jackets that they effectively acted as bookends on some of the biggest running stories of modern times.
>
> (Steinberg, 2005: A1)

This suggests the power of the three anchors to bestow significance to stories by their presence and the inseparability of anchors from the stories they covered. This point was also made by a *San Francisco Chronicle* columnist:

> These men with their sober aspects and grave voices matter more to our collective recording of events than we might recognize or acknowledge in the surging stream of today's 24-hour news cycle. They made us witness and remember, in a form that's been swept away by the more impatient delivery systems of all-news cable networks, Internet blogs and adversarial rants.
>
> (Winn, 2005: E1)

The comparison here between network television news and other news media forms highlights the powerful cultural role of Jennings, Brokaw and Rather both in securing attention and in shaping understandings of the news.

The memory work responding to these anchors establishes their cultural authority through their linkage to big stories. It suggests a role extending beyond merely conveying news to becoming part of the very events being covered. Over time, collective understandings of news events are closely bound up with their journalistic mediators. This may go against norms of detachment articulated within the objectivity paradigm of news, but it highlights the close attachment between television journalists and their viewers.

The television anchor as reporter

While commemorations of news anchors stressed their cultural significance and their close ties to viewers, they also responded to a persistent critique of the television news anchor as merely an attractive newsreader (Meltzer, 2009). The memory work around each deceased journalist stressed his involvement in constructing the news. David Brinkley, whose tenure in the early years of television preceded the mobility of his successors, was singled out by Dan Rather for his writing skills: 'David, unlike a lot of people in television then and now, wrote a great deal of his own material' (*Larry King Live*, CNN, 12 June 2003). By contrast, remembrance of Mike Wallace explained away his earlier entertainment-based work in television by noting his conversion to hard news. This included lauding his journalistic presence, marked by 'a voice that was shoe-leather tough and shoe-leather smooth' (*World News with Diane Sawyer*, ABC, 9 April 2012).

For longtime anchors Cronkite and Jennings, the emphasis was placed on their work as reporters. *60 Minutes* creator Don Hewitt stressed Cronkite's involvement beyond his on-camera appearances: 'Walter read assiduously. He talked to everybody who could possibly know something more about a story than he did. He was the newsman's newsman' (*Larry King Live*, CNN, 17 July 2009). Cronkite himself had titled his autobiography *A Reporter's Life* in an effort to stress active reporting over passive news reading. ABC News struck a similar chord by titling its two-hour retrospective on Jennings: 'Peter Jennings: Reporter' (10 August 2005): the program included ABC News president David Westin making this salient point: 'Even though Peter was such an outstanding anchor, he was never content just to remain in that anchor chair.' Meanwhile a *Denver Post* columnist played down the importance of Jennings's good looks and constant comparisons to James Bond by labeling him 'an overachieving journalist beyond being a handsome news reader' (Ostrow, 2005: F1).

The stress on these anchors as active news gatherers addresses a long-running criticism of television news personalities as more flash than substance. In this respect, these commemorations construct boundaries around the idealized news anchor as active in gathering and writing the news and not just in reading scripts in front of a camera. Such memories establish a tradition of the anchor as active, providing current and future practitioners with an argument for their authority as journalists.

Contrasting the past and the present

We argue that understanding memory work around deceased news workers requires contextualizing such commemoration within the conditions of the present. The journalists covered in this chapter all died amidst the ongoing transformation of the media environment. Their deaths came as network television news continued to wane in both its reach and significance. New journalistic practices signaled a more diverse news landscape than the homogeneity that reigned during the heyday of network television news from the 1960s through the 1990s. In response, journalists remembering their colleagues did so while establishing boundaries around preferred practices and disdaining new developments deemed to violate the core values that had undergirded network news.

Peter Jennings's death in 2005, coupled with Rather and Brokaw's respective departures from the anchor chair, was constructed negatively as a turning point. In an editorial, the *New York Times* contrasted the three network anchors as a force for quality journalism against current declining standards: 'because of their enormous fame, they were uniquely positioned to push for quality journalism and aggressive reporting, even as television turned steadily toward news as opinion or news as entertainment' (*New York Times*, 2005: A18). This statement clearly establishes a border between acceptable hard news and unacceptable forms of newscasting protected by the outsized power of three anchors to direct news coverage. The *Times* added that the passing of Jennings 'leaves behind a world in which network news operations are less well financed, less powerful and less likely to send an expensive team of cameras and producers to cover an overseas story.' Television news is viewed as worse off not merely because of larger changes but because of the loss of stewardship from Jennings. The *Philadelphia Inquirer* also used Jennings's death as an opportunity to editorialize about changes in news:

> Blogging, podcasting and instant messaging have made media messengers out of people with no training as journalists. Amid these developments, network news has become a less influential voice. Jennings' death is a reminder that a loss accompanies this brave news world: the loss of hearing the good and the bad from a person with a familiar voice, a voice you have come to trust.
>
> ('*Philadelphia Enquirer*,' 2005: A18)

This suggests a shift away from the authority of the news anchor toward the heterogeneity of a media landscape in which the border between professional and non-professional has continued to erode. Jennings's death provided a moment in which to lament this movement, and to advocate, however nostalgically, for a previous and more professional era.

Other speakers singled out objectivity as a casualty of the new media environment, lauding the deceased news anchors for their lack of opinions. CNN's John King made this clear while discussing Cronkite: 'We live in the age of cable, of Internet, of blogs. A lot of people on television voice their opinion, not the facts. And there is a fair amount of shouting that, I think it's fair to say, we both know Walter didn't like' (*Anderson Cooper 360*, CNN, 17 July 2009). Similarly, Ted Koppel saluted Jennings for possessing 'a determination to try at least to understand different aspects of an issue. To put cold facts in an intelligent and compassionate context. Peter was no ideologue of the left or the right' (*Nightline*, ABC, 8 August 2005). Fairness and objectivity were closely linked to civility. The *New York Times*'s Alessandra Stanley contrasted Jennings with unnamed others: 'in an era of chatty newscasters, jousting analysts and hyperactive commentators, he was a rare voice of civility' (Stanley, 2005: E1). In the *Washington Post*, Tom Shales similarly positioned David Brinkley against emergent trends: 'The qualities Brinkley embodied, though, are not exactly prized in broadcast journalism today. They belong to a more civilized, less frenzied time' (Shales, 2003: C1). In these examples, the discourse slips from the commemoration of an individual to the erection of boundaries around appropriate journalistic practices for television news. The unnamed other here is represented by pundit-driven programs on cable television and the growth of opinion media online.

The deceased as irreplaceable

We have seen above that memory work lauding deceased journalists constructs boundaries around acceptable practice, but commemorative discourse also highlights the singularity of individuals and their eras. Even if their work is promoted as positive, it is not always presented as a model for future work. This contrast points to the conflict in memory work. For example, the *St Louis Post-Dispatch* television columnist used the death of David Brinkley not to present him as a model but rather to signal the end of the news style he had cultivated: 'When David Brinkley and Chet Huntley signed on for NBC in 1956, their *Huntley-Brinkley Report* ushered in a new era in television news – an era that, five decades later, looks to be on its way out. ... There will never be another David Brinkley' (Pennington, 2003: A6). Brinkley's work as anchor had been praised, particularly his writing skills. Yet his era too was asserted to be almost over.

While Brinkley died decades after leaving the anchor chair, Jennings's quick death only months after his last television appearance – the program's full title remained *World News Tonight with Peter Jennings* – did not prevent similar assertions both of his irreplaceability and the passing of an era. A *Washington Post* editorial cited the development of new forms to argue for a sea change in television news: 'But well before these combatants [Jennings, Brokaw, and Rather] had departed, cable, satellite networks and the vast, chattering online universe had gone far to create a world in which no three men will ever again deliver the news to an entire nation with such Jovian authority' (*Washington Post*, 2005: A16). Such statements impose a mythic quality on these anchors while indicating the end of their applicability as models for news. Much of the argument for their irreplaceability lay in changes to the media landscape.

In discussing Cronkite, former news correspondent Sam Donaldson invoked the fragmentation taking place across television: '[Cronkite] had an audience so large, compared with the audiences today, why, prime-time shows would just give everything they had to have half of what Walter Cronkite had as a news audience in the late '60s and into the '70s' (*Campbell Brown*, CNN, 17 July 2009). This argument externalizes change beyond the scope of journalism, but it also reiterates the impossibility of another Cronkite because of these changes. Eroding audiences also meant tightened news budgets, which further distanced the deceased journalists from the realities of contemporary television news. The *Los Angeles Times* argued that the journalism represented by Mike Wallace was increasingly difficult to mount: 'Fewer news outlets are practicing the brand of investigative journalism that Wallace and *60 Minutes* helped to define. It is easier and cheaper for news outlets to turn to talking heads to fill air time' (James, 2012: D1).

Using the deaths of prominent journalists to assess the changing state of television journalism complicates the role of memory as boundary work. It is not just that the deceased are held to be models for contemporary practice. Instead, the qualities possessed by these eminent journalists are no longer those required by the larger context of a changing media landscape. This interpretive move transforms memory work from an individualized appreciation to a broader commentary about the state of television news.

Zombie boundary work: bringing Edward R. Murrow back to life

Commemoration of deceased anchors to accomplish authority-related boundary work has gone beyond drawing on the historical moment of their deaths. Bringing the memory of an anchor – and of his authority – back from the dead can also be used as a marker for defining appropriate journalistic performance in times when authority has been brought into question (Berkowitz and Gutsche, 2012). Such was the case when 'fake news' anchor Jon Stewart of the *Daily Show* took on the role of an activist journalist where it was perceived that journalism proper had failed to act. Stewart's actions were highlighted by the *New York Times* (Carter and Stelter, 2010), a revered guardian of journalistic authority in an article that invoked the soul of Edward R. Murrow to reposition its alignment with journalism's establishment boundaries.

In this case, Congress had reached stalemate in a debate about a federal healthcare bill for first responders to the 11 September 2001 attacks in New York. Stewart had invited a small group of these people onto his program to discuss the wide-ranging health problems they had faced. With the dilemma brought vividly home to his audience, legislators halted filibuster tactics and conceded support to responders' healthcare needs. What followed was a debate airing tensions between online journalists/bloggers and journalists working in traditional, mainstream media. With Stewart not falling cleanly into either camp, the *Times* article set up a journalism boundary debate where journalist/bloggers could gain ground in professional authority, while traditional journalists struggled to maintain their authority in light of yielding their responsibilities to Stewart.

Unlike the boundary work related to the other deceased anchors, the memory of Murrow was also capitalized upon by non-elite media, particularly bloggers with political or economic agendas. Through reference to Murrow as one of journalism's unconventional-yet-elite, bloggers could make what they wanted of the Jon Stewart comparison. In essence, the debate about Stewart's connection to the memory of Murrow was less related to Stewart himself and more about drawing new lines in the journalistic sand. The blog *Mind Your Own Damn Business*, for example, attempted to enhance its own authority by arguing that Stewart was a more responsible news reporter than actual mainstream news reporters:

> Thanks to Stewart, bloggers and many of the alleged 'news' organizations around the country jumped on Congress and as a result, Congress passed the bill. Thank you Jon Stewart for bringing this issue to my attention. And folks, in that is where We the People have a problem.
>
> (Siegel, 2010)

Likewise, the conservative blog *NewsBusters* made an effort to bolster its position, claiming that the *Times* had perpetuated – and attempted to engage with – the journalistic myth of Murrow through its comparison of Stewart:

> As it would only ever do for a liberal, the *Times* lauded Stewart as the exemplar of righteous journalistic advocacy. But if the *Times* revealed its bias by bestowing the honor upon Stewart, its counterfactual recollection of Murrow's legacy speaks to its willingness to take mythical journalistic folklore at face value.
>
> (Markay, 2010)

Mainstream media, though, had more to gain by quashing Stewart's journalistic credibility. An article on the ABC News website quoted Todd Gitlin, calling suggestions that Stewart was a journalist 'ignorant garbage.' To Gitlin, '[Stewart] is not a news person. He's a satirist and when he chooses to be blunt, he has the luxury of being blunt' (Marikar, 2010). Another mainstream media organization, the *Atlantic*, went a step farther, claiming that Stewart gained authority simply through the on-air persona he assumed each night on his own program:

> Stewart doesn't need to be the next Murrow to play a significant and laudable role in the public life of this country. The men, their deeds, and their times defy easy comparison. Stewart has become an eloquent and eminent prosecutor against much that is wrong about Washington (and sometimes the people who cover it).
>
> (Cohen, 2010)

The distinction between Stewart's satire and news work also occurred through suggestions of their mutual exclusivity. The *Orlando Sentinel* argued that comparisons to Murrow were detrimental to Stewart's authority: 'Stewart like Murrow? I can't believe that's what any comedian wants. Yes, it's nice to be compared to the serious, dignified, truth-seeking Murrow. But a comedian needs to be, well, funny' (Boedeker, 2010). Essentially, the *Sentinel* was arguing for yet another form of boundary work: that humor and seriousness should be held to be separate discursive modes, with a clear and wide boundary preserved in between.

In sum, the *Times*'s comparison of Jon Stewart to Edward R. Murrow served multiple aspects of boundary work, helping traditional journalism to maintain or even gain ground in the ongoing battle for journalistic authority. It presented an opportunity for non-elite media, especially bloggers, to stake their claim on a particular kind of authority and public service. This was also a chance for mainstream elite media to 'save face' after failing in their duty as society's watchdog. Bringing back Murrow from among the legions of dead anchors helped media organizations locate themselves in relation to their preferred boundaries of practice and re-establish or even expand their professional turf. For elite media and bloggers alike, memory became a way of drawing and redrawing journalistic lines through the authority that memory brings – the key here lies in what journalists selectively choose to remember.

Conclusion

We began this chapter by asking *how* television journalists commemorate their departed colleagues. The most straightforward answer would suggest that these journalists present their commemorations *respectfully*, aiming simply to recognize the immense contributions these anchors have made to their profession and to society. That kind of answer, however, would only be addressing superficial considerations. Below that surface lie considerations about the culture of journalism and its meanings. A more important question, then, is *why* television journalists chose to engage in these commemorations.

One form of meaning tied to the commemoration of deceased journalists is the effort to identify 'good' journalism practices and highlight responsibilities that the mainstream media hold dear. In this instance, commemoration becomes definitional. Once definitions of principles have been put in place, journalists can then assert their ties to those anchors, and by extension, claim legitimacy to their legacy. By commemorating legendary anchors, then, journalists re-validate their own work, regaining meaning for what they do each day. But the meaning of commemorating fallen journalistic heroes goes deeper yet, helping to define the boundaries that delineate those practitioners and forms of practice which can legitimately own a piece of that memory and those which do not deserve that recognition. Going further yet, mainstream journalists can use commemoration to break away from old forms of practice while affirming the values of current practice in the field. This notion appeared in commemoration of David Brinkley, Peter Jennings and most notably Walter Cronkite.

Commemorating the lives and work of anchors is not exclusively the domain of elite or mainstream media, as demonstrated by the widespread debate comparing the activist work of the Comedy Channel's 'fake journalist' Jon Stewart to the high impact social activism of legendary anchor Edward R. Murrow. There, bloggers found ways to leverage their own authority and stake out their own boundaries for what constitutes service to society. Although journalists actively construct memories of their predecessors, no one agent or community wholly controls discourse about journalism – particularly in an age in which new media have expanded the range of voices participating in the mediated public sphere.

In all, this chapter suggests cultural meanings for commemorating deceased anchors are only superficially about the anchors themselves. Although the commemorations we discussed certainly centered on those anchors, scrutiny about the meanings of these commemorations shows they were at least as much about the living anchors and their work, an opportunity to pause and restate the values they cling to in the present day and beyond.

References

Berkowitz, D. and Gutsche, R. (2012) 'Drawing Line in the Journalistic Sand: Jon Stewart, Edward R. Murrow, and Memory of News Gone By,' *Journalism and Mass Communication Quarterly*, 89, 643–56.

Berkowitz, D. and TerKeurst, J. (1999) 'Community as Interpretive Community: Rethinking the Journalist–Source Relationship,' *Journal of Communication*, 49, 125–36.

Bishop, R. (1999) 'From Behind the Walls: Boundary Work by News Organizations in Their Coverage of Princess Diana's Death,' *Journal of Communication Inquiry*, 23, 90–112.

Boedeker, H. (2010) 'Jon Stewart like Edward R. Murrow: Are you kidding?,' *Orlando Sentinel*, 28 December, available at http://blogs.orlandosentinel.com/ entertainment_tv_tvblog/2010/12/ jon-stewart-like-edward-r-murrow-are-you-kidding.html (accessed 12 July 2012).

Carlson, M. (2006) '"War Journalism and the 'KIA Journalist'": The Cases of David Bloom and Michael Kelly,' *Critical Studies in Media Communication*, 23, 91–111.

Carlson, M. (2007) 'Making Memories Matter: Journalistic Authority and the Memorializing Discourse Around Mary McGrory and David Brinkley,' *Journalism*, 8, 165–83.

Carlson, M. (2010) 'Embodying Deep Throat: Mark Felt and the Collective Memory of Watergate,' *Critical Studies in Media Communication*, 27, 235–50.

Carlson, M. (2012) 'Rethinking Journalistic Authority: Walter Cronkite and Ritual in Television News,' *Journalism Studies*, 13, 483–98.

Carlson, M. and Berkowitz, D.A. (2012) 'Twilight of the Television Idols: Collective Memory, Network News, and the Death of Walter Cronkite,' *Memory Studies*, 5, 410–24.

Carter, B. and Stelter, B. (2010) 'In "Daily Show" Role on 9/11 Bill, Echoes of Murrow,' *New York Times*, 27 December, B1.

Cohen, A. (2010) 'He's No Murrow, He's Stewart, and That's Plenty,' *Atlantic*, 29 December, available at http://www.theatlantic.com/entertainment/ archive/2010/12/hes-no-murrow-hes-stewart-and-thats-plenty/67000/ (accessed 12 July 2012).

Connerton, P. (1989) *How Societies Remember*. Cambridge: Cambridge University Press.

Eason, D. (1988) 'On Journalistic Authority: The Janet Cooke Scandal,' in J.W. Carey (ed.) *Media, Myths, and Narratives: Television and the Press*. Beverly Hills, CA: Sage, pp. 205–27.

Fish, S. (1980) *Is There a Text in This Class? The Authority of Interpretive Communities*. Cambridge, MA: Harvard University Press.

Gieryn, T.F. (1983) 'Boundary-Work and the Demarcation of Science from Non-Science: Strains and Interests in Professional Ideologies of Scientists,' *American Sociological Review*, 48, 781–95.

Gieryn, T.F. (1999) *Cultural Boundaries of Science*. Chicago, IL: University of Chicago Press.

Gitlin, T. (2011) 'A Surfeit of Crises: Circulation, Revenue, Attention, Authority, and Deference,' in R.W. McChesney and V. Pickard (eds) *Will the Last Reporter Please Turn Out the Lights*. New York: New Press, pp. 91–102.

James, M. (2012) 'Tough Guy at CBS News; Mike Wallace's Reporting Style on "60 Minutes" Was One of a Kind and Won't Likely be Matched,' *Los Angeles Times*, 9 April, D1.

Kantorowicz, E. (1957) *The King's Two Bodies*. Princeton, NJ: Princeton University Press.

Lewis, S.C. (2012) 'The Tension Between Professional Control and Open Participation: Journalism and its Boundaries,' *Information, Communication & Society*, 15(6), 336–66.

Marikar, S. (2010) 'Jon Stewart: Edward R. Murrow Incarnate, Or Something Else Entirely?' *ABC News*, 27 December, available at http://abcnews.go.com/Entertainment/jon-stewart-edward-murrow-incarnate/story?id=12485707#.UAdmGZHYHzM (accessed 12 July 2012).

Markay, L. (2010) 'Praising Jon Stewart, NYT Perpetuates The Myth of Murrow,' *Lachlan Markay's Blog*, 28 December, available at http://newsbusters.org/blogs/lachlan-markay/2010/12/28/praising-jon-stewart-nyt-perpetuates-myth-murrow#ixzz211oxwKtg (accessed 12 July 2012).

Meltzer, K. (2009) 'The Hierarchy of Journalistic Cultural Authority: Journalists' Perspectives According to News Medium,' *Journalism Practice*, 3, 59–74.

New York Times (2005) 'The Last Anchor,' 9 August, A18.

Ostrow, J. (2005) 'An Appreciation: Suave Jennings, A Reporter As Much As An Anchorman,' *Denver Post*, 9 August, F–01.

Pennington, G. (2003) 'The Era Brinkley Helped Launch Now Seems To Be On Its Last Legs,' *St Louis Post-Dispatch*, 13 June, A6.

The Philadelphia Inquirer (2005) 'Peter Jennings, 1938–2005: A Trusted Voice Silenced,' 9 August, A18.

Prior, M. (2007) *Post-Broadcast Democracy*. Cambridge: Cambridge University Press.

Project for Excellence in Journalism (2012) available at http://stateofthemedia.org/2012/network-news-the-pace-of-change-accelerates/network-by-the-numbers/ (accessed 12 July 2012).

Schudson, M. (1992) *Watergate in American Memory*. New York: Basic Books.

Schudson, M. and Anderson, C. (2009) 'Objectivity, Professionalism, and Truth Seeking in Journalism,' in K. Wahl-Jorgensen and T. Hanitzsch (eds) *Handbook of Journalism Studies*. New York: Routledge, pp. 88–101.

Selberg, T. (1993) 'Television and Ritualization of Everyday Life,' *Journal of Popular Culture*, 26, 3–10.

Shales, T. (2003) 'Good Night, David: America's Solid Anchor,' *Washington Post*, 13 June, C1.

Siegel, R.S. (2010) 'Jon Stewart; Comedian Did News Media's Job For News Media,' *Mind Your Own Damn Business Politics*, 27 December, available at http://mindyourowndamnbusinesspolitics.com/wordpress/2010/12/27/jon-stewart-comedian-did-news-media%E2%80%99s-job-for-news-media/ (accessed 12 July 2012).

Stanley, A. (2005) 'Among The Chatty Anchors, A Voice Of Civility,' *New York Times*, 9 August, E1.

Steinberg, J. (2005) 'Peter Jennings, Urbane News Anchor, Dies at 67,' *New York Times*, 8 August, A1.

The Washington Post (2005) 'Peter Jennings,' 9 August, A16.

Weber, M. (1947) *The Theory of Social and Economic Organization*, trans. and ed. by T. Parsons. New York: Free Press.

Williams, R. (1973) 'Base and Superstructure in Marxist Cultural Theory,' *New Left Review*, 82, 3–16.

Winch, S. (1997) *Mapping the Cultural Space of Journalism*. Westport, CT: Praeger.

Winn, S. (2005) 'Peter Jennings – A Calm, Cool Anchor In An Era When Being There Defined The News,' *San Francisco Chronicle*, 9 August, E1.

Zelizer, B. (1992) *Covering the Body*. Chicago, IL: University of Chicago Press.

Zelizer, B. (1993) 'Journalists as Interpretive Communities,' *Critical Studies in Mass Communication*, 10, 219–37.

13

American Journalism's Conventions and Cultures, 1863–2013: Changing Representations of the Gettysburg Address

Barry Schwartz

During the first three days of July 1863, the Battle of Gettysburg resulted in more than 50,000 casualties, to which the Union contributed almost 20,000 wounded and 3,155 dead. The toll was so great that President Abraham Lincoln agreed personally to dedicate a new cemetery for the Union's fallen soldiers.

Today, many believe that the Gettysburg Cemetery dedication gave President Lincoln an 'opportunity' to announce that his administration had changed its war goal from Union to emancipation, and that Gettysburg's fallen had died for this new cause. No interpretation could be more illogical, for without Union there could have been no emancipation; yet, during the past thirty years the academy and political left have embraced this interpretation tenaciously. To demonstrate that America's journalists have played a major role in this distortion is important not only for the light it throws on the changing meaning of the Gettysburg Address but also because it speaks to a more general problem: the relation between journalistic objectivity, generational experience and collective memory.

Collective memory

Memory is a necessary property of mind, a fundamental component of culture and an essential aspect of tradition. Although individuals alone possess the capacity to remember the past, they never do so singly; they do so with and against others situated in different groups and through the knowledge and symbols that predecessors and contemporaries transmit to them.

Collective memory differs from what individuals remember as eye witnesses. A variant of *public opinion*, collective memory refers to the *distribution* throughout society of what individuals know, believe and feel about past events, how they judge them morally, how closely they identify with them, and how much they are inspired by them as models for their conduct. The word 'distribution' is emphasized because its key property is variation, which denies the possibility of consensus. That every distribution also has a central tendency makes total dissensus equally impossible. The collective aspect of memory is evident in similar distributions of memory appearing among individuals widely dispersed and unknown to one another, and in memories reappearing across generations, linking the living and the dead. Thus, collective memory cannot result from individual memory because it is not included in it. Remaining after the individuals from whom it emerges disappear, collective memory is a 'collective representation' (Durkheim, 1974 [1898]: 1–34) which owes much of its resilience in literate societies to journalism. In Walter Lippman's words, 'ordinary citizens do not perceive the world directly but only through the set of forms and stereotypes provided by the press' (Lippman, 1922: 108). Lippman's statement requires three qualifications. First, press forms and stereotypes can simplify the complexity of real people and events, but they rarely arise independently of reality (Tajfel, 1968). Second, press forms and stereotypes are themselves modified as readers and other recipients pass them on to one another (Katz and Lazarsfeld, 1954). Third, journalism does more than inform; it exerts *social pressure* on readers and viewers to conform to community leanings and provides *social support* for doing so, thus reinforcing the impersonal representations that constitute collective opinion and memory.

The problem

As 'journalism continues to function as one of contemporary society's main institutions of recording and remembering, we need to invest more efforts in understanding how it remembers and why it remembers in the ways that it does' (Zelizer, 2008: 85). What one learns about collective memory, however, is affected by the specimen used to study it; to recognize this is the first step toward understanding its relation to journalism. In particular, no matter what Civil War archive one accesses, the Gettysburg Address is subject to comment. As the New Testament of American civil religion (Bellah, 1970: 176–9), it is almost universally recognizable:

> Four score and seven years ago our fathers brought forth on this continent, a new nation, conceived in Liberty, and dedicated to the proposition that all men are created equal.

Now we are engaged in a great civil war, testing whether that nation, or any nation so conceived and dedicated, can long endure. We are met on a great battle-field of that war. We have come to dedicate a portion of that field, as a final resting place for those who here gave their lives that that nation might live. It is altogether fitting and proper that we should do this.

But, in a larger sense, we can not dedicate – we can not consecrate – we can not hallow – this ground. The brave men, living and dead, who struggled here, have consecrated it, far above our poor power to add or detract. The world will little note, nor long remember what we say here, but it can never forget what they did here. It is for us the living, rather, to be dedicated here to the unfinished work which they who fought here have thus far so nobly advanced. It is rather for us to be here dedicated to the great task remaining before us – that from these honored dead we take increased devotion to that cause for which they gave the last full measure of devotion – that we here highly resolve that these dead shall not have died in vain – that this nation, under God, shall have a new birth of freedom – and that government of the people, by the people, for the people, shall not perish from the earth.

(Lincoln, 1953 [1863]: VII, 23)

From the turn of the twentieth century through the Korean War, journalists interpreted the Gettysburg Address as a call to honor the fallen, to continue struggle in the face of loss and suffering, and to save the world's only democratic government. During the civil rights movement, however, an 'adversary culture' superimposed itself upon journalists' acknowledgement of the ideal of objectivity. More than any previous generation, this culture, demonstrably left-leaning yet professing objectivity, has distorted public understanding of many aspects of the Civil War. To grasp why this distortion occurred when it did and what part of it resulted from journalism's conventions is the present problem.

Civil War press

The inverted triangle – lead, body, conclusion – is a longstanding journalistic convention. A second convention, formulated during a period of growing federal power, makes the President the key figure of any event in which he participates (Schudson, 1982: 9). During the Civil War, these conventions did not exist. Newspaper accounts of the Gettysburg Cemetery dedication contained no contextual preliminaries but went directly to the sequence in which local clergymen and officials participated. President Lincoln's comments, when mentioned, were subordinated to Edward Everett's two-hour oration.

Most literate Americans in 1863 never knew what Lincoln had said at Gettysburg, let alone how to interpret it. All 35 white-owned newspapers tracked, including Democratic and Republican, Southern and Northern, Eastern and Western papers, covered Edward Everett's two-hour oration, some reprinting it in its entirety, for it was the main event of the day, describing the details and ultimate meaning of the Gettysburg battles. Eleven, or about 31 percent of the total, made no mention of Lincoln's address. Seventeen newspapers, a little less than half, reprinted the Address without comment. The six newspapers that did assess Lincoln's words split along party lines.

Almost all city, town and village newspapers received subsidies from the political party with which they were locally affiliated, and all parties encouraged their members to become subscribers. Democratic newspapers accused Lincoln of exploiting the Gettysburg Cemetery dedication for political effect or pandering to abolitionists (criticisms evoked by his every presidential speech). Republicans extolled Lincoln's eulogy for the literary beauty with which it honored the dead and encouraged the living to fight to total victory.

New century

Lincoln's contemporaries had no reason to remember his Gettysburg speech. Not one lithograph or statue of Lincoln at Gettysburg appeared during or after the Civil War. Neither the press nor the public regarded the Address as a great oration; few intellectuals described it as such (Barton, 1930: 201; Dennet, 1934: 48). From post-Civil War reconstruction, through the Industrial Revolution and America's waging war against Spain, few had anything to say, one way or the other, about the Gettysburg ceremony. Not until the early twentieth century, when most of the Civil War generation had died and an industrial democracy had replaced a rural republic, was Lincoln's speech canonized.

If the nation's press at the turn of the century had remained as partisan as it had been in Lincoln's day, then interpretations of his Address would have been as divided. Political party subsidies, however, could no longer cover newspaper operating costs, especially in the larger cities, where they were replaced by new revenue sources, particularly department stores and other retail businesses. Because such businesses wanted their advertisements to reach the entire community, the criterion for good reporting shifted from political advocacy to the neutral collection, assessment and reporting of information. In this phase of the meaning of Lincoln's eulogy, journalists reached greater consensus than ever before.

Rapid industrialization and urbanization, a generation in which Civil War memories had faded, rising nationalism challenged by massive immigration – in this context an unprecedented enthusiasm for both Lincoln and his Gettysburg Address arose. In 1909 Major William H. Lambert (1909: 391–2, 399) told the Pennsylvania Historical Society that none of Lincoln's contemporaries saw unusual merit in his Gettysburg Address. 'It is difficult to realize that [the Address] ever had less appreciation than it does now.' 'The true applause' for the Address, added Charles E. Thompson, 'comes from this generation' (*New York Times*, Sec.5, 6 June 1913: 3). These comments are paralleled by the frequency with which the Address appeared in turn-of-the-century newspapers. When the number of newspapers referencing the Gettysburg Address per year is divided by the total number of newspapers archived (www. newspaperarchive.com), the proportion rises from 0.01, 0.02 and 0.01 in 1870, 1880 and 1890, then increases suddenly to 0.12, 0.36, 0.68 and 1.52 in the years 1900, 1910, 1920 and 1930.

The Gettysburg Address appeared regularly in the early twentieth-century printed media because it seemed as resonant with life in the 'progressive era' as in Lincoln's own generation. Lincoln's references to the equality of all men and to the government belonging to the people expressed America's hope of regulating growing inequities occasioned by the Industrial Revolution.

During late 1917 and 1918, Lincoln's image regained its original air in newspapers and articles about the Great War's challenges and costs. Cartoons linking President Woodrow Wilson and Lincoln abounded. Lines from the Gettysburg Address appeared in war propaganda, newspapers and periodicals (Schwartz, 2000: 225–55; see especially pp. 216, 239, 241, 247). Also, recitals of the Gettysburg Address became a traditional part of Memorial Day ceremonies – a practice that would continue through the 1960s.

How memory becomes newsworthy

The relevance and affective resonance of past events to present predicaments make history 'newsworthy' (Zandberg, Meyers and Neiger, 2012). This is why the media recovered the Gettysburg Address so suddenly during the progressive era. However, Zandberg and his associates' understanding of how relevance is itself invoked is incomplete.

Relevance is only realized when journalists succeed in pointing it out to their readers, but to do so is not a matter of straightforward description. As biblical scholar William Graham Scroggie (1903: 3) put it: 'The New is in the Old contained / The Old is in the New explained.' Many contemporary journalists sustain, enliven and often warp American memory on precisely this assumption. Unlike picture frames, which separate images from their surroundings, different journalistic frames establish different relations between present and past. Analogical thinking, as conceived above, is a common form of cognition, but to characterize it as 'reversed memory,' as do Zandberg et al. (2012), is an overgeneralization. In some cases, it is true, the past must be *revised* to make it relevant to the present. Such is the meaning of reversed, that is, 'presentist,' memory. In other cases, the reality of the past must be *affirmed* before it can articulate a current event. Japan's attack on Pearl Harbor, for example, was often mentioned in news stories about 9/11; but if the history of this attack were revised into a Japanese reaction to an unprovoked American oil blockade, leaving 240 rather than 2,402 dead, it would have lacked relevance to 9/11 and been useless as its historical prototype.

News conventions and domestic crises

The newsworthiness of the Gettysburg Address varied throughout the twentieth century, but the occasion for which Lincoln delivered it limited what later generations could make of it. When President Harding (1922) dedicated the Lincoln Memorial, he stressed that Lincoln went to war for no reason other than to save the Union (*Helena Daily Independent*, 31 May 1922: 2). Depression-era journalism magnified the Unionist theme. On Memorial Day 1930, after children had strewn flowers on the graves of Gettysburg soldiers, reporters listened closely to Herbert Hoover declaring that 'the Appeal for the unity of our people and the perpetuation of the fundamentals of our democracy is as vital today in our national thinking as it was when Lincoln spoke' (*Bismarck Tribune*, 31 May 1930: 2).

But something new had occurred: a realignment of history, journalism, commemoration and memory. As the Great Depression intensified, disillusion over World War I set in, and fewer believed that facts spoke for themselves. The unprecedented shock and complexity of events made their interpretation urgent. According to Edwin Emery (1972: 562), the rise of interpretive reporting was the most important development in journalism of the 1930s and 1940s. For many, objectivity and unbiased interpretation were synonymous with self-deception, but if plausible interpretation were indistinguishable from implausible, what would give journalism its authority? Walter Lippman (1920) had seen only one solution: to make journalism more professional. This required the institutionalization of objectivity: making false documentation illegal, requiring identification of sources in all stories, and facilitating the creation of non-partisan domestic and international research institutes and news agencies. The upgrading of journalism required a discipline 'in which the ideal of objective testimony is central' (Lippman, 1920: 82). If objectivity is to mean anything, however, its object must be significant; on the other hand, significance is precisely what makes interpretation – the *subjective* identification of present meaning and relevance – imperative.

Existential threats

When the United States entered World War II, the original dual sense of the Gettysburg Address – consolation and renewal of militancy – reemerged. Newspaper and radio journalists knew the Axis threat was existential; prospects of defeat affected their tastes for historical analogies: 'A new birth of freedom' meant military victory (*New York Times*, 19 March 1943: 22); that democratic government 'shall not perish from the earth' now meant it would prevail over fascism (editorial entered into *Congressional Record*, House, November 1941: A819). Simultaneously, 'In this tremendous war,' the *New York Times* (1943) editor noted, 'whose every day adds to the number of our dead, Mr. Lincoln's words of eighty years ago are as strong, inspiring and immediate as if they were heard today for the first time' (14 April 1943: 92). An eerie but relevant reality accompanied these words as the Gettysburg Cemetery reopened to embrace the bodies of the returning dead of World War II. Meanwhile, the will of the home front, always prone to lassitude, had to be stiffened. On the anniversary of the Gettysburg Address, the Cumberland (MD) *Evening Times* editor announced: 'Let the words of Abraham Lincoln, coming down through the years, be inspiration for greater effort on the part of those at home, to crown with success the heroic struggle of those who are fighting for us on foreign fields' (19 November 1943: 4).

Lincoln at Gettysburg remained newsworthy during the early years (1945–55) of the Cold War, when 'anxious humanity still yearned for a new birth of freedom.' World War II and Cold War journalists, thus, saw in the Gettysburg Address the concerns that Lincoln's generation saw in it. Civil rights-era journalists saw in this Address something very different.

Civil rights movement and the new Gettysburg Address

In 1978, Gaye Tuchman demonstrated that many young reporters assigned to cover demonstrations and campus unrest during the 1960s were moved and radicalized by what they witnessed. Reporters were attracted rather than repelled because their liberal leanings (Weaver et al., 2007) inclined their sympathy toward the weak and vulnerable, and led them to attribute the plight of minorities to external circumstances rather than internalized values and motives (Felson, 1991). These tendencies find dramatic expression in both contemporary victim theory and revision of Americans' understanding of President Lincoln's motives for going to war.

On 19 November 1963, in the midst of civil rights strife and a polarizing Civil War centennial, newspapers throughout the country reported on Secretary of State Dean Rusk observing how 'Lincoln's reaffirmation of the American commitment to the "proposition that all men are created equal" had been preceded by the Emancipation Proclamation.' William Scranton, Republican Governor of Pennsylvania, amplified Rusk's comments by including the civil rights issue in his official centennial address:

> Today, a century later, our nation is still engaged in a test to determine if the United States, conceived in liberty and dedicated to the proposition that all men are created equal, can long endure. Blood has been shed in the dispute over the equality of men even in 1963.
> (*Gettysburg Times*, 19 November 1963: 1, 4).

For Lincoln, then, it seemed emancipation was only a first step toward racial justice.

By the last decade of the twentieth century, historians and journalists had achieved a wholesale revision of Lincoln's eulogy, one that conformed to the goals of the civil rights movement, not the one that Gettysburg attorney David Will had in mind when he invited Lincoln to make a few remarks by the graves of the soldier dead. The transformation resulted from a new *perspective* that de-emphasized the themes of sacrifice, death and the sacredness of the Union, not from the accumulation of new *evidence*.

Garry Wills's (1998) Pulitzer Prize-winning *Lincoln at Gettysburg: The Words That Changed America* was the first comprehensive articulation of this new perspective. Wills meant his subtitle to be taken literally. Distinguishing between a Declaration of Independence affirming the equality of all men and a Constitution legitimating slavery, Wills claimed that Lincoln invoked the former to 'cleanse' the latter (Wills, 1998: 38). Lincoln knew that the Declaration's 'all men are created equal' referred to the equality of Englishmen in the colonies and mother country. He also knew that the 'new birth of freedom' implied the old birth of freedom that occurred in 1776 and ended in secession 85 years later. Concealing these truths, Lincoln, in an 'open-air sleight of hand,' transformed America into an egalitarian nation (Wills, 1998: 38). Wills's work received widespread and enthusiastic reviews from newspapers, whose book editors could not, or would not, see its miscalculations, one of which is evident in its very subtitle. What if Lincoln had failed to speak 'the words that changed America'? What if he had fallen ill on his way to Gettysburg, or before, or for some other reason failed to deliver his address? What would have become of the 'unchanged' America? Would it have become a fascist state? Socialist? Totalitarian? No newspaper reviewer bothered to ask. Meanwhile, Wills's unchallenged conclusions were piously reiterated in the academy's history and social science classes.

Journalists regularly interview proponents of the 'new' Gettysburg Address on public television and C-Span. Historian James Horton declared in the Great American Writers Series (C-Span 2, 18 June 2001) that Lincoln at Gettysburg put the Emancipation Proclamation into different words, highlighted the Declaration of Independence's celebration of equality, and redefined the Constitution in terms of it. The leading Lincoln scholars of the day made similar claims, revealing a likemindedness that reverberated upon itself. On 'Lincoln at Gettysburg,' an episode of the *Civil War Journal* (1994), one expert historian after another explained that Lincoln used the Gettysburg Address to tell the nation what the war was about. Their words, systematically paired with visual images, made the point unmistakably. The phrase 'conceived in liberty and dedicated to the proposition that all men are created equal' (quoted intermittently throughout the documentary) was accompanied by pictures of slaves and black soldiers. Verbal references to 'a new birth of freedom' accompanied the same images of the same African Americans.

Documentary journalism has done as much or more than any other medium to revise American memory of the Civil War. Consider the television documentary 'Abraham and Mary: A House Divided' (2001). After a voice read the Gettysburg Address, Professor Margaret Washington explained that Lincoln's words expressed the great catharsis that the American people had achieved. That Professor Washington felt no need to document her implausible claim about Lincoln's expressing Americans' sense of being purified of their inner racism exemplifies television journalism's commemorative bias.

Frequent media references to 'the unfinished work' to which Lincoln referred at Gettysburg bear mention in this regard. When national samples of Americans in 2000 and 2001 were asked to explain Lincoln's presidential greatness, the overwhelming proportion reflected journalism's Lincoln by mentioning emancipation and racial justice; only a small minority mentioned Lincoln's role in preserving the Union.

One of the most dramatic revisions of the Gettysburg Address accompanied the presidential inauguration of Barack Obama. As a 'media event' or 'high holiday of mass communication' (Dayan and Katz, 1992), the 2009 inauguration was framed by the regular invocation of Lincoln and the Gettysburg Address. On his way to Washington, the President-elect, never out of sight of the press, traced Lincoln's route from Springfield, Illinois. The night before the inauguration, Obama and his family made a point to visit the Lincoln Memorial. He wove the phrase 'New Birth of Freedom,' the inauguration's official theme, into many of the day's ceremonies (Lisi, 2009), which included his taking his oath on Lincoln's Bible, and a luncheon consisting of the food Lincoln enjoyed, served on replicas of plates purchased by First Lady Mary Lincoln (Ruane and DeBose, 2008). Three weeks later, on the bicentennial of Abraham Lincoln's birth, the Emancipation Proclamation and Gettysburg Address were read *sequentially* to Obama and the rest of the Ford's Theater audience (Marks, 2009).

The transformation of the Gettysburg Address could have resulted from: (1) new information, (2) proof that multiple versions of the Address are equally true, or (3) proof that the phrases emphasized in the Address today had approximately the same meaning as they did for Lincoln and his contemporaries. These hypotheses have yet to be validated. No additional information on Lincoln's motives for writing the Address has been discovered; instead, selected portions of the Address – most commonly, 'all men are created equal,' 'unfinished work,' and 'new birth of freedom' – have been sanctified. Multiple truths (as opposed to multiple perceptions) are unconvincing given evidence on what the occasion obligated Lincoln to say.

Journalists have always pressed the meaning of old facts to the service of new problems, but in the minority rights context (Skrentny, 2002) these facts had to be utterly distorted in order to be made relevant. Such is the failing of journalism's 'redactional culture' (Jones, 2009: 133): reinterpretation of established facts trumps the discovery of new ones.

During the twentieth century, journalism produced two versions of the Gettysburg Address – an early version that consecrated the 3,155 Union dead by invoking the ideals of Union and democracy, and a later revision that depicts Lincoln at Gettysburg eulogizing the fallen as martyrs for emancipation. That the emancipationist account of the Gettysburg Address corresponds to an abrupt rise in articles on slavery is therefore no coincidence. The Lexis-Nexis evidence is abundant, but one source, the *Washington Post*, is representative. In 1980 and 1985, a total of 11 articles on American slavery appeared; in 1990 and 1995, 37 articles; in 2000 and 2005, 94 articles. In 2010 alone 51 articles appeared. Rising interest in slavery and emancipationist interpretations of the Gettysburg Address are aspects of the new journalism's celebration of diversity, racial equality and inclusion.

Context and truth

Adjudicating between emancipationist and traditional versions of the Gettysburg Address requires recognition of journalism's traditional shortcoming, namely, failure to contextualize properly the events on which it reports. A touching speech that affirms the equality of all men makes sense to a society that disdains invidious distinctions of race, ethnicity and religion, but it would have made no sense to Abraham Lincoln's society where such distinctions were the very foundations of social order. It would have made no sense to the political officials sharing the Gettysburg Cemetery platform with Lincoln – particularly governors representing states with strong Democratic constituencies: Governor Horatio Seymour of New York, Governor Joel Parker of New Jersey, Governor William Denison and former Governor David Tod of Ohio, and Governor Augustus Bradford of Maryland. Soldiers from these four states, largely antiwar and at best neutral toward slavery, filled 41 percent of Gettysburg's graves.

Lincoln had no reason to torment his listeners by expressing a conviction they did not share. He was not prepared to tell them, in the midst of thousands of fresh graves, that they had been tricked, that the purpose of the war was different from what they believed it to be. Most soldiers believed they were fighting to save the Union, and the last thing Lincoln wanted to do, especially in south-central Pennsylvania – a 'stronghold of rebel sympathizers' (*Indianapolis Daily Journal*, 23 November 1863: 2) – was to give the impression to bereaved families that he had manipulated their young men into dying to free blacks for whom they had no interest, let alone compassion. To do so would have transformed a solemn event which unified a grieving people into a partisan rally that divided people by exploiting rather than honoring their dead. That Lincoln knew as much, that he wrote a eulogy that would please the Democratic and Republican press alike but hide his true abolitionist feelings, is a comforting thought today, but it is inconsistent with the fact that he was prepared on more than one occasion to renege on his Emancipation Proclamation if President Jefferson Davis would have abandoned his secession plans (Lincoln, 1953 [1863], 6: 410; Pease and Randall, 1925 [1850–64]).

Adversary culture

From the early to the mid-twentieth century, journalists interpreted Lincoln's Address as a call to honor the fallen, continue to fight in the face of suffering, and perpetuate democratic government. Not until the civil rights movement did historians imagine that Lincoln's goal at Gettysburg was to redefine the war as a fight for emancipation. This revision, the least authentic stage of interpretation, occurred in the context of significant changes in all American institutions, including journalism. Journalistic conventions of objectivity dominating the first half of the twentieth century remained during the second half, but the journalistic values that underpinned the establishment of those conventions did not. An adversarial culture of two complementary orientations emerged: (1) skepticism toward the nation's government, tradition, mores and privileged strata and (2) sympathy for the poor and for racial and other excluded minorities. Michael Schudson's (2008) commentary on *Why Democracies Need an Unlovable Press* embodies the adversary position. Democracies, he contends, need 'journalists who get in the face of power'. Decontextualizing events, fixating on conflict and distrusting politics enable the press 'to maintain a capacity for subverting established power' and promoting appreciation of minority rights, alternative viewpoints, and the lives of other people, 'especially those less advantaged than themselves' (Schudson, 2008: 100, 50, 12). Gettysburg Address revisionism is symptomatic of this adversary movement, for its newest reading gets 'in the face of power,' and promotes appreciation of those 'less advantaged than ourselves.'

Conclusion

As a repository of facts, journalism's relation to memory is archival. As an interpreter of facts, journalism's relation to memory is cultural. Journalism as a cultural system inherits and/or revises traditional conceptions in terms of which people develop their perspectives on and knowledge about life (Geertz, 1973: 89). National crises express best how journalistic culture works. During World War II, for example, the press drew on Lincoln's words to legitimate war against Germany and Japan, to explain the immediate reasons for fighting it, clarify the values at stake, console the bereaved and inspire others to sustain the fight. To say that journalists write the first draft of history is therefore to say too little; rather, they explain the meaning of history for their readers and for their respective generations. This point takes us into deeper waters.

Whether or not print capitalism is a sufficient condition of nationhood, as Benedict Anderson (1991) claims, journalism, with or without the word capitalism, is a primary carrier of national memory. Journalism is a time machine not only because it preserves *contemporary* events for posterity but also because it brings to presence the experiences of the *past*. Having traced the way successive generations of media have represented the Gettysburg Address, one is struck that previous generations of journalists interpreted the Address as Lincoln's listeners understood it, but selectively in light of some predicament, while the present generation has undertaken wholesale revision rather than selective reinterpretation of the original. If distortion were merely a problem of different generations getting different parts of the story right and the rest wrong, it would be a simple matter of synthesizing partial truths. However, journalism's adversary culture differs from that of previous generations, inducing journalists, no less than historians, to undertake, without documentation, the wholesale warping of American memory.

Two concepts, 'framing' and 'keying' (Goffman, 1974), are the means by which journalism, revisionist and conservative alike, conducts its memory-work. Journalists invoke a primary framework when they select an event preceding the one they interpret and identify the latter's meaning by keying it to the former. For example, newspaper and television commentators assigned historical meaning to President John Kennedy's assassination and funeral by keying them to Lincoln's. Journalism makes this transformation public: Lincoln becomes a nineteenth-century Kennedy; Kennedy, a twentieth-century Lincoln. The framing-keying relation realizes its function by a literal crossing of ideational wires – a forced juxtaposition such that the story of one event is an appropriate frame through which to interpret another.

In the present case, 'forced juxtaposition' results from a six-step keying process: (1) *selection:* to sustain the drive to racial equality, a specific event, the Gettysburg Address, is invoked as a primary framework; (2) *scanning*: the content of the Gettysburg Address is scrutinized with a view to finding the words and phrases most relevant to the issue of African Americans' distress; (3) *event alignment*: emphasis on relevant similarities and ignoring of dissimilarities allow Lincoln's Address to be read as foreshadowing the civil rights and racial equality movements; (4) *identification*: contemporary journalists deploy Lincoln at Gettysburg as a model for their efforts to publicize and gain sympathy for the black struggle; (5) *values alignment*: journalists conceive their writings and Lincoln's eulogy as efforts toward the same moral goal; and (6) *idealization*: they conceive the Gettysburg Address to be akin to a sacred scripture, commanding recognition of black suffering and participation in efforts to hasten reform. This six-step process generalizes readily to many other if not most cases of journalism and collective memory. The power of this process, undertaken by print and video journalism, is indicated by the extent to which readers and viewers believe it authentic, feel and judge it appropriate, and see themselves in it.

The Gettysburg Address is at present unique because adversary journalists must revise it thoroughly, or report historians' revisions, before keying into it any current predicament. The adversary culture with which these journalists have affinity arose during an antinomian era hostile to ethnic, racial, gender and class boundaries. Leftward-leaning journalists are adversary culture's leading agents, and they have enlarged the collective memory by revealing heretofore ignored historical information; but they have distorted at least as much as they have uncovered. As the reformist strain of adversary culture asserts itself, the notion of truth, once essential to the understanding of journalism and collective memory, 'appears to have fallen off the agenda of communication scholars' (Tenenboim-Weinblatt, 2009: 101). Accordingly, journalists can now say, with little fear of contradiction, that on 18 November 1863, in the midst of the carnage of war, Abraham Lincoln left his work, his desperately ill son, and his fragile wife for two days in order to make a speech at Gettysburg Cemetery – not to recognize massive Union casualties (all white men) but to affirm the ideal of racial equality. For adversary journalism, then, the cost of affirming racial equality in the present is to distort a eulogy for the war dead delivered 150 years ago.

References

Anderson, B. (1991) *Imagined Communities: Reflections on the Origin and Spread of Nationalism*. London: Verso.

Barton, W. (1930) *Lincoln at Gettysburg*. Indianapolis: Bobbs-Merrill.

Bellah, R. (1970) *Beyond Belief*. New York: Harpers and Row.

Dayan, D. and Katz, E. (1992) *Media Events: The Live Broadcasting of History*. Cambridge, MA: Harvard University Press.

Dennett, T. (1934) *John Hay: From Poetry to Politics*. New York: Dodd, Mead & Co.

Durkheim, E. (1974 [1898]) 'Collective Representations,' in T. Parsons (ed.) *Sociology and Philosophy by Emile Durkheim*. New York: The Free Press, pp. 1–34.

Emery, E. (1972) *The Press and America*. Englewood Cliffs: Prentice Hall.

Felson, R. (1991) 'Blame Analysis: Accounting for the Behavior of Protected Groups,' *American Sociologist*, 22, 5–23.

Geertz, C. (1973) *The Interpretation of Cultures*. New York, Basic Books.

Goffman, E. (1974) *Frame Analysis: An Essay on the Organization of Experience*. New York: Harper and Row.

Jones, J. (2009) 'Believable Fictions: Redactional Culture and the Will to Truthiness,' in B. Zelizer (ed.) *The Changing Faces of Journalism: Tabloidization, Technology, and Truthiness*. London: Routledge, pp. 127–43.

Katz, E. and Lazarsfeld, P. (1954) *Personal Influence: The Part Played by People in the Flow of Mass Communications*. Glencoe, IL: Free Press.

Lambert, W. (1909). 'The Gettysburg Address: When Written, How Received, Its True Form,' *Pennsylvania Magazine*, 33, 385-408.

Lincoln, A. (1953 [1863]) *The Collected Works of Abraham Lincoln*. 9 vols. ed. R. Basler. New Brunswick: Rutgers University Press.

Lippman, W. (1920) *Liberty and the News*. New York: Harcourt, Brace, and Hone.

Lippman, W. (1922) *Public Opinion*. NY: The Macmillan Company.

Lisi, C. (2009) 'O to Arrive in a "Lincoln" – Inaugural Themes Will Harken Back to Great Emancipator,' *New York Post*, 13 January.

Marks, P. (2009) 'Ford's Gala Does Justice to 16's Legacy,' *Washington Post*, 12 February.

Pease, T. and Randall, J. (eds) (1925 [1850–64]) 'The Diary of Orville Hickman Browning,' *Collections of the Illinois State Historical Library*, 20. Springfield, IL: Illinois State Historical Library.

Ruane, M. and DeBose, T. (2008) 'Words of Lincoln will be Woven into Obama Inaugural Activities,' *Washington Post*, 6 November.

Schudson, M. (1982) 'The Politics of Narrative Form: The Emergence of News Conventions in Print and Television,' *Daedalus*, 3, 97–112.

Schudson, M. (2008) *Why Democracies Need an Unlovable Press*. Cambridge: Polity.

Schwartz, B. (2000) *Abraham Lincoln and the Forge of National Memory*. Chicago: University of Chicago Press.

Scroggie, William Graham (1903) *The Unity of the Old and New Testaments*. Denton, TX: Charles E. Stolfus.

Skrentny, J. (2002) *The Minority Rights Revolution*. Cambridge, MA: Harvard University Press.

Tajfel, H. (1968) 'Social and Cultural Factors in Perception,' in G. Lindzey and E. Aronson (eds) *The Handbook of Social Psychology*, Vol. 3, 2nd edn. Reading, MA: Addison-Wesley, pp. 315–94.

Tenenboim-Weinblatt, K. (2009) 'Rethinking Truth Through Truthiness,' in B. Zelizer (ed.) *The Changing Faces of Journalism: Tabloidization, Technology, and Truthiness*. London: Routledge, pp. 101–3.

Tuchman, G. (1978) *Making News: A Study in the Construction of Reality*. New York: Free Press.

Weaver, D., Beam, R., Brownlee, B., Voakes, P. and Wilhoit, G. (2007) *The American Journalist in the 21st Century: U.S. News People at the Dawn of a New Millennium*. Mahwah, NJ: Erlbaum Associates.

Wills, G. (1992) *Lincoln at Gettysburg: The Words That Changed America*. New York: Simon & Schuster.

Zandberg, E., Meyers, O. and Neiger, M. (2012) 'Past Continuous: Newsworthiness and the Shaping of Collective Memory,' *Critical Studies in Media Communication*, 29, 65–79.

Zelizer, B. (2008) 'Why Memory's Work on Journalism does not Reflect Journalism's Work on Memory,' *Memory Studies*, 1, 79–87.

14

Historical Authority and the 'Potent Journalistic Reputation': A Longer View of Legacy-Making in American News Media

Carolyn Kitch

The peak moment of American journalism's power and prestige is debatable, but many observers would be likely to place it somewhere in the middle decades of the twentieth century, a time when a handful of high-profile newsmen and major news institutions had the visibility, resources and reach to make them important historic actors. In his 1969 book *The Kingdom and the Power*, Gay Talese described the influence of the one news institution he held above all:

> ... each day, barring labor strikes or hydrogen bombs, it would appear in 11,464 cities around the nation and in all the capitals of the world, 50 copies going to the White House, 39 copies to Moscow, a few smuggled into Beijing, and a thick Sunday edition to the foreign minister in Taiwan, because he required the *Times* as necessary proof of the earth's existence, a barometer of its pressure, an assessor of its sanity. If the world did indeed still exist, he knew, it would be duly recorded each day in the *Times*.
>
> (Talese, 1969: 72)

This tribute to the *New York Times* is recited in the narration of *Page One: Inside the New York Times*, a 2011 documentary film by Andrew Rossi in which the newspaper's media reporters discuss the current 'crisis' in newspaper journalism. Talese's words are read over film from a 1954 episode of Alistair Cooke's weekly television program *Omnibus*, which he introduces by saying: 'This is the beehive, the central office, the city room. Here, an avalanche of news is shaped into Monday morning's newspaper.' We see *Times* reporters and editors gather around a table at what is presumably a page-one meeting in 1954, a scene that will be repeated seven minutes later into the film, a page-one meeting in 2010. In an interview conducted for this segment, Talese remembers the power of the newspaper when he worked there during the 1950s and 1960s: 'NBC, CBS, ABC – the first thing they'd do in the morning, the directors of their shows would look at *The New York Times*, and if *The New York Times* had a story about such-and-such in a faraway place, the networks would think, "Ah, now we'll send Walter Cronkite over there"' (*Page One*, 2011).

Here is a memory not only of a great institution in its glory days, but also of a historic moment when newspapers were threatened by a new medium, television, which would challenge the authority and viability of print journalism. The *Times* weathered that threat, Talese reminds us, by continuing to influence all other news sources, even Walter Cronkite. Just as its documentary filmmakers are compared to Talese's 'behind-the-scenes look' at this newspaper four decades earlier, *Page One* is less about the current crisis facing journalism in general than it is a tribute to the *Times*: in ways that will be discussed later in this chapter, it is a memory text meant to shape future recollection of the *Times*'s place in history right now.

A growing body of scholarship contends that ideas about the past are central to ideas about journalistic authority. This chapter suggests, more specifically, that they underlie branding strategies and boundary-drawing at times of competitive flux in the news industry, and, more generally, that they do so in ways that use *ideas about time* (not only the past) in sometimes complex ways. In today's climate, proud references to yesterday are often really about tomorrow, a prescriptive future into which certain kinds of reporting *should* endure.

Within today's 'crisis' dialogue, 'legacy' news media increasingly turn to history – their own and the world's – as confirmation of their lasting importance in a fractured and uncertain media landscape. Yet this is not a new phenomenon. Indeed, it was through claims of historic significance that many such institutions established their legacies in the first place.

This chapter considers how memory has served American news media over time in related and yet evolutionary ways. In the early republic, as the function and form of journalism were still emerging, newspapers and magazines made frequent references to both the future and the past, describing an 'American history' that was in fact quite recent. This content was common in the periodicals that most successfully established major news brands within an expanding race for mass-circulation audiences. The twentieth century saw the rise and dominance of what we still recognize as today's mainstream news media, whose authority and influence were symbolized by iconic reporters and broadcasters. In recent years, however, those same institutions have turned to summary journalism and reminiscence about their own great pasts as their technological and economic models are failing; in the meantime, new forms of journalism are staking their own claims to public memory and historic importance.

Surveying two centuries of American journalism, this chapter offers a longer view of the strategic uses of memory by news media, first, during an initial pursuit of cultural and commercial prominence, second, throughout a period of influence and dominance, and finally, in the present struggle for relevance and survival.

The quest for prominence: branding memory and nation in a new commercial marketplace

Early American newspapers and magazines frequently contained historical essays, in part because of their didactic purpose. Yet content that drew upon shared memory also became a way for emerging periodicals to establish their editorial authority by defining a new national identity – and, as the press became an industry like others during the Industrial Revolution, to establish their brand names and sell their products.

In his study of the civic functions of journalism in early America, David Nord identifies one early date when newspapers drew upon the country's brief history in order to characterize 'American' identity: 4 July 1826, the fiftieth anniversary of the signing of the Declaration of Independence and the day on which both Thomas Jefferson and John Adams died. 'This "double apotheosis" of "twin sons of liberty", this "setting of two suns" on the same historic day, was an astonishingly providential and national event,' Nord writes. 'As the news slowly spread from Quincy and Monticello throughout the land, Americans were awakened by their own past' (2001: 89). In their own study of nineteenth-century American journalism, Betty Winfield and Janice Hume found extensive references to the country's past, telling 'an American story worth remembering at a time of nation-building' (2007: 120). The relationship between news and history was a symbiotic one: 'History served a newsworthy purpose,' they observe (2007: 151).

Historic content also served a commercial purpose, during a 'market revolution ... [that] encouraged the press to sell itself in new ways, and newspapers began to market and promote themselves aggressively,' becoming 'arguably the first branded commodities' (Barnhurst and Nerone, 2001: 106, 71). As Barnhurst and Nerone note, the most prominent national brands in the mid-nineteenth century represented a new form of journalism, 'illustrated news,' made possible by techno-logical advances in printing and engraving. By the end of the American Civil War, nearly a quarter of a million readers 'saw' the great events of their day through the illustrations of *Harper's Weekly*, which called itself, in its nameplate, 'A Journal of Civilization.' Its ornate imagery, suitable for framing, made heavy memorial gestures, from the radiant, wheat-bearing, winged angel on its cover titled 'Peace: Fourth of July, 1865' (8 July 1865) to its four-color 1897 'Inauguration Number' cover after the election of President William McKinley (13 March 1897). When McKinley was assassinated four years later, another winged angel reached out between busts of Lincoln and Garfield to welcome him to the 'Hall of Martyrs' (14 September 1901: 909).

By the turn of the twentieth century, competition for mass audiences drove New York City's daily newspapers into a 'moral war,' pitting 'decent' papers against William Randolph Hearst's *New York Journal* and Joseph Pulitzer's *New York World*. In particular, the *New York Times*, resuscitated by Adolph Ochs, 'used them as a foil in promoting itself .... with the slogan "It does not soil the breakfast cloth"'(Schudson, 1978: 112). Yet if the *Times* ultimately won the moral war, its competitors during this era won the commercial war, in part through grand gestures toward nation-building and memory. Among Pulitzer's various editorial campaigns was an 1885 fundraising appeal to complete a base so that the Statue of Liberty could, in Pulitzer's words, 'stand upon an American pedestal, and then be referred to for a very long time with more senti-ment than we can now dream of.' Biographer James McGrath Morris adds that this 'public service also turned out to be good for business. The *World*'s circulation soared. ... its Sunday edition was the largest in size and in circulation of any newspaper published in the United States' (2010: 236–7).

The 'yellow papers' each reached a daily circulation of nearly a mil-lion during their sensational coverage of the 1898 sinking of the USS Maine. This well-traveled tale in journalism history – 'You furnish the pictures, and I'll furnish the war,' publisher William Randolph Hearst supposedly cabled to his illustrator, Fredric Remington – 'almost cer-tainly is apocryphal,' writes W. Joseph Campbell (2001: 16). Within this folklore, however, is a very real example of the strategic use of memo-rial rhetoric by news media vying for a mass audience. Fueled by the newspapers' erroneous reports that Spain had torpedoed the ship and by their somber tributes to the dead, a cottage industry of memorial emerged, as the phrase 'Remember the Maine!' circulated in songs and speeches and on postcards, paperweights and collectible plates.

Fifteen years later, newspapers recalled the brief Spanish-American War as the unifying force that had healed the sectarian divisions of the Civil War. This point was made in coverage of the 1913 reunion of some 50,000 Union and Confederate soldiers in Gettysburg, PA, on the fiftieth anniversary of the battle that had taken place there. 'What had been, in 1863, a battle in which the country was perhaps the most divided it had ever been, became, 50 years later, a vivid example of military valor – a gift to posterity,' writes Jared Brey, adding, 'the very soldiers who had tried to kill each other half a century before ... were accompanied by reporters, who covered their every conversation and handshake' (2011: 3–4). Those reporters rewrote the story of the war, celebrating rituals that recast all of the soldiers as patriotic. Such uncontroversial memory served the commercial interests of the newspapers while creating a sense of national stability in a modern era.

The era's top-circulation magazine, the *Saturday Evening Post*, similarly hoped to inspire 'a sense of nationalism strong enough to override America's regional differences' (Cohn, 1995: 2) at a time of intense competition for national audiences within the booming magazine industry. In its articles, fiction and artwork, the weekly *Post* regularly ran historical features, recounted national folklore and offered nostalgic imagery of small-town and rural life. In 1916, editor George Lorimer hired a young illustrator named Norman Rockwell who became key to this enterprise, and in 1918 the *Post* became the first magazine to pass the two-million circulation mark.

Such popular nostalgia competed on newsstands with a new kind of magazine journalism that would also employ grand ideas about history – and American identity – in its editorial favor. Based on the premise that, in the modern era, there was too much news to keep up with and too little 'time which busy men are able to spend on simply keeping informed,' the new *Time* magazine promised to 'organize the world's news and give it to readers in short, easily digestible doses' (Tebbel and Zuckerman, 1991: 160). From its 1923 launch, *Time* functioned as an 'aggregator' (Skok, 2012: 47) while also summarizing and repackaging its own content. It initiated its 'Man of the Year' tradition in 1927, choosing aviator Charles Lindbergh 'as a way to justify a reprise of the biggest news story of the year' (Elson, 1968: 167).

In the early 1930s, *Time* began extending its brand through other media, producing programs titled *The March of Time* in radio and newsreel formats. 'On a thousand fronts the history of the world moves swiftly forward,' began the 6 March 1931 debut of the weekly radio series (Elson, 1968: 178). The prospectus for the newsreel series, launched in 1935, lent *Time*'s brand reputation to a lesser medium: 'the status of the Newsreel can be revolutionized,' wrote editor Henry Luce with ceremonious capitalization, 'as soon as the public realizes that the Newsreel has become a product of Journalism, produced and morally and intellectually underwritten by one or more potent Journalistic reputations' (Elson, 1968: 230–1).

Figures of dominance: the mythic twentieth-century newsman as 'witness to history'

Time's 'Man of the Year' (later to become 'Person of the Year') issues formalized a narrative trend that had begun in mass-circulation magazines such as *McClure's* and *The Saturday Evening Post*: telling history in terms of the 'great men' who made it. Interestingly, this gallery of popular history-makers quickly came to include not only those who made the news, but also the men who covered the news – who 'brought history' to a national audience. This conflation was especially striking during World War II, although it survived into the later twentieth century.

Journalism's own historical narrative is peppered with characters – prescient publishers, crusading muckrakers and courageous eyewitnesses – who are widely understood to have been historical agents themselves. Because of their unusual foresight into the country's future or their unflinching documentation of its unfolding present, these people are remembered as having 'made' history or changed the course of history. Such news heroes can become 'archetypical figures' who are representative of the lasting meaning of 'critical incidents' that enable 'journalists [to] redefine boundaries of professional practice' (Zelizer, 1992: 67).

Henry Luce was one such archetypal figure, drawing attention to himself and his various news media by making bold proclamations about America's role in the world. He did so most famously in an editorial he published in February 1941 in *Time*'s corporate sibling, the weekly picture-magazine *Life*. Titled 'The American Century', this essay contended not just that the country must enter the European war but that the time had come 'to be the powerhouse from which [American] ideals spread throughout the world' (Luce, 1944: 65). *Life*'s cultural authority was established during that war, when it published photographs that today are taken for granted as iconic, including staff photographer Robert Capa's blurry pictures of soldiers in the water during the D-Day landings of June 1944, in which he himself took part. Later that summer, *Life*'s cover contained a different kind of iconic image of the war which would also survive in memory: an anonymous American soldier grasping his rifle and gazing determinedly upward (the caption read 'In Normandy', *Life*, 14 August 1944). Like Capa's documentary images, this symbolic image would be reprinted in later anniversary and summary journalism, including *Life*'s own commemorative issue (2004), co-produced by the History Channel and marking the sixtieth anniversary of D-Day.

Throughout the war, American journalism constructed a memory ideal of the typical soldier, and out of this news rhetoric would emerge a new, heroic type of newsman as well. Both figures would feature in the mid-twentieth-century reporting of news organizations that were trying either to maintain or to gain authority in an increasingly diverse media world.

Like Robert Capa, Scripps-Howard newspaper reporter Ernie Pyle and *Stars and Stripes* cartoonist Bill Mauldin experienced the war alongside American infantrymen. Mauldin, who was a soldier, comically sketched the miserable conditions of soldiers' day-to-day lives through two cartoon characters named Willie and Joe, while Pyle described his companions as 'the mud-rain-frost-and-wind boys ... the guys that wars can't be won without' (1943). Pyle's descriptions of infantrymen were not glorious – he wrote of their 'inhuman exhaustion' – but, like Mauldin's drawings, they were always tributes to the ordinary soldiers' extraordinary courage. Pyle himself became a celebrated hero and was widely mourned when he was killed in Japan just four months before the war's end. Both men won the Pulitzer Prize for their wartime work, which was quickly republished in book form; Pyle's book, *Brave Men*, also became the basis for a 1945 Hollywood film, *The Story of G.I. Joe*. Appearing in hundreds of newspapers, these syndicated columns and cartoons were central to the construction of public memory even while the war was still under way. Their popularity reaffirmed the importance and impact of newspaper journalism at a time when that industry was threatened by competition from radio news (Jackaway, 1995).

Yet radio's credibility as a news medium also increased during the war, in part due to the reporting of Edward R. Murrow, who braved the Blitz to report live from London, and flew on Allied bombing missions; a decade later, he huddled in the cold with soldiers stationed at the front during the Korean War for the Christmas 1952 episode of his weekly television news program *See It Now*. Murrow is a key figure in journalistic professional memory chiefly because of the 1954 episode in which he castigated Senator Joseph McCarthy, concluding with an editorial that drew on memory and national ideals: quoting Shakespeare and invoking the patriots of the American Revolution, he urged viewers to 'dig deep into our history and our doctrine, and remember that we are not descended from fearful men' (Murrow, 1954). This scene has survived in popular memory and was dramatically reenacted by actor David Strathairn half a century later in the 2005 Hollywood biopic *Good Night and Good Luck*, named for Murrow's sign-off line.

During the 1960s, 'And that's the way it is' was the phrase that closed the *CBS Evening News* in its new half-hour nightly format anchored by Walter Cronkite. In his own era, Cronkite helped to establish the credibility and power of television news by 'bringing' to audiences the great events of history; in later memory, as Matt Carlson notes, Cronkite became 'fused ... with the events he covered into a common experience shared by millions of viewers' (Carlson, 2012: 492). Long after he was off the air as a newsman, Cronkite appeared in historical documentaries, one titled *Walter Cronkite: Witness to History*, and provided audio-essays of reminiscences for National Public Radio. When he died in 2009, the *New York Times* called him 'a proxy for a nation' and editorialized that 'his death is like losing the last veteran of a world-changing war' (Klinkenborg, 2009: A18). Curiously, that metaphor drew on a memory narrative that had been popularized not by Cronkite but by one of his successors, NBC News anchor Tom Brokaw.

Brokaw's rhetorical star rose, initially, alongside that of President Ronald Reagan, whose frequently televised speeches were threaded with nostalgia, references to historic figures and patriotic tributes to heroes. When in 1984 he saluted the Allied troops on the fortieth anniversary (and on the site) of the D-Day landings, Reagan's words echoed the homespun language of Ernie Pyle. Also in Normandy for this reunion of soldiers was Brokaw, who interviewed survivors and narrated an hour-long special titled *D-Day – Plus 40 Years*. Most of that program was a historical account of the invasion, but it ended with Brokaw's summary of the lasting meaning of the event. Standing in the American Cemetery above Omaha Beach, he said of the veterans:

> The passage of time has softened those memories, even the painful memories. The terrible personal sacrifices were cushioned by a common purpose, shared values unquestioned. What comes through is the innocence, the goodness of those days. The war was not the same after D-Day, and neither were we.
>
> (NBC, 1984)

This report was made only two years after Brokaw had become NBC's evening news anchor and just a year after the end of Cronkite's career.

Brokaw would carry this historic banner forward for more than two decades. He spoke on behalf of history in coverage of other major events of the 1980s, such as the fall of the Berlin Wall in 1989 (NBC, 1989), when he anchored a program titled *Freedom Night*. But it was his series of tributes to the veterans of World War II – another special report on the fiftieth anniversary of D-Day, his 1998 bestselling book *The Greatest Generation*, later the basis for a television program, and two further books – that transformed him into a national public historian. Brokaw's non-fiction characters, real veterans, were paralleled in fiction by the characters of Steven Spielberg's blockbuster film *Saving Private Ryan*. Debuting in the same year, these two texts together reconstructed Ernie Pyle's 'mud-rain-frost-and-wind boys.' When the veterans reunited on the National Mall in 2004 for the dedication of the World War II Memorial, they were saluted jointly by Tom Brokaw and Tom Hanks, the actor who had played the everyman-soldier who saved Private Ryan. At the start of the twenty-first century, the paired symbolic figures of the ordinary soldier and the authoritative newsman were once again in the foreground of public memory.

The battle for survival: elite voices in the construction of future memory

Within the journalism industry, however, the dominance of the twentieth century's major players was eroding, the outcome of factors including changes in news-media ownership and news-consumption patterns as well as competition from a new technology, the Internet. In television news, this shift was temporarily masked by the continuing prominence of famous newsmen, all of whom had been at the anchor desk since the early 1980s. Kimberly Meltzer notes that even though 'Brokaw, Jennings and Rather presided over the greatest erosion in network evening news ratings ever .... [t]heir long tenures presented a veneer of stability to what otherwise was a period of unprecedented change in the national news landscape' (2010: 178).

In fact, during the 1980s and 1990s, the national broadcast news networks faced new competition from 24-hour cable news channels, while their budgets and bureaus were slashed. Afternoon newspapers began folding, chain ownership became the norm, and circulation was declining steadily, prompting one media consultant to warn that 'something fundamental is happening to many American newspapers' (Morton, 1999: 96). Meanwhile, *Time* magazine had 'lost its leading role in opinion leadership' as its focus shifted toward 'covers on cats, cholesterol or cocktails,' contends James Baughman (1998: 121, 123). *Life* had ceased to be a news weekly, transitioning to a feature-photo monthly and then folding in 2000, even though its famous brand continued to appear on historical books and on special issues designated as 'commemorative.'

Given its vast photo archives, *Life* was especially well suited to the creation of memory products looking back on the twentieth century, issuing two hardcover books, titled *Our Century in Pictures* and *Century of Change*. Their editor, Richard Stolley, who as a young reporter had been instrumental in the magazine's coverage of the Kennedy assassination, described the first book as 'a keepsake, a provoker of memories' and as 'a personal photo album' (2000: vii). Century summaries were abundant across legacy media organizations, some of which worked together and lent authority to each other. CBS broadcast a series of programs presenting the historic figures named by *Time* magazine as the most important people of the century; when this, too, became a book, *People of the Century*, CBS anchor Dan Rather wrote in the introduction that 'the rough draft of history now has a smoother, more definitive shape' (Rather and Isaacson, 2000: 19). For ABC News, Peter Jennings anchored a set of special programs, collectively titled *The Century*, recalling iconic events that had 'defined' America; these were later broadcast on the History Channel (ABC's corporate sibling) and inspired a book.

Such productions were evidence of twin imperatives driving the major players in American journalism as they entered the twenty-first century: to assert their professional and cultural status by enlisting high-profile journalists to explain key events and define national identity, and to extend their corporate brands. These are related concerns: the brand certifies the authority of legacy news media in the current competitive environment, yet it was the previous authority of those news media that built the brand. Thus today's legacy news organizations recycle and repackage their past work, and their current journalism is full of references to their own institutional history, as well the great moments of history more generally.

As they have in the past, these strategies escalate in coverage of disasters, wars and national ceremonies. In a special report on Hurricane Katrina on 9 September 2005, *Dateline NBC* closed with remarks from Tom Brokaw, who recalled that New Orleans had manufactured the 'Higgins boats' that had gone ashore in Normandy on D-Day and concluded that the city's recovery 'will require the same spirit that prevailed in World War II – sacrifice and common purpose.' Historic references and commemorative products poured forth from America's leading news organizations in 2009 when Barack Obama was inaugurated as the first African-American US President. Both the *Washington Post* and the *New York Times* reprinted their own coverage in hefty hardcover books. In his introduction to the *Times*'s commemorative offering, titled *Obama: The Historic Journey*, editor Bill Keller – in phrasing reminiscent of Henry Luce's embrace of the newsreel – called the company's multi-media coverage 'one organic journalistic endeavor, produced by the same expert cast' (2009: 16). The television news networks similarly repackaged their coverage in DVDs with titles such as *A Moment in History* (ABC). Within weeks of taking the oath of office, Barack Obama was already in the history books – the popular ones – bearing the logos of the nation's leading news organizations.

Six months later, Obama returned the favor, serving as mourner-in-chief at the televised memorial service for Walter Cronkite in 2009. Surrounded by the dignitaries of American journalism, the President credited Cronkite with 'calmly and authoritatively telling us what we needed to know' and providing 'a voice of certainty' conveying 'the truth, unvarnished and accompanied by theater or spectacle.' He contrasted Cronkite's 'simple values' with the current 'age of dwindling attention spans and omnipresent media' and wondered: 'Would he have been able to cut through the murky noise of the blogs and the tweets and the sound bites to shine the bright light on substance?' (CBS News, 2009).

Much as Norman Rockwell's cover art had recalled a pastoral nine-teenth century in the distressingly urban early twentieth century, Obama's eulogy recalled a more 'certain' and central kind of journalistic authority in the distressingly fragmented media world of the early twenty-first century. His comparison was an unflattering statement about current journalism, and he made it to a large crowd of journalists, but his remarks were enthusiastically applauded. This audience was, after all, full of the country's top news people from its most elite institutions. Obama's criticism was not of those legacy media but of their competitors, and he ended his eulogy with a call for 'the kind of journalism [Cronkite] embodied', urging journalists to 'stand up and demand it and resolve to value it once again' (CBS News, 2009).

Across journalism, eulogies to Cronkite were threaded with nostalgia, note Matt Carlson and Dan Berkowitz, who conclude that 'journalists confronted with change cling nostalgically to a glorified and overly sim-plified past' (2012: 422). Yet this nostalgia did not indicate a wish to return to the past; it was a wish to bring the past into the present. Journalism's history was recalled in order to take back journalistic authority – by dis-tinguishing, in the present, between the truth and 'spectacle,' between the calm 'voice of certainty' and the 'murky noise' of pretenders.

The tributes to Cronkite are further evidence of the extent to which current professional discourse, while nostalgic, is full of pointed references to elite journalism's greatest moments. For the tenth anniversary of the September 11th attacks, NBC News reconvened its reporters who had covered that day to remember their role as journalists in the telling of this story over time. This program, titled 'In Our Own Words,' is still available for purchase online, as are nearly all of the Obama and century-summary products. Brokaw's 'Greatest Generation' books and DVDs are available in the online NBC Store alongside a DVD titled *Deep Throat: The Full Story of Watergate*, in which, according to the on-site blurb, 'Tom Brokaw goes straight to the source: *Washington Post* reporter Bob Woodward' to provide 'a definitive look at a crucial moment in American history'. In 2012, on the fortieth anniversary of the Watergate break-in, *The Washington Post* republished its Watergate coverage as an e-book for the Kindle, with a new foreword written by Bob Woodward and Carl Bernstein.

Bernstein resurfaces in the *Page One* documentary, which begins with clips of television news reports of the deaths of newspapers across the country and the question posed by *Times* media reporter David Carr of 'what's going to happen at *The New York Times*?' Carr is among the paper's present-day journalists who speculate about the future of newspapers while also debating how they should handle the media-related stories that they are covering at the time. The latter episodes provide a fascinating mix of dismissals of other news providers. Throughout the film we see Carr working on a story that will topple the Tribune Company CEO, a former radio advertising executive who expressed open contempt for his newspaper journalists in Chicago and Los Angeles. In other segments, *Times* journalists compare the paper's decision to publish the Wikileaks documents to its 1971 publication of the Pentagon Papers, and they criticize the NBC Nightly News for broadcasting an unconfirmed report that the United States was ending combat operations in Iraq ('If it is a story, it's that television decided to declare it a dramatic moment,' says Washington Bureau Chief Dean Baquet). And then suddenly Carl Bernstein is on camera, recalling Watergate, a seeming non sequitur in a documentary about the *New York Times*. He is followed by yet another outsider, *New Yorker* editor David Remnick, speaking about the subsequent 'diminishment' of the *Washington Post* and adding, 'if that were to happen in any serious way to *The New York Times*, that would be a terrible tragedy' (*Page One*, 2011). The film ends on a positive note, in a newsroom scene somewhat reminiscent of the ending of *All the President's Men*, as editor Bill Keller ascends stairs to announce the paper's receipt of Pulitzer Prizes for 2010. 'Journalism', he tells his assembled staff, 'is alive and well.'

Conclusion: the possible futures of legacy-making

In the end, *Page One* is itself fundamentally a memory text, a story ostensibly about the present that really is about future memory of the present when it is the past. Not only its historic segment but also its elite interviewees marshal memory in service of journalism's most elite institution. Should the *Times*, or its paper version, not survive the crisis, the present moment in history may indeed one day be recalled as a 'tragedy', its passing heralded as – in the *Times*'s own words in its eulogy of Cronkite – the death of 'the last veteran of a world-changing war.'

Or by then the sands of authority may have shifted in favor of other news brands that manage to acquire (in Henry Luce's wording) their own 'potent journalistic reputations.' Ironically, the seeming nemeses of today's legacy news media, digital news platforms, are, as a result of their storage and design capacities, especially well-suited to the preservation and communication of memory and history. The circulation of their content can blur authorship, and therefore authority as well. Yet certainly the media technologies we still call 'new' already have proven to be powerful 'eyewitnesses to history,' which they can redistribute indefinitely; they have also become adept at calling upon shared memories to draw audiences to their brands.

Twitter and Facebook, which began as purely social media, are now increasingly accepted as vehicles for journalism, especially after their widely acknowledged 'historic' role in covering the revolutions of the 2011 'Arab Spring.' Public mourning and memorial after tragedies – once the province of major newspapers, national news magazines and evening television news specials ceremoniously featuring famous anchors – now occur online, where photo galleries and remembrance books are archived. Nevertheless, most Americans still access online news through the websites of the legacy news institutions which rose to prominence and dominance in the previous century (Pew, 2012).

Tomorrow's dominant brands in journalism may include familiar names as well as new ones. And even in the face of rapid technological change, the past landscape of media memory suggests that those news organizations' success will lie partly in their ability to stake a claim to 'history,' to provide authoritative explanations of the passage of time. Like *Harper's Weekly* a century and a half ago, they will need to offer audiences a new definition of 'Civilization' as they construct repositories and communities of memory for the future.

References

Barnhurst, K.G. and Nerone, J. (2001). *The Form of News: A History.* New York: Guilford Press.

Baughman, J.L. (1998) 'The Transformation of *Time* Magazine,' *Media Studies Journal*, 12(3), 120–7.

Brey, J.D. (2011) '"The Dead Issues of a Dead Past": Newspaper Commemorations of the Battle of Gettysburg,' paper presented to the American Journalism Historians Association, 7 October, Kansas City, MO.

Campbell, W.J. (2001) 'You Furnish the Legend, I'll Furnish the Quote,' *American Journalism Review*, 23(10), 16.

Carlson, M. (2012) 'Rethinking Journalistic Authority: Walter Cronkite and Ritual in Television News,' *Journalism Studies*, 13(4), 483–98.

Carlson, M. and Berkowitz, D. (2012) 'Twilight of the Television Idols: Collective Memory, Network News, and the Death of Walter Cronkite,' *Memory Studies*, 5(4), 410–24.

CBS News (2009) 'Obama's Tribute to Cronkite,' 9 September, available at http://wwww.cbsnews.com/video/watch/?id=5297808n (accessed 21 June 2012).

Cohn, J. (1995) *Covers of* The Saturday Evening Post*: Seventy Years of Outstanding Illustration from America's Favorite Magazine*. New York: Viking.

Elson, R.T. (1968) *Time Inc.: The Intimate History of a Publishing Enterprise, 1923–1941*. New York: Atheneum.

Jackaway, G.L. (1995) *Media at War: Radio's Challenge to the Newspapers, 1924–1939*. Westport, CT: Praeger.

Keller, B. (2009) 'Introduction,' *The New York Times: Obama: The Historic Journey*. New York: Callaway, pp. 16–19.

Klinkenborg, V. (2009) 'Walter Cronkite,' *New York Times*, 20 July, A18.

Luce, H.R. (1944) 'The American Century,' *Life*, 17 February, 61–5.

Meltzer, K. (2010) *TV News Anchors and Journalistic Tradition: How Journalists Adapt to Technology*. New York: Peter Lang.

Morris, J.M. (2010) *Pulitzer: A Life in Politics, Print, and Power*. New York: HarperCollins.

Morton, J. (1999) 'Bad News about Newspaper Circulation,' *American Journalism Review*, 21(6), 96.

Murrow, E.R. (1954) 'A Report on Sen. Joseph R. McCarthy.' *See It Now*, CBS, 9 March.

NBC (1984) 'D-Day – Plus 40 Years.' 6 June, available at http://tvnews.vanderbilt.edu (accessed 19 July 2012).

NBC (1989) 'The Berlin Wall Falls 1989 NBC Coverage Pt2,' YouTube, uploaded 10 November 2009, available at http://www.youtube.com/watch?v=y-9_uQx6IsQ&feature=relmfu (accessed 19 July 2012).

Nord, D. (2001) *Communities of Journalism: A History of American Newspapers and Their Readers*. Urbana and Chicago: University of Illinois Press.

The Pew Research Center's Project for Excellence in Journalism (2012) 'State of the News Media 2012: An Annual Report on American Journalism,' available at stateofthemedia.org (accessed 22 December 2012).

Pyle, E. (1943) 'The God-Damned Infantry,' Indiana University School of Journalism, 2 May, available at http://journalism.indiana.edu/resources/erniepyle/wartime-columns/the-god-damned-infantry/ (accessed 25 June 2012).

Rather, D. and Isaacson, W. (2000) *People of the Century: One Hundred Men and Women Who Shaped the Last One Hundred Years.* New York: Simon & Schuster.

Schudson, M. (1978) *Discovering the News: A Social History of American Newspapers.* New York: Basic Books.

Skok, D. (2012) 'The Wide Web of Innovation: Aggregation is Deep in Journalism's DNA,' *Nieman Reports*, 66(1), 47.

Stolley, R. (ed.) (2000) *Life: Our Century in Pictures.* New York: Bulfinch Press.

Talese, G. (1969) *The Kingdom and the Power.* New York: World Publishing.

Tebbel, J. and Zuckerman, M.E. (1991) *The Magazine in America, 1741–1990.* New York: Oxford University Press.

Winfield, B.H. and Hume, J. (2007) 'The Continuous Past: Historical Referents in Nineteenth-Century American Journalism,' *Journalism and Communication Monographs*, 9(3), 119–74.

Zelizer, B. (1992) 'CNN, the Gulf War, and Journalistic Practice,' *Journal of Communication*, 42(1), 66–81.

15
Argentinean Torturers on Trial: How Are Journalists Covering the Hearings' Memory Work?

Susana Kaiser

Buenos Aires, August 2011, I am attending a hearing. The witness testifying warns: 'The only way for you to enter into a concentration camp and travel to those times is through our memories. And they are imprecise.'[1] This powerful and emotional statement acknowledges the limitations and imprecision of survivors' memories while recognizing that in the absence of confessions from torturers and assassins, the hazy memories of survivors are our only window into what happened inside Argentinean torture chambers three decades ago. Who dares to challenge this statement? The impact of the testimony is obvious in the courtroom. I look around; there aren't many people present and I wonder why all of Argentina isn't here to witness these testimonies. Will people who are not in the courtroom ever know about what is unfolding here? Are journalists covering these trials?

The last Argentine dictatorship (1976–83) left a legacy of 30,000 disappeared people. The systematic abduction, torture and killing of political activists and the kidnapping of babies born in captivity characterized the dictatorship's reign of terror. Human rights abuses included torture of pregnant women and 'death flights' in which living prisoners were thrown into the ocean. The return to civilian rule set precedents with a Truth Commission (1983–84) and trials for members of the military juntas (1985), but these were followed by legalized impunity (1986–87) and presidential pardons (1989–90) for many perpetrators.[2] Unyielding campaigns for justice continued; in 2005 the Supreme Court nullified the impunity laws and hundreds of criminals are now on trial.

I argue that these trials are public spaces for the ongoing writing of memory, arenas for memory battles, and forums where new knowledge and perspectives on state terrorism continually emerge. The testimonies of survivors offer new insights into the human rights violations that occurred and how the repressive apparatus worked. Listening to those who suffered and witnessed atrocities transports us back to the scenes of the crimes, like a time machine propelled by the urgency and unreliability of memory – as the quoted survivor reminds us.

This chapter discusses the performance of memory at the trials and explores how journalists are covering them. Two major questions guide my research: (1) What memory work takes place at the hearings? (2) How do journalists use this raw material of memory? I am interested in the ways in which journalists are capitalizing on this historic opportunity to write revised drafts of a well-known history that is continually being updated. What unfolds at the hearings broadens our understanding of society's complicity in the crimes, including the involvement of the Catholic hierarchy, corporations and civil society. By examining the role of journalists as memory agents, I seek to assess how coverage of the hearings promotes or ignores the memory work taking place. I look at how coverage is influenced by factors including the personal interests and political ideologies of the journalists, the editorial policies and conventions of the media, the newsworthiness of events that happened three decades ago, and the challenges and restrictions journalists face in covering the trials. I explore why coverage is the way it is and what this case study can tell us about the relationship(s) between journalism and memories of state terrorism.

I focus on two trials that took place in the city of Buenos Aires. First, *Megacausa* ESMA 1 ('ESMA 1'), the case against those accused of crimes committed at ESMA (Navy Mechanics School), one of the most notorious centers for torture and extermination; it is estimated that only 200 of the approximately 5,000 people taken there survived. The ESMA 1 trial began in December 2009; the accused were sentenced in October 2011.[3] Second, I examine *Plan Sistemático de Apropiación de Menores* (Systematic Plan for the Appropriation of Children, 'Plan Sistemático'), the case against those responsible for seizing an estimated 500 children as spoils of war. Some were toddlers kidnapped with their parents, but most were born in captivity to prisoners who later disappeared. As of August 2012, the Grandmothers of the Plaza de Mayo, an organization of activist women searching for their grandchildren, had recuperated 106 children. The *Plan Sistemático* trial began in February 2011; the perpetrators were sentenced in July 2012.[4]

These trials take place within a specific historic, mnemonic and political environment that determines their newsworthiness and shapes a new wave of remembering: in these times of rampant impunity, mass human rights abusers being brought to justice is rare. Unlike trials in the International Criminal Court, these trials are taking place where the crimes were committed; criminals are tried for atrocities that happened three decades ago, at great temporal remove, but in a milieu where memories of state terrorism have been under construction for many years.

In spite of their relevance, there is a general media silence around the trials, with coverage usually limited to the lead-up, sentencing and a few key testimonies. This silence matters because without media coverage, the only way to know what happens at the hearings is to be in the courthouse when they are taking place. Broadcasting restrictions contribute to this silence. In 1985, military officers on trial and survivors' accounts were newsworthy, but there was no live broadcasting. News programs showed three minutes of images with a voice-over. Politicians and/or the military imposed the boundaries of media coverage and determined the scope of society's mediated participation. There are also limitations on the current trials. A Supreme Court resolution guarantees the right to broadcast the beginnings and endings of the trials, but allows judges to decide how public the rest of the trials should be. Tribunals may interpret this as permission to allow cameras during testimonies or to prohibit them, as happened in the trials discussed here. This restriction is another example of crimes against humanity being tried without the potential of becoming a media event.

In my examination of the media coverage of the trials I analyzed five Buenos Aires publications, including *La Nación*, the establishment newspaper, and *Clarín*, the largest circulating daily. I also examined three pro-human rights publications – the *Página 12* newspaper which celebrated its twenty-fifth anniversary in 2012; *Tiempo Argentino*, a daily founded in 2010; and *Miradas al Sur*, a weekly launched in May 2008. I interviewed five journalists who specialize in human rights issues and work as investigative journalists, editors, authors, professors, bloggers and film producers. They are uniquely qualified to discuss the interactions between journalism and the trials. Alejandra Dandan is the lead reporter covering the trials for *Página 12*, the publication with the best human rights reporting; Julia Izumi is political editor for *Tiempo Argentino*, which allocates two pages daily to coverage of human rights issues; Claudio Martiniuk writes for *Clarín*, teaches the philosophy of law, and has authored a book about ESMA; Ricardo Ragendorfer writes about state terrorism and the trials for *Miradas al Sur* and has worked on numerous films as a researcher and writer; Horacio Verbitsky, a lawyer and top investigative journalist, writes for *Página 12*, has published several books about the dictatorship, and is the director of the Center for Legal and Social Studies (CELS), one of Argentina's leading human rights organizations. Our conversations were not limited to the trials I discuss here or the media where the journalists work, but focused on coverage of the trials in general.

I based my analysis on: (1) ethnographic observation during the ESMA 1 and *Plan Sistemático* hearings in 2010 and 2011; (2) an assessment of these five publications' coverage; and (3) interviews with the journalists. I first introduce the concepts framing my analysis and then discuss what takes place at the hearings. Finally, I look at the coverage in the five publications and conclude with a discussion of journalism's relationship to the trials.

Framing the discussion

Conceptually, I explore the trials as part of a dynamic and ongoing collective memory construction process in which journalists are mediators in the 'witnessing chain,' connecting what happens at the hearings with 'removed recipients' (Blondheim and Liebes, 2009: 112–13); as mediators, they write and shape memories of state terrorism. Central to my analysis is the concept of bearing witness to this historical process. I focus on layers of witnessing and how they shape our reactions to what we witness.

I propose that witnessing as a process demanding action operates according to Liberation Theology's basic schema for assessing what needs to be done – See, Judge, Act. Witnessing has both a passive 'seeing' face and an active 'saying' one (Peters, 2001: 709); several factors determine the judging and acting aspects of witnessing.

Seeing. Peters (2001: 720–1) highlights the relevance of spatial and temporal frameworks, stating that an event's relative distance in space and time determines our perspective on witnessing and how we see. There are multiple perspectives on seeing the trials, including presence in time and space (being there at the courthouse); presence in time but absence in space (watching a simultaneous broadcast of the hearings); and a double absence in space and time (reading a newspaper article or watching a recording of the hearings). Hearings thus have multiple audiences belonging to a 'double-layered structure' of publics – 'local' and 'imagined' (Thomas, 2009: 102). The local public at the courthouse includes judges, lawyers, journalists and the general public; it directly witnesses the testimonies and vicariously witnesses the ordeals of those tortured, assassinated, or disappeared, as remembered by witnesses. Imagined publics witness vicariously through the media, both what happened three decades ago and at the courthouse the day before.

Judging and acting. Witnessing means becoming aware, and it has political consequences: now that you know, what do you do? What motivates people to act rather than to remain passive is critical to analyzing the process of witnessing (Ellis, 2009; Peters, 2001; Rentschler, 2004; Zelizer, 2002). Witnessing traumatic accounts can affect the ways in which both local and imagined publics remember state terrorism. Moreover, layers of witnessing may shape how we recognize and act on our responsibilities in these situations.

Authors (Keats, 2005; Rentschler, 2004; Zelizer, 2002) have theorized about forms of vicarious witnessing, including bearing witness to suffering and imagining the trauma of others through mass mediated representations. If broadcast television is an effective form of communication which turns 'citizens into witnesses of the events of their time' (Ellis, 2009: 73) we need to explore how witnessing state terrorism's atrocities through media affects viewers. Blondheim and Liebes (2009: 125) question whether distance allows viewers to feel free from responsibility for suffering but note that audiences may demand action if they feel closely connected to those whose suffering they witness. In assessing potential effects, we should note that without broadcasts, coverage of the trials discussed is absent in space and time, representing 'layers of non-presence' (Frosh, 2009: 53).

In re-living their trauma, survivor witnesses speak of what they passively observed three decades ago. Publics, local and imagined, passively witness their remembering and may actively communicate what they witness in the form of journalistic coverage, films, or research projects. Witnessing the trials may offer society a better understanding of what happened under state terrorism and why, leading people to reconsider human rights abuses and reflect on their responsibility in the process of accountability.

The potential impact on society is speculative, but we can ask how journalists assume responsibility as witnesses. The legal practice of witnessing has become part of journalism, turning journalists into heirs of legal witnessing (Thomas, 2009: 107; Blondheim and Liebes, 2009: 113). On-site reporters covering the trials are professional witnesses (Ashuri and Pinchevski, 2009: 139), reinforcing a conceptualization of journalism as the practice of bearing witness (Rentschler, 2009: 170).

Journalism's coverage is one mode in which 'seeing' becomes 'saying,' but how does memory enter into what journalists say? Zelizer (2008: 83) argues that journalism invites memory when the past is used to engage with the present and there is simultaneous discussion of present and past, a concept that it is useful to apply when analyzing coverage of the trials. Journalism can focus on the event itself (the trial) with minimal engagement with the past, or it can invite memory to contextualize the reporting, simultaneously addressing the present – the hearings – and the past – the events that occurred under the dictatorship. If journalists write first drafts of history and also its rewrites (Edy, 1999: 71), reporting on the trials combines the writing of both first and revised drafts. What is known about state terrorism is updated by new information and revealed in the memories on which journalists report. By exercising journalism's authority in writing history and memory, journalists can choose to ignore or amplify the memory work that takes place at the hearings and, through their reporting, reinforce particular memory frames. Exploring the coverage reveals how journalists act as professional witnesses and memory agents.

What happens at the hearings?

The trials are public. Anybody can attend. Perpetrators on trial aren't the only ones to blame for 30,000 disappearances. Calveiro (1998) argues that torture chambers are not rare aberrations isolated from the society in which they emerge. We could apply to many Argentineans what Arendt (2004: 97) highlighted in her reporting of Eichmann's trial: 'the degree of responsibility increases as we draw further away from the man who uses the fatal instrument with his own hands.' Through the testimony of witnesses and the defenses of the accused, layers of guilt and responsibility continually emerge; society's interactions and complicities with state terrorism become public – the priest baptizing a baby born in a torture center, the corporate managers denouncing union activists.

The witnesses are survivors, relatives of victims, activists and other people with useful information. They remind us of a terrified and paralyzed society and apparent 'normality' under a state of fear (Kaiser, 2005: 43–81). Torture centers were located in highly populated areas. Survivors mention the 'sounds of normal life' surrounding them, like the noises during breaks at ESMA's next-door trade school. Several testimonies reaffirm the complicities and insanity, in the pathological sense of the term, of the repression – prisoners sharing a barbecue with the torturers' families, the survivor under monitored freedom forced to accompany torturers on a pilgrimage to the Sanctuary of Our Lady of Lourdes, a 'liberated' woman settling in Spain and reporting to an overseas 'parole officer' who owned the most famous disco in Buenos Aires.

Shameless and arrogant perpetrators smile and wave to their supporters. To prove their innocence, lawyers acknowledge the crimes and the conditions under which prisoners were held, and then challenge survivors' testimonies, claiming that victims were blindfolded and unable to observe anything. The lawyers confirm that decisions about who would disappear in the weekly 'death flight' were made on Tuesdays but insist that their clients were not at ESMA during those years. Erasing the phrase 'my client wasn't there' from the record might reveal detailed confessions of the crimes by the perpetrators' own lawyers.

Hearings become political arenas for competing memories, in which survivor witnesses challenge denials and fabrications from the accused. They reveal specifics about sectors that ignored, condoned, or profited from state terrorism, and they create a comprehensive account of what went on inside the torture chambers and their many links with the outside.

How are journalists covering the trials?

As the primary means for society to access what unfolds at these trials, the press has both an opportunity and a responsibility. Here, I discuss its performance by examining coverage of the hearings in *Clarín, La Nación, Página 12, Tiempo Argentino* and *Miradas al Sur*.

Generally, the media speak about the repression without openly defending the dictatorship or directly objecting to the trials, but the production of news implies a selection and encoding process. The various media are distinguishable by the dominant frames of reporting and memories of the dictatorship that they reinforce. Events can be covered with or without alluding to the past or inviting memory to contextualize the significance of the hearings.

Página 12, Tiempo Argentino and *Miradas al Sur* are pro-human rights publications and strong supporters of policies aimed at ending the cycle of impunity. Their coverage of the trials complements other content focused on human rights and the dictatorship and its legacies, but their circulation is much smaller than that of the mainstream newspapers. While *Clarín's* Sunday circulation is around 600,000, *Página 12* sells fewer than 50,000 copies,[5] meaning that powerful human rights messages reach a limited public.

An assessment of the reporting in these publications reveals major differences in the number of articles, the style of coverage, and the way in which articles about the trials are contextualized. I searched the publications' websites using a combination of terms that retrieved articles that referred directly to the trials. I excluded those that mentioned the cases but not the trials themselves. This makes it difficult to identify and evaluate the number of articles. Within these limitations, one example suffices: between 1 November 2009, a month before ESMA 1's start, and 31 October 2011, the month of the sentencing, 162 articles were published in *Página 12*, thirty-one in *Clarín* and twenty-nine in *La Nación*.

Other factors merit consideration. The pro-human rights publications started after the dictatorship was over, so they had no past interactions with state terrorism. Most mass media had a relationship with the dictatorship, either supporting its policies or maintaining silence about its crimes. This complicity is linked to the growth and increased profits of some media conglomerates. Relations with the Kirchner administration, under which the trials are taking place, may also influence journalistic decisions, ranging from avoiding implicating media owners to omitting content that could benefit the government. Dandan (2012a), from *Página 12*, spoke of 'restrictive gazes,' reflected in silences about trials covering issues that incriminated these media.

With exceptions, *Clarín* and *La Nación* offer coverage characterized by wire service style without much analysis. Many articles are unsigned. For Dandan (2012a), the journalist vanishes and the individuality of the reporter attending the hearing becomes a fissure in the medium or is buried by information that doesn't support covering the trials. Martiniuk (2012) however, who writes for *Clarín*, noted that there is no apparatus of editorial censorship and respected journalists often make their points. How *Clarín* and *La Nación* cover sentencing in a particular trial may be shaped more by the specific journalist than by the newspaper's editorial policies.

La Nación may be reviving the 'Two Demons' theory – an explanation that argues that state violence was a response to guerrilla violence. This reinforces an ideological memory frame in which there was a war and both sides committed atrocities. Verbitsky (2012), who writes for *Página 12*, explained that editorials questioning the judicial process argue that leaders of what they call terrorist organizations should also be judged. Editorials and letters to the editor amplify the voices of the perpetrators. Martiniuk (2012) referred to instances in which *La Nación* echoed defense lawyers' arguments that the trials are a farce. *Clarín*'s coverage of a Catholic university professor who participated in torture, for example, reveals a lack of analysis – the article reported important information about a civilian perpetrator but failed to explore the implications of a professor moonlighting as a torturer.

The articles in pro-human rights publications also illustrate major differences.

Miradas al Sur discusses the complicity of corporations such as Editorial Atlántida, a leading publisher, by reprinting magazine articles published during the terror, including one arguing that a toddler captured with her parents (who disappeared) was abandoned by careless subversive parents. This girl, now an adult, explains that publishing this article was the military's condition by which she was given to her biological relatives. There is also the story of ESMA prisoners being hidden on an island owned by the Catholic Church, appropriately named 'The Silence,' during a visit to Argentina by the Inter-American Commission on Human Rights.

Tiempo Argentino emphasizes civilian and corporate complicity. As its political editor Izumi (2012) explained, this prevents the discussion from being limited to the military and what happened inside the torture chambers. There are accounts of a high-ranking Ministry of Economics functionary participating in torture sessions; survivors naming journalists, priests and businessmen who regularly visited ESMA; and corporations such as Ford participating in the torture and disappearance of workers. Reports also focus on testimonies that create precedents for future prosecutions based on the torture of children, sexual violence and rape as crimes against humanity.

Página 12's outstanding coverage is unmatched in terms of number of articles and depth of analysis. Alejandra Dandan, *Página 12*'s main reporter on ESMA 1 and *Plan Sistemático*, regularly attended the hearings. In her articles, ethnographic observations are contextualized by invited memories and investigative journalism. Her work addresses gender and sexual violence, covering testimonies of female prisoners forced to accompany their torturers to restaurants, discos and even on 'vacations' in Mexico; evidence of multiple links between the Catholic hierarchy, military juntas and ESMA's torturers; and discussions of perpetrators combining denials, forgetting and vindications of 'the war they won' in their arguments. Her articles also discuss another facet of society's participation – resistance and solidarity. We know very little about the neighbors who witnessed a military operative and, in spite of their fear, challenged the mandate not to get involved by daring to observe what was happening.

Pro-human rights publications amplify the memory work taking place at the hearings and remind the public of the battles between conflicting versions of the past. Links on their websites weave a net of interrelated articles that expand on the presence of the trials in the daily news. Content is matched by a reporting style that transports readers to the courtroom, allowing them to experience what it's like to 'be there' and overcome layers of absence.

Journalism's relationship with the trials

My interviews with journalists focused on how they fulfill their responsibility in covering the trials, the tasks of activist journalism, restrictions on media coverage, how simultaneous broadcast could change coverage, and the potential use of images.[6] I was also interested in exploring perceptions of how the disclosure of atrocities might affect journalists and audiences, how layers of witnessing shape action, and how coverage of the trials contributes to the writing of memories.

Fulfilling a historical responsibility

Interview subjects agreed that the trials are unveiling extremely important information about the most atrocious crimes in Argentine history but that journalism's response has been relativistic, insignificant and bureaucratic, leading to minimal representation in mass media. They further noted that journalists, as social actors, have a political responsibility to build memory but few fully assume it, instead staying quiet and failing as witnesses to history.

Mainstream media are ignoring the human rights and memory issues highlighted by the trials. Coverage focuses on transcribing the most relevant testimonies and verdicts. For Ragendorfer (2012), from *Miradas al Sur*, this is a missed opportunity. Martiniuk (2012) noted that certain reporting is mediocre, mean, or simply absent, revealing a lack of interest on the part of journalists and the readers they address, including sectors of society for whom human rights are a peripheral concern. The normalization of the judicial process might also contribute to the limited coverage. Verbitsky (2012) mentioned society's acceptance of the fact that crimes of state terrorism are very grave and that those responsible must be judged. The exceptional status of the 1985 trials has passed, reducing the newsworthiness of current trials – except for those in provinces where the process is taking place for the first time and local media coverage is significant.

The lack of coverage means that society, particularly the younger generation, has no access to crucial information. Few are addressing this layer of witnessing. Izumi (2012) noted that the trials open a Pandora's box. They are not just about judging those at the top; a wealth of information is being uncovered, doors are opening, and details keep emerging, particularly from new witnesses. Men who served in the military at the time are being encouraged to speak about what they saw. Neighbors are talking. Dandan (2012a) observed that people testifying for the first time about events that took place in their neighborhoods three decades ago are symbolically opening the door that they obediently closed during military operations. The same state that terrified them, locked them in their homes, and forced them to become accomplices, is now asking them to testify. They sit in the same chairs as the victims and, in some way, accuse the perpetrators from the victims' position. They are actively saying what they once passively saw.

Activist journalism

Covering the trials as a professional witness demands close involvement and commitment and carries responsibility. As already discussed, witnessing the disclosure of atrocities affects journalists covering the hearings – a burden I have felt after a long day of witnessing. These traumatizing effects are similar to those observed in Rentschler's (2009: 167) analysis of journalists as first responders covering disasters, suggesting that 'to witness is to be subject to trauma.' While sensitivity to what we witness doesn't necessarily diminish, the effects on young journalists covering trials for the first time – as first responders in their first encounters with horror – seem to be particularly devastating, reflected in reports that 'bleed' (Dandan, 2012a).

Committed journalists assume the moral responsibility of bearing witness, acting upon it and turning news-making into an 'act of moral responsibility' (Rentschler, 2009: 175) and a 'kind of testimony' (Frosh and Pinchevski, 2009: 2). Interviewees reflected on 'Activist Journalism,' questioning impartiality. Dandan (2012a) quoted Jorge Massetti, founder of *Prensa Latina*, an alternative news organization created in the 1960s: 'We are objective but not impartial. We consider that impartiality is cowardice because you cannot be impartial between good and evil.' This statement guides activist journalists and sets clear parameters for covering the trials. For Dandan, journalists must define the position from which they speak and write. She reports from the perspective of human rights organizations as a contribution to the justice and memory construction processes.

Izumi (2012) believes committed journalists cannot be objective about this genocide; there are no moderate positions on what happened. She insists that it is necessary to cover what is emerging because the media were complicit, with few exceptions, in the generalized silence that prevailed before the impunity laws were nullified. Silence, without a doubt, attests to ideological positions promoting amnesia.

Media witnessing provides many people with primary access to what happens at the hearings; activist journalists are challenged to make people feel like they are in the courtroom. The task is finding ways 'to perforate the courthouse's walls and reach those who would never enter it' (Dandan, 2012b: 16). Activist work includes lobbying for the elimination of broadcast restrictions, applying pressure by being at the courthouse and attesting to the relevance of what happens there, and alerting other journalists when something important is going to occur.

Restrictions on media coverage

We discussed the restrictive way in which the tribunals interpreted the Supreme Court's broadcast resolution. Interviewees mentioned several factors, including the judges' need for total control and their desire not to be observed, which they may believe could impair their authority, and the persistence of anti-democratic practices inherited from the dictatorship. In spite of some gems in the Supreme Court and many brilliant judges, the structure of the judiciary is authoritarian, with pre-democratic ideology and obscure work standards. Judges avoid exposure and can be seen falling asleep during hearings and asking inarticulate questions. Rather than preserving democratic transparency they preserve themselves from public scrutiny. The legal practice of prohibiting witnesses from listening to each other's testimonies is here a bureaucratic excuse. As Verbitsky (2012) noted, many testifying survivors were locked together in the same torture centers and have participated in the same protest marches over the years. It is unlikely that one witness would alter her testimony based on another survivor's testimony.

The mainstream media did nothing to demand broadcasts of the hearings. Without surprise, indignation, or repudiation, they accepted the restrictions. There are different tribunals for each trial; the media could have applied pressure to each one, but such requests have been the sole work of human rights organizations, which lobbied to guarantee and sustain the right of media outlets to broadcast segments of the trials.

Simultaneous broadcast?

How would the media react to a lifting of the broadcast ban? Would television stations cover trials? How might such coverage impact audiences? We discussed many issues, including the media interest in capitalizing on the opportunity presented by the hearings and what they would produce and broadcast.

To Izumi (2012), lifting the broadcast ban would mean that television stations could collect images for a precious archive. Interviewees doubted that networks would broadcast complete trials. Simultaneous broadcasting poses many challenges – hearings are long and can be boring; live coverage might only interest educational channels and specialized cable stations. Verbitsky (2012) speculates that television would broadcast fragments of whatever they considered newsworthy. Dandan (2012a) wondered about possible chain effects if one channel starts broadcasting; if people were given the opportunity to watch and listen to the twenty-three young witnesses, stolen babies who recuperated their identities and testified in *Plan Sistemático,* the impact of these powerful testimonies might persuade the mainstream networks to pay attention.

Would people watch broadcasts? What are the potential effects? Audiences would definitely see sleepy judges and defense lawyers checking their Facebook pages, something I observed, but testimonies witnessed via television could also be very powerful. We know that people forge personal connections with traumatic public pasts (Zelizer, 2002: 697). Society's attitude toward the dictatorship – an old story for many – influences the potential audience for broadcasts of the hearings. Dandan (2012a) argues that those who say 'we've had enough' are the ones who would witness the testimonies and feel ashamed because most of them have never bothered to ask what happened.

The National Institute of Cinematography is filming the trials. We discussed how television programs and documentaries could be powerful carriers for memory. Dandan (2012a) says she would adapt the footage of the trials for television. She proposes focusing on one victim, reconstructing events and gathering testimonies generated around this person, including the stories of new witnesses like friends and neighbors. Izumi (2012) suggested selecting a moving story and building a narrative around one person's testimony, which could be a starting point for different stories, bringing the issues close to the audience in a more engaging way. Journalists committed to witnessing this historic process and assuming responsibility for taking action know what needs to be done, why, and how, and what the potential impact of improved media coverage could be.

Concluding remarks

Coverage of the trials tells us several things about the relationship between journalism and memories of state terrorism. It suggests that in instances of mass human rights violations in polarized societies ideology shapes editorial policies, and the responsibility of bearing witness to history and acting upon it is assumed unevenly.

Trials provide spaces to gain new information. Thirty thousand people don't disappear because a group of military officers take over. By detailing the functioning of state terrorism, activist journalists, as professional witnesses, amplify what unfolds at the hearings, constantly inviting memory to contextualize new information and counter denials with proven facts. These rewrites of history expose the networks of complicities and multiple levels of responsibility, focusing attention on actors beyond those standing trial. In doing so, they also scrutinize society, revealing inconvenient truths for many.

Trials help break silences, and this is why media coverage matters. We need to explore how those who witness vicariously through the media may be prompted to make their memories of this traumatic past public. New testimonies could trigger an overdue discussion of how millions experienced state terrorism. More voices may produce new data to help identify the guilty and responsible and fill in incomplete accounts, adding new patches to the 'quilt of the nation's collective memory' (Gelman, 1998).

Trials are spreading across Argentina. Despite the three decades that have passed, trials in the provinces are generating media interest. In small towns the local newspaper headlines focus on the trials. How this impacts the memory process is a topic for further research. These trials provide case studies for understanding the complexity of the multiple relationships between journalism and memory and exploring how imagined publics decode and use journalists' reports, for we know very little about this layer of witnessing.

As Ernest Renan noted, 'the essence of a nation is that all individuals have many things in common, and also that they have forgotten many things' (in Anderson, 1983: 199). In contemporary Argentina, and in relation to state terrorism, determining what is to be remembered and forgotten is an ongoing struggle in which journalism plays a key role.

Notes

Thanks to Alejandra Dandan, Julia Izumi, Claudio Martiniuk, Ricardo Ragendorfer and Horacio Verbitsky for sharing their expertise and to Andrew Shaffer for his research assistance.

1. Testimony of Miguel D'Agostino, *Plan Sistemático* Trial, 1 August 2011.
2. Law No. 23493, 'Full Stop' (12/23/86) and Law No. 23521, 'Due Obedience (6/4/87); Decrees of pardon Nos. 1002-05 (10/7/89) and Nos. 2741–43 (12/30/90).
3. ESMA 1 tried and convicted 18 perpetrators on 86 counts.
4. Eight perpetrators tried and convicted for 35 cases.

5. IVC figures (entity certifying circulation): *Clarín*: Monday–Sunday, June 2012: 271,147; Sunday, June 2012: 596,443. *La Nación*: Monday–Sunday, July 2012: 167,605; Sunday, July 2012: 359,818. *Miradas al Sur*: Sunday, June 2012: 12,739. The other two publications are not affiliated with IVC so these figures are an average of estimates from different sources. *Página 12*: Monday–Sunday: 35,000; Sunday: 80,000. *Tiempo Argentino:* Monday–Sunday: 6,000; Sunday: 10,000.
6. This section is based on interviewees' opinions. Unless I quote or paraphrase a specific statement, I summarize what I was told, as there was considerable concurrence around several issues.

References

Anderson, B. (1983) *Imagined Communities: Reflections on the Origin and Spread of Nationalism*. New York: Verso.

Arendt, H. (2004) 'From Eichman in Jesusalem: A Report on the Banality of Evil,' in N. Scheper-Hughes and P. Bourgois (eds) *Violence in War and Peace*. Oxford: Blackwell, pp. 91–100.

Ashuri, T. and Pinchevski, A. (2009) 'Witnessing as a Field,' in P. Frosh and A. Pinchevski (eds) *Media Witnessing*. Basingstoke: Palgrave Macmillan, pp. 133–57.

Blondheim, M. and Liebes, T. (2009) 'Archaic Witnessing and Contemporary News Media,' in P. Frosh and A. Pinchevski (eds) *Media Witnessing*. Basingstoke: Palgrave Macmillan, pp. 112–32.

Calveiro, P. (1998) *Poder y Desaparición: Los Campos de Concentración en la Argentina*. Buenos Aires: Colihue.

Dandan, A. (2012a) [Interview by author] Buenos Aires, 9 August.

Dandan, A. (2012b) 'El ojo de la cámara,' *Página 12*, 22 July, 16–17.

Edy, J.A. (1999) 'Journalistic Uses of Collective Memory,' *Journal of Communication*, 49(2), 71–85.

Ellis, J. (2009) 'Mundane Witness,' in P. Frosh and A. Pinchevski (eds) *Media Witnessing*. Basingstoke: Palgrave Macmillan, pp. 73–88.

Frosh, P. (2009) 'Telling Presences: Witnessing, Mass Media, and the Imagined Lives of Strangers,' in P. Frosh and A. Pinchevski (eds) *Media Witnessing*. Basingstoke: Palgrave Macmillan, pp. 49–72.

Frosh, P. and Pinchevski, A. (2009) 'Introduction,' in P. Frosh and A. Pinchevski (eds) *Media Witnessing*. Basingstoke: Palgrave Macmillan, pp. 1–22.

Gelman, J. (1998) 'Del Silencio,' *Página 12*, 13 August, Contratapa.

Izumi, J. (2012) [Interview by author] Buenos Aires, 26 July.

Kaiser, S. (2005) *Postmemories of Terror: A New Generation Copes with the Legacy of the 'Dirty War'*. New York: Palgrave Macmillan.

Keats P.A. (2005) 'Vicarious Witnessing in European Concentration Camps: Imagining the Trauma of Another,' *Traumatology*, 11(3), 171–87.

Martiniuk, C. (2012) [Interview by author] Buenos Aires, 24 July.

Peters, J.D. (2001) 'Witnessing,' *Media, Culture & Society*, 23(6), 707–23.

Ragendorfer, R. (2012) [Interview by author] Buenos Aires, 17 July.

Rentschler, C. (2004) 'Witnessing: US Citizenship and the Vicarious Experience of Suffering,' *Media, Culture & Society*, 26(2), 296–304.

Rentschler, C. (2009) 'From Danger to Trauma: Affective Labor and the Journalistic Discourse of Witnessing,' in P. Frosh and A. Pinchevski (eds) *Media Witnessing*. Basingstoke: Palgrave Macmillan, pp. 158–81.

Thomas, G. (2009) 'Witness as a Cultural Form of Communication: Historical Roots, Structural Dynamics, and Current Appearances,' in P. Frosh and A. Pinchevski (eds) *Media Witnessing*. Basingstoke: Palgrave Macmillan, pp. 89–111.

Verbitsky, H. (2012) [Skype interview by author] 3 July.

Zelizer, B. (2002) 'Finding Aids to the Past: Bearing Personal Witness to Traumatic Public Events,' *Media, Culture & Society*, 24(5), 697–714.

Zelizer, B. (2008) 'Why Memory's Work on Journalism Does not Reflect Journalism's Work on Memory,' *Memory Studies*, 1(1), 79–87.

Epilogue

Paul Connerton

Four nodal points, either explicitly addressed or at least touched upon in this collection, might provoke fruitful discussion in the immediately foreseeable future. They are: the question of globalized memories; the problem of generational memory; the relationship between time and memory; and the representation of death in the news media.

Globalized memories

Volkmer and Lee (Chapter 3) argue that one of the most important lessons journalism has to learn from the contemporary workings of memory is the acknowledgement that journalists now perform their work within a transnational global public sphere. Olick (Chapter 1) agrees that memory in the contemporary period transcends the 'container' of the nation-state, and cites the memory of the Holocaust as an example of the now 'global' or 'cosmopolitan' memory. Contemporary news coverage, however, bears the shadow of past practices; thus Hoskins, in Chapter 11, sees the media coverage of 9/11 as defined by the topos of the Japanese attack on Pearl Harbor in the Second World War in its iconographic rhetoric.

In Chapter 15, a study of trials of those involved in torture under the Argentinean dictatorship, Kaiser indicates how these trials provided a public space where one generation was able to bear witness to the behavior of an earlier generation. Here journalists could capitalize on the historic opportunity of producing a revised draft of a well-known history, even if few journalists in practice fully assumed the task of bearing witness to the crimes of an earlier generation. By contrast with the confrontation of an earlier generation by a later generation, Edy (Chapter 4) observes the incompatibility of memory in the 'same' generation. For, as she points out, it is unlikely that many Americans are aware that Japanese memory of the Second World War is one of victimhood: as their military were preparing to defend their homeland against invasion, their civilians were devastated by a weapon unleashed by white people against non-white people. Here, too, memory communities exist side by side, largely unaware of each other, in part at least because they share no medium in common. Within the smooth functioning of a single national medium, Kitch demonstrates in Chapter 14 the extent to which the work of foremost news journalists provided a focus for a generation's memory: long after he was off the air as a newscaster, Walter Cronkite continued to appear in historical documentaries, and when he died in 2009 the *New York Times* spoke of him as 'a proxy for the nation' and said that 'his death was like losing the last veteran of a world-changing war.' Even the initial establishment of memory studies itself is part of a generational memory. When Zelizer (Chapter 2) speaks of the 'foundational period' of memory studies in the late nineteenth and early twentieth centuries, she cites Halbwachs in sociology, Freud in psychoanalysis, Bartlett in psychology, Bergson and Husserl on the phenomenology of time, Benjamin in literary studies and Warburg in art history: to which cluster of remarkable names one might add that of the French psychologist Pierre Janet, who, on the basis of his study of soldiers who had been involved in the First World War, made an important distinction between narrative memory and traumatic memory.[1] What Zelizer speaks of as the foundational period of memory studies is in fact a generational phenomenon. Just as Joachim Ritter argued, in a seminal article, that the emergence of the historical sciences in the nineteenth century was a form of cultural 'compensation' for the process by which the advance of industrialization consigned earlier traditions to the realm of obsolescence,[2] so one might argue that the foundational period of memory studies, in the late nineteenth and early twentieth centuries, was a further moment of 'compensation' or, perhaps better, a 'reply,' to a later stage in the development of scientific-technical civilization.

In Chapter 7 of this book, Neiger, Zandberg and Meyers make an important intervention on the relationship of memory and time based on their interpretation of the news media coverage of Israel's Holocaust Remembrance Day, established in 1951, which has become over the years one of the dominant rituals of Israel's civil religion. Whereas we commonly think of collective memory as, on the one hand, dealing with shared pasts 'there and then,' and of news, on the other hand, as focusing on information concerning the present 'here and now,' Neiger, Zandberg and Meyers see here an example of a case where temporality works in a contrary direction, since it moves, not from past to present, but from present to past. They speak of this narrative device, therefore, as 'reversed memory.' Reversed memory makes possible the creation of narratives that qualify both as news items and as commemorative tools; here, shared manifestations of the past become an essential ingredient in the 'see it now' discourse of current events news coverage.

The observations of Hariman and Lucaites in Chapter 8 concentrate on photojournalism. Photographic images of leadership, they note, involve hands: hands that vote, salute and pledge allegiance. They also, particularly in representations of dissent, involve hands (or arms) and feet (and boots or shoes). These frequently provide the main focus of photographed demonstration, which ensures that these events are perceived as shaped by the gestural economy of populist movements striving to communicate what would otherwise be unvoiced and unheard. Deceased journalists are also rescued from possible oblivion, as Carlson and Berkowitz observe, by the professional rite in which journalists revisit the careers of their late colleagues through montages of past stories and personal recollections (Chapter 12). The commemoration of deceased journalists provides an opportunity to highlight responsibilities which the mainstream media hold dear; in addition to which the significance of Walter Cronkite was seen in his role as the voice through which so many people were united into an imagined community, as they experienced in common the Kennedy assassination, the moon landing and Watergate.

Cultural memory used to be much discussed in the context of the nation-state. Benedict Anderson (1991) and Ernest Renan (1882) were prominent in these debates. The former argued that print culture, and therefore newspapers, was crucial in the consolidation of national identities; the latter argued, much earlier, that a shared forgetting was at least as important as a shared remembering in integrating a nation. It has become evident more recently, however, that news media act as agents of memory not only in a national setting but also when addressing global events. Bayart (2007: 51) writes that we 'need to grasp' how 'post-national points of reference are the political site of the practices of memory'; and Beck and Beck-Gernsheim (2009: 25) observe that 'the sphere of experience can no longer be understood as nationally bound but is determined by global dynamics.' Yet it is only recently, as Erll (2008: 2) has remarked, that memory studies has begun to address 'forms of remembering across nations and cultures.' 9/11 was one such event; it was perceived and remembered as a global event which continually resurfaces in public contexts where people living in different locations all over the globe perceive the same event through journalism.

The Treaty of Westphalia, which brought the Thirty Years' War to an end in 1648, established a European system of nation-states which was to last for about three centuries. But it would be wrong to infer from this that the members of nation-states remembered in common events that occurred within their borders. As Schwartz observes in this volume (Chapter 13), most literate Americans in 1863 never knew what Lincoln had said at Gettysburg, and it was only between 1945 and 1955, during the early years of the Cold War, that his address came to be viewed as fully newsworthy. Again, despite the opinion, held by many, that France was a homogeneous nation from the time of the French Revolution onwards, France remained riven by provincial heterogeneity throughout the nineteenth century. During that century certain provinces of France were repeatedly compared to overseas colonies (Weber, 1977). In 1843 Adolphe Blanqui compared the people of France's Alpine provinces to those of Kabylia and the Marquesas; in Franche-Comté, even in the twentieth century, people claimed that for many years they had themselves buried face down as a protest against the region's annexation by France; and as late as 1914, Camille Le Mercier d'Erm, in a book on Brittany compared that region to such other oppressed and vanquished nations as Ireland, Bohemia, Finland and Poland. Perhaps, therefore, we should devote more attention to investigating the persistence of *provincial* memories – for example, in France, Germany and Italy – during the period when we have come to think of the nation-state as fully established.

Generational memory

We also need to distinguish between globalized memories and *international* memories. For centuries before it became fashionable to speak about globalization, there had existed in Europe, at least among the educated strata, an international culture and an international memory. Jacob Burckhardt (1852; 3050) was referring to the demise of that culture when he lamented the decay of ancient rhetoric; he characterized the nineteenth century as a time of linguistic formlessness in which 'barely one in a hundred of our scholars' still know 'anything about the real art of constructing periods.' He was only partly correct; it was still possible in the mid-nineteenth century to witness and enjoy the spectacle of Roman rhetoric in the speeches delivered in the British House of Commons by such luminaries as Disraeli and Gladstone, Peel and Palmerston, all of whom had been trained in the classics. In a magisterial work, *European Literature and the Latin Middle Ages* (1953), Ernst Robert Curtius examined with unsurpassed erudition the long survival of that international culture. He showed that, for many centuries, the substance of antique culture was never destroyed; that Latin remained a learned language throughout the Middle Ages; that the encyclopedia of the great seventh-century scholar Isidore of Seville served the entire Middle Ages as a basic book, and that during the Renaissance, Erasmus of Rotterdam was familiar with the works of Plautus, Terence, Lucretius, Cicero, Sallust, Horace and Virgil.

Karl Mannheim (1952) proposed that shared memory was a generational phenomenon, and that each generation's world-view was influenced particularly strongly by the public events that occurred in their early adulthood. In the light of this it is worth reflecting on the careers of Pope John Paul II and George Soros. Pope John Paul II was born in 1920, George Soros in 1930. This means that Pope John Paul II would have been nineteen when in 1939 Hitler and Stalin colluded to carve up Poland, and that George Soros would have been twenty-six when the abortive Hungarian revolution of 1956 was crushed by the Russian army. From the time when he became Pope in 1978, Pope John Paul II continued to enjoy great influence in the cultural life of Poland, the weakest link in the Soviet Empire, through repeated discussions with Lech Walesa and tumultuous appearances in Poland. During the 1980s, George Soros drew upon his vast financial resources to establish scholarships for Russian and East European students to travel abroad; the Russians later went on to play, on the whole, relatively ineffectual lives in Russia, whereas the East European students became the leaders of the European revolutions of 1989. There is surely an element of *ressentiment* here for the events of 1939 and 1956. The world-views of Pope John Paul II and George Soros were evidently influenced by the public events that had occurred in their early adulthood. There must surely be many more cases – cases it would be worth examining in detail – where the memories of early adulthood affected the behavior of influential individuals in their later public lives.

Nevertheless, the idea of generational memory may not be as straightforward as Karl Mannheim appears to think it is. This becomes evident when we reflect on the historical novel as a genre. Historical novels – for example, those of Scott, Fenimore Cooper, Gogol, Pushkin and Lampedusa – frequently feature intimate contact between two regions, or two ages, which ostensibly belong to one and the same 'generation,' but which are radically *at odds* with one another in their customs and in their memories. In *The Pioneers*, Fenimore Cooper portrays a time-conflict between the indigenous native American Indians, who respect nature and its times, and the European settlers, who squander natural resources by violating the centuries old growth of forests and slaughtering migrating birds. In *Waverley*, Scott observes that 'so little was the condition of the Highlands known at all at that period, that the character and appearance of their population, while thus sallying forth as military adventurers, conveyed to the south-country Lowlanders as much surprise as if an invasion of African negroes or Esquinaux Indians, had issued forth from the northern mountains of their own native country' (Scott, 1814: 97). In *The Leopard*, when Lampedusa comes to portray the difficulties encountered by Garibaldi in seeking to conquer Sicily for the Risorgimento, he compares Sicily to a 'centenarian being dragged in a bath-chair round the Great Exhibition in London, understanding nothing and caring about nothing, whether it's the steel factories of Sheffield or the cotton spinneries of Manchester and thinking of nothing but drowsing off again on beslobbered pillows with a pot under the bed' (Lampedusa, 1958: 146).

Time and memory

Patterson (1998: 56) observes that ' time affects the work of every institution, but few so substantially as the news media.' In Chapter 6 of this volume Tenenboim-Weinblatt remarks that journalists increasingly struggle to meet the demands of accelerating news cycles; and Schudson (Chapter 5) notes that concepts such as debt, loyalty, commitment, shame, guilt and justice all emphasize a moral continuity over extended time-spans, which contrasts with the accelerated tempo of current news circulation. Both would agree, surely, with Schweizer (2008: 1), who says that 'waiting seems to be almost universally denigrated and should be avoided at all costs.' Yet, as Schweizer and Tenenboim-Weinblatt (Chapter 6) also emphasize, waiting is not only an inconvenience, but can be understood as a creative space. One of the most famous plays of the twentieth century – Samuel Beckett's *Waiting for Godot* – contains waiting in its title and in its subject matter; and one of the reasons that many present-day students find it difficult to watch the films of Antonioni is that waiting figures prominently in them and that they are shot at a slow pace to which contemporary students have become utterly unaccustomed.

A society which finds no place for *slowness* – in relationships, in meals, in reflection – is a deeply disturbed society. We need to rediscover slowness. In his short book, *Slowness*, Milan Kundera comments on the absurdity of contemporary accelerated and abbreviated news time. News reporters, he writes, do not reflect nearly as much as they should do on the fact that the situations which history stages 'are floodlit only for the first few minutes. No event remains news over its whole duration, merely for a quite brief span of time, at the very beginning.' He conveys the eerie quality of this strangeness in an arresting image. 'The way contemporary history is told,' he writes, 'is like a huge concert where they present all of Beethoven's one hundred and thirty eight opuses one after the other, but actually only play just eight bars of each. If the same concert were given again in ten years, only the first note of each piece would be played, thus one hundred and thirty eight notes for the whole concert, presented as one continuous melody' (Kundera, 1996: 79, 80). Once we reflect on the matter, it is obvious that news reporters are only one particular social group among many, and that since there are different social groups, there are different types of time and correspondingly different types of memory (Halbwachs, 1925). There are, for instance, women's times, family times, the time of peasants, the time of aristocrats, the time of merchants, the time of the church. It would be worth examining in detail the *contrasts* between and the *intersections* between, these different times and memories.

Representations of death

Photojournalism during the Second World War remained noticeably reticent in the depiction of dead soldiers. Such scenes were rarely represented (Zelizer, 1998). Increasingly, however, as Andén-Papadopoulos (Chapter 9) and Reading (Chapter 10) observe in this volume, death and dying are captured through the witnessing of ordinary citizens who produce a visual record on their mobile phones and then transmit these images to mainstream news organizations. Part of the value of such activity is that it disrupts one of photojournalism's strongest conventions, which is to withhold documentary scenes of death from public view.

There appears to be a paradox here. Contemporary photojournalism and television present repeated visual *representations* of dying to an unprecedented extent, yet it is also one of the most evident features of contemporary society that it does everything possible to *repress* our acknowledgement of the elementary fact – the one fact about which we can all be completely certain – that we shall die. No one really wants to think at length about this, nor did most people ever. As Rochefoucauld wrote, 'Neither the sun nor death can be looked at steadily.' This is as true of our century as of his. But in our century something new has happened. In *The Loneliness of the Dying* (1985), Norbert Elias sees the repression of the fact of death as one more aspect of that long-term historical process, stretching from at least the fifteenth to the nineteenth century in Europe, which he previously analyzed in his magisterial work, *The Civilising Process* (1978), in which he argued that all elemental aspects of life, of which eating is one and dying another, were subjected to a gradually increasing regulation, an ever more differentiated form of control. If, in encountering this process of repressing the phenomenon of death, we come across yet one more stage in the civilizing process, it is a fact, nonetheless, that we chance upon a strange asymmetry of perception. Everyone knows that around six million people were killed in the Holocaust, yet few people now know that thirty-six million people were killed in the Second World War between 1939 and 1945. Why do we lament the first fact so publicly and so overtly, yet apparently pay so little attention to the second?

The attempt to repress any acknowledgement of the fact of death – which now coexists with an unprecedented visual public representation of the process of dying – may perhaps have its most fundamental origin in the fact that we seek to repress the cultural memory of something which was evidently so horrible, and which, as T.S. Eliot would have put it, would entail us acknowledging 'too much reality which we cannot bear': that is to say the colossal loss of human life during the twentieth century – in the First World War, in the Second World War and in the horrendous toll exacted by the repeated genocides of the century.

Notes

1. Pierre Janet, *L'Évolution de la mémoire et de la notion du temps* (Paris, 1928) For a study of Janet in his historical context see Ruth Leys, 'Traumatic Cures: Shell Shock, Janet, and the Question of Memory,' in *Trauma: a Genealogy* (Chicago and London, 2000) 83–119. For a study of the rivalry between Janet and Freud see Campbell Perry and Jean-Roch Laurence, 'Mental Processes Outside of Awareness: The Contributions of Freud and Janet,' in K.S. Bowers and Donald Meichenbaum (eds) *The Unconscious Reconsidered* (New York, 1984) 9–48.
2. Joachim Ritter, 'Die Aufgabe der Geisteswissenschaften in der modernen Gesellschaft,' *Schriften der Gesellsschaft zur Förderung der Westfälischen Wilhelms-Universität zu Munster* (1963).

References

Anderson, Benedict, *Imagined Communities* (London and New York, 1991)

Bayart, Jean-François, *Global Subjects* (Cambridge, 2007)

Beck, Ulrich and Beck-Gernsheim, Elisabeth, 'Global Generations and the Trap of Methodological Nationalism. For a Cosmopolitan Turn in the Sociology of Youth and Generation', *European Sociological Review* 25(1) (2009) 25–36

Burckhardt, J., *Die Zeit Constantins des Grossen* (1852)

Cooper, James Fenimore, *The Pioneers* (New York, 1823)

Curtius, Ernst Robert, *European Literature and the Latin Middle Ages* (Eng. tr. London, 1953)

Elias, Norbert, *The Civilising Process* (Eng. tr. Oxford, 1978)

Elias, Norbert, *The Loneliness of the Dying* (Eng. tr. New York and London, 1985)

Erll, Astrid, *Cultural Memory Studies: an International and Interdisciplinary Handbook* (Berlin, 2008)

Halbwachs, Maurice, *Les Cadres Sociaux de la Memoire* (Paris, 1925)

Kundera, Milan, *Slowness* (Eng. tr. London and Boston, 1996)

Lampedusa, Giuseppe di, *The Leopard* (Milan, 1958)

Mannheim, Karl, 'The Problem of Generations', in Kecskemeti, Paul (ed) *Essays on the Sociology of Knowledge* (London, 1952) 276–320

Patterson, T.E., 'Time and News: The Media's Limitations as an Instrument of Democracy', *International Political Science Review* 19(1) (1998) 55–68

Renan, Ernest, 'Qu'est-ce que une nation?' in *Oeuvres Completes* (Paris, 1947–61) Vol 1 pp.887–906

Rochefoucauld, François de la, *Reflections; or Sentences and Moral Maxims* (Paris, 1665–1678).

Scott, Walter, *Waverley* (London, 1814)

Schweizer, H., *On Waiting* (London and New York, 2008)

Weber, Eugen, *Peasants into Frenchmen: The Modernisation of Rural France, 1870–1914* (London, 1977)

Zelizer, Barbie, *Remembering to Forget. Holocaust Memory through the Camera's Eye* (Chicago and London, 1998)

Index

Connerton, Paul, 43, 44
Conrad, Sebastian, 23
contested memories, and collective
    memory, 69–70
contingency, 166, 167
convergent journalism, 148
Cooke, Alistair, 227
Corlett, William, 143
cosmopolitan memory, 23, 51, 259
Cronkite, Walter, 11, 195, 198, 199,
    201, 203, 204, 207, 228, 234, 237,
    260, 261
crowd-sourced video
    and aesthetics of, 158–9:
        hypermobility, 154–5; non-
        narrativity, 155–6; opacity, 155;
        raw audio, 156
    and authenticity, 149, 152:
        aesthetics of, 154–6
    and authority of, 159
    and challenges to journalistic
        standards, 151–2, 160
    and concerns over, 159–60
    and de-authorization of, 160
    and democratizing nature of, 149,
        154
    and ethics of, 156–8, 159: affectivity,
        157; partisanship, 158;
        subjectivity, 156–7
    and impact on journalism, 152,
        159
    and increasing use of, 151
    and interdependence of moral and
        aesthetic values of, 150, 159
    and limitations as mnemonic
        record, 150
    and news organizations' reliance
        on, 151
    and political impact of, 159
    and role in shaping news, 151
    and shooting of Neda Agha Soltan,
        150–1, 154, 155, 156, 157, 158,
        159, 160
    and status assigned to, 148
    and witnessing of death, 167–8
cultural authority, and journalism,
    196–7, 198
cultural memory, *see* collective
    memory

cultural production and consumption,
    166
Curtius, Robert, 262
cyber warfare, 186, 187

Danchev, Alex, 184–5
Dandan, Alejandra, 244, 249, 250,
    251–2, 253, 254
databasing of the world, 188
David, Shay, 188
Davis, Jefferson, 222
Dayan, Daniel, 22
death
    and representation of, 265
    and repression of fact of, 265–6
    and witnessing of, 167–8
Deffner, Florian, 59
Demosthenes, 35
Denison, William, 221
Derrida, Jacques, 30
Der Zeitung, 173–4
Descartes, René, 37
digital media, *see* new media
digital witnessing, 165–6
digitization, 165, 166
    and impact on journalism, 180–1
    and mediality of images, 181
directive discourse, and time-counting,
    108–9
Disraeli, Benjamin, 262
dissent
    and citizen journalism, 158
    and feet or hand images, 137, 261
domains, and memory, 3, 6–12
dominant memory
    and collective memory, 70
    in post-broadcast world, 70
Donaldson, Sam, 204
Douglas, Mary, 46
Durkheim, Emile, 24, 212
Dutch Revolt (1568), 36

Editorial Atlántida, 249–50
Edy, J.A., 70, 75
Egypt, 89
Einstein, G.O., 109
Elias, Norbert, 265
Eliot, T.S., 266
Ellis, John, 167, 246

Printed and bound in the United States of America